SMALL IS BEAUTIFUL

small is beautiful

ECONOMICS AS IF PEOPLE MATTERED

25 years later . . . with commentaries

E.F. SCHUMACHER

Hartley & Marks
PUBLISHERS

Published by Hartley & Marks Publishers Inc, 1999

PO Box 147	3661 W. Broadway
Point Roberts, WA	Vancouver, BC
98281	V6R 2B8

Published by Hartley and Marks
by arrangement with HarperCollins.

LIBRARY OF CONGRESS CATALOGING-IN-PUBLICATION DATA

Schumacher, E.F. (Ernst Friedrich), 1911–1977
Small is beautiful : a study of economics as if people mattered /
E.F. Schumacher.
p. cm.
Originally published: London : Blond and Briggs, 1973
Includes bibliographical references and index.
ISBN 0-88179-169-5
1. Economics. I. Title.
HB171.S384 1998
330.1—dc21 98-28470
CIP

Design & composition by
Hartley & Marks Publisher's Inc.
Set in Scala

Printed in the United States

Few can contemplate without a sense of exhilaration the splendid achievements of practical energy and technical skill, which, from the latter part of the seventeenth century, were transforming the face of material civilisation, and of which England was the daring, if not too scrupulous, pioneer. If, however, economic ambitions are good servants, they are bad masters.

The most obvious facts are the most easily forgotten. Both the existing economic order and too many of the projects advanced for reconstructing it break down through their neglect of the truism that, since even quite common men have souls, no increase in material wealth will compensate them for arrangements which insult their self-respect and impair their freedom. A reasonable estimate of economic organisation must allow for the fact that, unless industry is to be paralysed by recurrent revolts on the part of outraged human nature, it must satisfy criteria which are not purely economic.

—R.H. Tawney
Religion and the Rise of Capitalism

By and large, our present problem is one of attitudes and implements. We are remodeling the Alhambra with a steam-shovel, and are proud of our yardage. We shall hardly relinquish the shovel, which after all has many good points, but we are in need of gentler and more objective criteria for its successful use.

—Aldo Leopold
A Sand County Almanac

CONTENTS

ABOUT THE AUTHOR

ERNST FRIEDRICH SCHUMACHER (1911–1977) is best known for his critique of Western economics and his solutions calling for human-scale, decentralized, and appropriate technologies. When *Small is Beautiful* was first published in 1973, its message was immediately adopted by many people who were disaffected by current patterns of development and global economics, and were actively seeking a better way. His book was translated into many languages and Schumacher himself was launched into international touring for lectures and consulting until his death. In that short time he had been honored with awards and degrees in North America, England, and Europe, and met with leaders of many nations and multinational corporations.

German-born and the son of a professor of economics, Fritz attended universities in Germany, the United States, and England, and earned a diploma in economics. During World War II he lived in England, in opposition to Hitler's regime, and was interned as an enemy alien. After the war he served as economic advisor with the British Control Commission and then with the British National Coal Board for 20 years. In the meantime, he founded the Intermediate Technology Development Group in 1966, traveling throughout the Third World to speak with leaders and policy-makers about creating self-reliant economies by using appropriate technologies. As well, he had become a trustee of the Scott Bader Commonwealth, and in 1970, president of the Soil Association. Throughout this time he wrote reports and pamphlets and contributed articles to magazines such as *The Economist* and *Resurgence*.

Schumacher retired early from the Coal Board to write several books, including *A Guide for the Perplexed* and *Good Work,* published after his death. When Fritz died during a lecture tour in Switzerland, he was mourned as a prophet standing against the tide and a man who asked the right questions at the right time. In the words of his daughter, Barbara Wood, author of *E.F. Schumacher: His Life and Thought,* "His words were directed always at reality, at those who would translate them because they demanded a personal response, an awakening of the heart." His work, she explained, "was for the people, and it was the people, as individuals and small groups who, he knew, would ultimately turn the tide to sanity."

PREFACE

"THE TASK OF OUR GENERATION, I have no doubt, is one of metaphysical reconstruction." This is surely the key to Schumacher's thinking: we need to reconstruct the meaning of ideas like wealth, knowledge, work, economics, development, and progress.

We who knew Schumacher and now support Schumacher Circle organizations—including Schumacher College, Schumacher Societies in Britain and the U.S.A., Intermediate Technology, Soil Association, and New Economics Foundation—have been powerfully influenced by the range and depth of *Small is Beautiful*. But we recognize that its message has not yet shaped the mainstream agendas that govern our use of land, energy, and other resources, our technologies and industries, our national and international institutions and policies, the scale on which we organize our activities, and our own lifestyles.

Why is this? Was the message lacking in some respects?

For example, Schumacher said that "women, on the whole, do not need an 'outside' job, and the large-scale employment of women in offices or factories would be considered a sign of economic failure" by a Buddhist economist. Did he have too little to say about the changing role of women in society, the rise of feminine consciousness, and the possibility that male domination is at least partly responsible for what is wrong with the modern world?

Again, was he too focused—as a trained economist—on the prospect of stable equilibrium, rather than on the evolving processes of change? Are contemporary ideas about the evolution of consciousness, and the challenge of breaking through to a new age of ecology and spiritual awareness at odds with his commitment to eternal Catholic verities?

Peter Etherden (in "The Schumacher Enigma," *Fourth World Review*, 1999:93) has recently pointed out that *Small is Beautiful* says virtually nothing about money. Many people in the new economics movement now believe that the existing systems of money and finance, taxation and public spending are root causes of the damage suffered by people and the earth. They see monetary and financial reform as a top priority. So why was Schumacher, who worked with J.M. Keynes and J.K. Galbraith after World War II and was internationally recognized as an up-and-coming young expert on international finance and currency reform, silent about it in his later years? Why, after long experience as a senior Coal Board official, did he pay so little attention to the more general point that institutions (including money) help to determine how people and organizations behave? Had he really concluded that institutional reconstruction was much less important than metaphysical reconstruction?

I knew Fritz Schumacher personally and much admired him. A copy of his last book, *A Guide for the Perplexed*, reached me in the mail with the author's compliments just after I was told of his death. I had been privileged to speak on the same platform with him more than once. After his death I was asked to take on some engagements arranged for him in Canada. Today I am sure he would be glad that those who stand on his shoulders are celebrating *Small is Beautiful*. But I think he would also hope we would read it again critically and constructively, in order to build more effectively.

James Robertson
Cholsey, Oxfordshire, England
April 30, 1999

INTRODUCTION

F OR SOME OF THE CONTRIBUTORS to this 25th anniversary edition, *Small is Beautiful* was the most important book of their life. For others, it was pivotal to their education or intellectual development. When first released 25 years ago, the impact was enormous. Coming on the heels of a deep worldwide recession, the OPEC oil crisis, and a near quadrupling of commodity prices, *Small is Beautiful* was both diagnostic and prescriptive. It explained the chaos of world and domestic events while pointing to intuitively obvious solutions. At Portola Institute in Menlo Park, California, publisher of the *Whole Earth Catalogs, Small is Beautiful* became canon. Here in one book was an organizing framework for an emerging group of decentralist ideas, technologies, and social movements that, though highly progressive, were still inchoate. The infectious excitement that quickly attached itself to the man and the ideas has not been seen since.

Unlike the writings of other economic theorists such as Adam Smith, Karl Marx, or John Maynard Keynes, Schumacher's essays did not surprise us because of their originality—they enlightened us because of the breadth of their sensibility. For many, it was a synthesis that had been begging to be articulated, yet none had. While many of the concepts presented were being talked about amongst small groups of academicians, leftists, activists, and nongovernmental organizations, it took a respectable gentleman in pin-stripes and a black homburg, a man who had worked diligently as the chief economist for the National Coal Board of Britain for 20 years to announce to the world that neo-classical economics was dead and inhumane, that more production of goods would not make people happy, that large-scale technologies were dehumanizing and morally wrong, and that "man is small, and, therefore, small is beautiful."

I met Schumacher twice, and heard him speak to different venues in England, New York, and California. In Palo Alto, California, he spoke to a diverse audience ranging from students, political activists, and environmentalists on one hand, and academic deans, economists, and executives from high-tech companies on the other. He was able to establish rapport across the spectrum of listeners for three reasons: his humility, his erudition, and his sense of humor. At the time, the inevitability of his ideas appeared overwhelming in the face of the failure of Western governments' environmental, energy, and social policies. But that was not to be the case. While myriad movements grew out of or were empowered by his work, the world as a whole has moved powerfully towards consolidation, gigantism, and globalization.

Does this mean his ideas are invalid, outdated, or impractical? Inside this volume is a wealth of commentaries by writers, teachers, and organizers, heirs to Schumacher's thinking, who believe quite the opposite. But it is for each reader to decide. If we conclude that good ideas are those easily taken up by mainstream society, then *Small is Beautiful* is an outdated shibboleth. But there is another possibility—that Schumacher articulated truths that are fundamentally true regardless of time, culture, or prevailing economic system. One of the important ideas, synonymous with the title, is that there is an optimal human scale, size, or relationship inherent in economic activity, a geometry of life that is independent of economic theory, even his own. Schumacher was not suggesting a return to another age as he was sometimes accused. Rather, in both his monastic retreats and in the rhythm of Burmese village life, he made an observation that was both heretical and edifying: There are inherent thresholds in the scale of human activity that, when surpassed, produce second- and third-order effects that subtract if not destroy the quality of all life.

If Schumacher had only brought forth the concept of human scale, which in itself was an amplification of Leopold Kohr's writings, we would be eternally grateful. But Schumacher was fundamentally a systems thinker, and saw the world not in terms of problems, but in patterns or relationships. From this one volume arose tenets, issues, and timeless themes that inform thousands of institutions in the world today. These include the right to have humanizing work that is dignified and meaningful—right livelihood as it is known in Buddhist terms; the idea of nature as both mentor and spiritual sanctuary, a concept that now encompasses movements as diverse as "biomimicry" and eco-feminism; the economic concept of natural capital, natural resources, both renewable and non-renewable, as well as the integrity and flow of ecosystem services flowing into civilization from living systems; the concern that no economic system that externalized its costs could endure or sustain itself, voiced today in TOES (The Other Economic Summit) and the International Society of Ecological Economics (ISEE); the growing and widespread destruction of the environment and the toll it is taking on society; the concept of what is enough, which has taken root in the writings of Alan Thein Durning at the Northwest Environment Watch, Betsy Taylor's work at the Center for the New American Dream, and the book *Your Money or Your Life* by Vicki Robin and Joe Dominguez; a clear delineation of the destructiveness of man-over-nature models of thinking, organization, and development; and the idea that we are trying to satisfy non-material needs with material goods, a concept brilliantly brought forth by Manfred Max-Neef.

Without question, the most exciting work today is not creating another business (there are over 100 million in the world), but what is called "social entrepreneurship," the extraordinary act of bringing people together to transform the institutions that rule, harm, and overwhelm the nature of human existence and our relationship to living systems. There are today over 30,000 nongovernmental organizations in the United States and perhaps another 70,000 worldwide that are actively working towards one or more of the ideas presented within this book. The tens of thousands of organizations that are working towards a sustainable world are, on the whole, diverse, local, underfunded, and tenuous. Scattered across the globe, from Denmark to Chile to Kenya to Bozeman, Montana, people and institutions are organizing to defend human life and the life of the planet. They address a broad array of issues including environmental justice, ecological literacy, public policy, conservation, women's rights and health, population, renewable energy, corporate reform, labor issues, climate change, trade agreements, ethical investing, ecological tax reform, water, and much more. These groups conform to both of Ghandi's imperatives: Some resist while others create new structures, patterns, and institutions that are humane in scale and nature.

Knowingly or unknowingly, these socially entrepreneurial organizations are informed by Schumacher's work and depth of humanity. Although uncoordinated and mostly disconnected, the mandates, directives, principles, declarations, and other statements of purpose drafted by these groups are extraordinarily consonant. They are creating conventions and frameworks for civilization that are remarkably in accord with *Small is Beautiful*. These groups include the International Forum on Globalization, the Grameen Bank, Society for Ecological Restoration, Worldwatch Institute, Friends of the River, Development Alternatives (Delhi), Land Stewardship Council, Institute for Agriculture and Trade Policy, The Just Transition Consortium, The Instituto de Ecologia Politica (Santiago, Chile), American Farmland Trust, The Cenozoic Society, Indigenous Environmental Network, Friends of the Earth, and many more. Never before in history have independent groups from around the world derived frameworks of knowledge that are utterly consonant and in agreement. It is not that they are the same; it is that they do not conflict. This hasn't happened in politics, not in religion, not in psychology, and not in economics. As worldwide conditions continue to change and worsen socially, environmentally, and politically, organizations working towards sustainability increase, deepen, and multiply. Some day, these dots are going to be connected.

While one might despair that Schumacher's work has not been more fully taken up by mainstream economists and educational institutions, I find hope in the work of awakening citizens who are beginning to realize that they must now actively participate to create a world that is worth passing on to the next generation. In this vibrancy and steadfastness, embodied by millions of people working towards a just and humane world, the work and words of Schumacher have been both seed and inspiration. I once had a Buddhist teacher who did not think much about spending one's life reading books. When asked which books I should read, he replied, "Read the books that save you from reading others." *Small is Beautiful* is and has always been one of those rare books—a book that can inform a lifetime.

Paul Hawken
Sausalito, California
May 30, 1999

PART I

THE MODERN WORLD

CHAPTER I

THE PROBLEM OF PRODUCTION

ONE OF THE MOST fateful errors of our age is the belief that "the problem of production" has been solved. Not only is this belief firmly held by people remote from production and therefore professionally unacquainted with the facts—it is held by virtually all the experts, the captains of industry, the economic managers in the governments of the world, the academic and not-so-academic economists, not to mention the economic journalists. They may disagree on many things but they all agree that the problem of production has been solved; that mankind has at last come of age. For the rich countries, they say, the most important task now is "education for leisure" and, for the poor countries, the "transfer of technology."

That things are not going as well as they ought to be going must be due to human wickedness. We must therefore construct a political system so perfect that human wickedness disappears and everybody behaves well, no matter how much wickedness there may be in him or her. In fact, it is widely held that everybody is born good; if one turns into a criminal or an exploiter, this is the fault of "the system." No doubt "the system" is in many ways bad and must be changed. One of the main reasons why it is bad and why it can still survive in spite of its badness, is this erroneous view that the "problem of production" has been solved. As this error pervades all present-day systems there is at present not much to choose between them.

The arising of this error, so egregious and so firmly rooted, is closely connected with the philosophical, not to say religious,

Most of the environmental movement takes a utilitarian ecology approach, that we must protect the environment because it is useful and beneficial to human beings. Schumacher's approach was that we must take care of the environment out of our deep reverence for it. I call the Schumacherian approach to the environment "reverential ecology."

Reverential economy and ecology say that you must know your limits and learn to live within them. Then everything will be recycled and regenerated. Mahatma Gandhi said there is enough in the world for everyone's need, but not enough for anyone's greed. Our modern dinosaur society has become a greedy society and we don't know when enough is enough.

—SATISH KUMAR

changes during the last three or four centuries in man's attitude to nature. I should perhaps say: *Western* man's attitude to nature, but since the whole world is now in a process of westernisation, the more generalised statement appears to be justified. Modern man does not experience himself as a part of nature but as an outside force destined to dominate and conquer it. He even talks of a battle with nature, forgetting that, if he won the battle, he would find himself on the losing side. Until quite recently, the battle seemed to go well enough to give him the illusion of unlimited powers, but not so well as to bring the possibility of total victory into view. This has now come into view, and many people, albeit only a minority, are beginning to realise what this means for the continued existence of humanity.

The illusion of unlimited powers, nourished by astonishing scientific and technological achievements, has produced the concurrent illusion of having solved the problem of production. The latter illusion is based on the failure to distinguish between income and capital where this distinction matters most. Every economist and businessman is familiar with the distinction, and applies it conscientiously and with considerable subtlety to all economic affairs—except where it really matters: namely, the irreplaceable capital which man has not made, but simply found, and without which he can do nothing.

A businessman would not consider a firm to have solved its problems of production and to have achieved viability if he saw that it was rapidly consuming its capital. How, then, could we overlook this vital fact when it comes to that very big firm, the economy of Spaceship Earth and, in particular, the economies of its rich passengers?

One reason for overlooking this vital fact is that we are estranged from reality and inclined to treat as valueless everything that we have not made ourselves. Even the great Dr. Marx fell into this devastating error when he formulated the so-called "labour theory of value." Now, we have indeed laboured to make some of the capital which today helps us to produce—a large fund of scientific, technological, and other knowledge; an elaborate physical infrastructure; innumerable types of sophisticated capital equipment, etc.—but all this is but a small part of the total capital we are using. Far larger is the capital provided by nature and not by man—and we do not even recognise it as such. This larger part is now being used up at an alarming rate, and that is why it is an absurd and suicidal error to believe, and act on the belief, that the problem of production has been solved.

Let us take a closer look at this "natural capital." First of all, and most obviously, there are the fossil fuels. No one, I am sure, will deny that we are treating them as income items although they are undeniably capital items. If we treated them as capital items, we should be concerned with conservation; we should do everything in our power to try and minimise their current rate of use; we might be saying, for instance, that the money obtained from the realisation of these assets—these irreplaceable assets—must be placed into a special fund to be devoted exclusively to the evolution of production methods and patterns of living which do *not* depend on fossil fuels at all or depend on them only to a very slight extent. These and many other things we should be doing if we treated fossil fuels as capital and not as income. And we do not do any of them, but the exact contrary of every one of them: we are not in the least concerned with conservation; we are maximising, instead of minimising, the current rates of use; and, far from being interested in studying the possibilities of alternative methods of production and patterns of living—so as to get off the collision course on which we are moving with ever-increasing speed—we happily talk of unlimited progress along the beaten track, of "education for leisure" in the rich countries, and of "the transfer of technology" to the poor countries.

The liquidation of these capital assets is proceeding so rapidly that even in the allegedly richest country in the world, the United States of America, there are many worried men, right up to the White House, calling for the massive conversion of coal into oil and gas, demanding ever more gigantic efforts to search for and exploit the remaining treasures of the earth. Look at the figures that are being put forward under the heading "World Fuel Requirements in the Year 2000." If we are now using something like 7,000 million tons of coal equivalent, the need in twenty-eight years' time will be

The term natural capital, introduced to a broad audience by Schumacher in Small is Beautiful, *was not immediately taken up by economists or academics. The term seemed to lay dormant until the past decade. Today, it is being used commonly, certainly in environmental circles and writings.*

Schumacher defined natural capital both narrowly and amorphously: fossil fuels and the tolerance margins of nature and human subsistence. Today we understand natural capital as the sum total of renewable and non-renewable resources, including the ecological systems and services that support life. It is different from conventionally defined capital in that natural capital cannot be produced by human activity. What was unimaginable 25 years ago was the speed with which the loss of natural capital would affect humankind.

—PAUL HAWKEN

There is a fundamental difference between production in the economy and production in nature. Because they are essentially self-producing, and use only dispersed (high entropy) substances for their growth and maintenance, green plants are called primary producers. By contrast, humans are strictly secondary producers. We use enormous inputs of high-grade energy and material resources extracted from the rest of the ecosphere to produce and maintain our bodies and all the products of our factories. In short, all production by the human enterprise involves the consumption of a much larger quantity of energy and material first produced by nature. From this material perspective, economic activity is more an inefficient conversion process than it is a productive process.

—WILLIAM REES

three times as large—around 20,000 million tons! What are twenty-eight years? Looking backwards, they take us roughly to the end of World War II, and, of course, since then fuel consumption has trebled; but the trebling involved an increase of less than 5,000 million tons of coal equivalent. Now we are calmly talking about an increase three times as large.

People ask: Can it be done? And the answer comes back: It must be done and therefore it shall be done. One might say (with apologies to John Kenneth Galbraith) that it is a case of the bland leading the blind. But why cast aspersions? The question itself is wrongheaded, because it carries the implicit assumption that we are dealing with income and not with capital. What is so special about the year 2000? What about the year 2028, when little children running about today will be planning for their retirement? Another trebling by then? All these questions and answers are seen to be absurd the moment we realise that we are dealing with capital and not with income: fossil fuels are not made by men; they cannot be recycled. Once they are gone they are gone forever.

But what—it will be asked—about the income fuels? Yes, indeed, what about them? Currently, they contribute (reckoned in calories) less than four per cent to the world total. In the foreseeable future they will have to contribute seventy, eighty, ninety per cent. To do something on a small scale is one thing: to do it on a gigantic scale is quite another, and to make an impact on the world fuel problem, contributions have to be truly gigantic. Who will say that the problem of production has been solved when it comes to income fuels required on a truly gigantic scale?

Fossil fuels are merely a part of the "natural capital" which we steadfastly insist on treating as expendable, as if it were income, and by no means the most important part. If we squander our fossil fuels, we threaten civilisation; but if we squander the capital represented by living nature around us, we threaten life itself. People are waking up to this threat, and they demand that pollution must stop. They think of pollution as a rather nasty habit indulged in by careless or greedy people who, as it were, throw their rubbish over the fence into the neighbour's garden. A more civilised behaviour, they realise, would incur some extra cost, and therefore we need a faster rate of economic growth to be able to pay for it. From now on, they say, we should use at least some of the fruits of our ever-increasing productivity to improve "the quality of life" and not merely to increase the quantity of consumption. All this is fair enough, but it touches only the outer fringe of the problem.

To get to the crux of the matter, we do well to ask why it is that all these terms—pollution, environment, ecology, etc.—have so *suddenly* come into prominence. After all, we have had an industrial system for quite some time, yet only five or ten years ago these words were virtually unknown. Is this a sudden fad, a silly fashion, or perhaps a sudden failure of nerve?

The explanation is not difficult to find. As with fossil fuels, we have indeed been living on the capital of living nature for some time, but at a fairly modest rate. It is only since the end of World War II that we have succeeded in increasing this rate to alarming proportions. In comparison with what is going on now and what has been going on, progressively, during the last quarter of a century, all the industrial activities of mankind up to, and including, World War II are as nothing. The next four or five years are likely to see more industrial production, taking the world as a whole, than all of mankind accomplished up to 1945. In other words, quite recently—so recently that most of us have hardly yet become conscious of it—there has been a unique quantitative jump in industrial production.

Partly as a cause and also as an effect, there has also been a unique qualitative jump. Our scientists and technologists have learned to compound substances unknown to nature. Against many of them, nature is virtually defenceless. There are no natural agents to attack and break them down. It is as if aborigines were suddenly attacked with machine-gun fire: their bows and arrows are of no avail. These substances, unknown to nature, owe their almost magical effectiveness precisely to nature's defencelessness—and that accounts also for their dangerous ecological impact. It is only in the last twenty years or so that they have made their appearance *in bulk*. Because they have no natural enemies, they tend to accumulate, and the long-term consequences of this accumulation are in many cases known to be extremely dangerous, and in other cases totally unpredictable.

In other words, the changes of the last twenty-five years, both in

Much so-called economic activity is really human ecology and both economists and ecologists agree that humans are consumer organisms. Actually, ecologists classify humans as macro-consumers. In general, macro-consumers are largish animals that consume green plants or other animals directly to satisfy their metabolic needs. However, human ecologists also have to account for our industrial metabolism, the consumption demands of our manufactured capital. All our toys and tools, factories, and infrastructure (our exosomatic organs) require continuous flows of energy and material from and to nature for their production, maintenance, and operation. Economists talk about increasing output, of maximizing resource or labor productivity, but the reality is that no matter how efficient the economy becomes, economic production requires material consumption.
—WILLIAM REES

the quantity and in the quality of man's industrial processes, have produced an entirely new situation—a situation resulting not from our failures but from what we thought were our greatest successes. And this has come so suddenly that we hardly noticed the fact that we were very rapidly using up a certain kind of irreplaceable capital asset, namely the *tolerance margins* which benign nature always provides.

Now let me return to the question of "income fuels" with which I had previously dealt in a somewhat cavalier manner. No one is suggesting that the world-wide industrial system which is being envisaged to operate in the year 2000, a generation ahead, would be sustained primarily by water or wind power. No, we are told that we are moving rapidly into the nuclear age. Of course, this has been the story for quite some time, for over twenty years, and yet, the contribution of nuclear energy to man's total fuel and energy requirements is still minute. In 1970, it amounted to 2.7 per cent in Britain; 0.6 per cent in the European Community; and 0.3 per cent in the United States, to mention only the countries that have gone the furthest. Perhaps we can assume that nature's tolerance margins will be able to cope with such small impositions, although there are many people even today who are deeply worried, and Dr. Edward D. David, President Nixon's Science Adviser, talking about the storage of radioactive wastes, says that "one has a queasy feeling about something that has to stay underground and be pretty well sealed off for 25,000 years before it is harmless."

However that may be, the point I am making is a very simple one: the proposition to replace thousands of millions of tons of fossil fuels, every year, by nuclear energy means to "solve" the fuel problem by creating an environmental and ecological problem of such a monstrous magnitude that Dr. David will not be the only one to have "a queasy feeling." It means solving one problem by shifting it to another sphere—there to create an infinitely bigger problem.

Having said this, I am sure that I shall be confronted with another, even more daring proposition: namely, that future scientists and technologists will be able to devise safety rules and precautions of such perfection that the using, transporting, processing and storing of radioactive materials in ever-increasing quantities will be made entirely safe; also that it will be the task of politicians and social scientists to create a world society in which wars or civil disturbances can never happen. Again, it is a proposition to solve one problem simply by shifting it to another sphere, the sphere of everyday human behaviour. And this takes us to the third category of "natural capital" which we are recklessly squandering because we treat it as if it were income: as if it were something we had made ourselves and could easily replace out of our much-vaunted and rapidly rising productivity.

Is it not evident that our current methods of production are already eating into the very substance of industrial man? To many people this is not at all evident. Now that we have solved the problem of production, they say, have we ever had it so good? Are we not better fed, better clothed, and better housed than ever before—and better educated? Of course we are: most, but by no means all, of us: in the rich countries. But this is not what I mean by "substance." The substance of man cannot be measured by Gross National Product. Perhaps it cannot be measured at all, except for certain symptoms of loss. However, this is not the place to go into the statistics of these symptoms, such as crime, drug addiction, vandalism, mental breakdown, rebellion, and so forth. Statistics never prove anything.

I started by saying that one of the most fateful errors of our age is the belief that the problem of production has been solved. This illusion, I suggested, is mainly due to our inability to recognise that the modern industrial system, with all its intellectual sophistication, consumes the very basis on which it has been erected. To use the language of the economist, it lives on irreplaceable capital which it cheerfully treats as income. I specified three categories of such capital: fossil fuels, the tolerance margins of nature, and the human substance. Even if some readers should refuse to accept all three parts of my argument, I suggest that any one of them suffices to make my case.

And what is my case? Simply that our most important task is to get off our present collision course. And who is there to tackle such a task? I think every one of us, whether old or young, powerful or powerless, rich or poor, influential or uninfluential. To talk about

Despite reams of press about the state of the environment and a raft of laws attempting to prevent further loss, the stock of natural capital is plummeting as are vital life-giving services that flow from it. Having inherited a 3.8-billion year store of natural capital, at present rates of use and degradation, there will be little left by the end of the next century. Thus, as Herman Daly has written, natural capital is rapidly becoming the limiting factor to human development, an event that will topple the wobbly supports of neoclassical economics. In the face of this relentless loss of living systems, fractious political conflicts over laws, regulations, and business economics appear petty and small.

It is not that these issues are unimportant, but that they ignore the larger context. Are we or are we not systematically reducing life and the capacity to recreate order, the source of economic value? This is the level on which our discourse ➡

➡ *should take place as Schu-macher so clearly saw, for it is here that a framework for both understanding and action can be formulated. In spite of what such signals as the gross domestic product or the Dow Jones Industrial Average indicate, it is ulti-mately the capacity of the photosynthetic world and its nutrient flows that determine the quality and the quantity of life on earth.*
—PAUL HAWKEN

the future is useful only if it leads to action *now*. And what can we do *now*, while we are still in the position of "never having had it so good"? To say the least—which is already very much—we must thoroughly understand the problem and begin to see the possibility of evolving a new life-style, with new methods of production and new patterns of consumption: a life-style designed for permanence. To give only three preliminary examples: in agriculture and horti-culture, we can interest ourselves in the perfection of production methods which are biologically sound, build up soil fertility, and produce health, beauty and permanence. Productivity will then look after itself. In industry, we can interest ourselves in the evolu-tion of small-scale technology, relatively nonviolent technology, "technology with a human face," so that people have a chance to en-joy themselves while they are working, instead of working solely for their pay packet and hoping, usually forlornly, for enjoyment solely during their leisure time. In industry, again—and, surely, industry is the pace-setter of modern life—we can interest ourselves in new forms of partnership between management and men, even forms of common ownership.

We often hear it said that we are entering the era of "the Learn-ing Society." Let us hope this is true. We still have to learn how to live peacefully, not only with our fellow men but also with nature and, above all, with those Higher Powers which have made nature and have made us; for, assuredly, we have not come about by acci-dent and certainly have not made ourselves.

The themes which have been merely touched upon in this chap-ter will have to be further elaborated as we go along. Few people will be easily convinced that the challenge to man's future cannot be met by making marginal adjustments here or there, or, possibly, by changing the political system.

The following chapter is an attempt to look at the whole situa-tion again, from the angle of peace and permanence. Now that man has acquired the physical means of self-obliteration, the question of peace obviously looms larger than ever before in human history. And how could peace be built without some assurance of perma-nence with regard to our economic life?

CHAPTER 2

PEACE AND PERMANENCE

THE DOMINANT MODERN BELIEF is that the soundest foundation of peace would be universal prosperity. One may look in
vain for historical evidence that the rich have regularly been more
peaceful than the poor, but then it can be argued that they have
never felt secure against the poor; that their aggressiveness
stemmed from fear; and that the situation would be quite different
if everybody were rich. Why should a rich man go to war? He has
nothing to gain. Are not the poor, the exploited, the oppressed most
likely to do so, as they have nothing to lose but their chains? The
road to peace, it is argued, is to follow the road to riches.

This dominant modern belief has an almost irresistible attraction, as it suggests that the faster you get one desirable thing the
more securely do you attain another. It is doubly attractive because
it completely by-passes the whole question of ethics: there is no
need for renunciation or sacrifice; on the contrary! We have science
and technology to help us along the road to peace and plenty, and all
that is needed is that we should not behave stupidly, irrationally,
cutting into our own flesh. The message to the poor and discon-
tented is that they must not impatiently upset or kill the goose that
will assuredly, in due course, lay golden eggs also for them. And the
message to the rich is that they must be intelligent enough from
time to time to help the poor, because this is the way by which they
will become richer still.

Gandhi used to talk disparagingly of "dreaming of systems so
perfect that no one will need to be good." But is it not precisely this
dream which we can now implement in reality with our marvellous

What seemed so evident to early readers of Small is Beautiful *still seems painfully opaque to the world today. When the book was first published, many thought that change would come about through insight, logic, compassion, and reason. Increasingly, it seems that change will come about after we have exhausted every other theory of greed and gain, and the winds of change are no longer metaphorical, but force five hurricanes destroying whole regions. That the world should become so immune to its own losses seemed inconceivable 25 years ago. Now that we have re-learned how remarkably obtuse humankind can be when dazzled by monetary and material gain, we must shine the light all the brighter on the singularity and prescience of Schumacher's work and vision.*

—PAUL HAWKEN

powers of science and technology? Why ask for virtues, which man may never acquire, when scientific rationality and technical competence are all that is needed?

Instead of listening to Gandhi, are we not more inclined to listen to one of the most influential economists of our century, that great Lord Keynes? In 1930, during the world-wide economic depression, he felt moved to speculate on the "economic possibilities for our grandchildren" and concluded that the day might not be all that far off when everybody would be rich. We shall then, he said, "once more value ends above means and prefer the good to the useful."

"But beware!" he continued. "The time for all this is not yet. For at least another hundred years we must pretend to ourselves and to every one that fair is foul and foul is fair; for foul is useful and fair is not. Avarice and usury and precaution must be our gods for a little longer still. For only they can lead us out of the tunnel of economic necessity into daylight."

This was written forty years ago and since then, of course, things have speeded up considerably. Maybe we do not even have to wait for another sixty years until universal plenty will be attained. In any case, the Keynesian message is clear enough: Beware! Ethical considerations are not merely irrelevant, they are an actual hindrance, "for foul is useful and fair is not." The time for fairness is not yet. The road to heaven is paved with bad intentions.

I shall now consider this proposition. It can be divided into three parts:

First, that universal prosperity is possible;
Second, that its attainment is possible on the basis of the materialist philosophy of "enrich yourselves";
Third, that this is the road to peace.

The question with which to start my investigation is obviously this: Is there enough to go round? Immediately we encounter a serious difficulty: What is "enough"? Who can tell us? Certainly not the economist who pursues "economic growth" as the highest of all values, and therefore has no concept of "enough." There are poor societies which have too little; but where is the rich society that says: "Halt! We have enough"? There is none.

Perhaps we can forget about "enough" and content ourselves with exploring the growth of demand upon the world's resources which arises when everybody simply strives hard to have "more." As we cannot study all resources, I propose to focus attention on one type of resource which is in a somewhat central position—fuel.

More prosperity means a greater use of fuel—there can be no doubt about that. At present, the prosperity gap between the poor of this world and the rich is very wide indeed, and this is clearly shown in their respective fuel consumption. Let us define as "rich" all populations in countries with an average fuel consumption—in 1966—of more than one metric ton of coal equivalent (abbreviated: c.e.) per head, and as "poor" all those below this level. On these definitions we can draw up the following table (using United Nations figures throughout).

TABLE I (1966)

	Rich	(%)	Poor	(%)	World	(%)
Population (millions)	1,060	(31)	2,284	(69)	3,384	(100)
Fuel Consumption (million tons c.e.)	4,788	(87)	721	(13)	5,509	(100)
Fuel Consumption per Head (tons c.e.)	4.52		0.32		1.65	

The average fuel consumption per head of the "poor" is only 0.32 tons—roughly one-fourteenth of that of the "rich," and there are very many "poor" people in the world—on these definitions nearly seven-tenths of the world population. If the "poor" suddenly used as much fuel as the "rich," world fuel consumption would treble right away.

But this cannot happen, as everything takes time. And in time both the "rich" and the "poor" are growing in desires and in numbers. So let us make an exploratory calculation. If the "rich" populations grow at the rate of $1^1/4$ per cent and the "poor" at the rate of $2^1/2$ per cent a year, world population will grow to about 6,900 million by 2000 A.D.—a figure not very different from the most authoritative current forecasts. If at the same time the fuel consumption *per head* of the "rich" population grows by 2^1/$_4$ per cent, while that of the "poor" grows by 4^1/$_2$ per cent a year, the following figures will emerge for the year 2000 A.D.

TABLE II

	Rich	(%)	Poor	(%)	World	(%)
Population (millions)	1,617	(23)	5,292	(77)	6,909	(100)
Fuel Consumption (million tons c.e.)	15,588	(67)	7,568	(33)	23,156	(100)
Fuel Consumption per Head (tons c.e.)	9.64		1.43		3.35	

The total result on world fuel consumption would be a growth from 5.5 billion tons c.e. in 1966 to 23.2 billion in the year 2000—an increase by a factor of more than four, half of which would be attributable to population increase and half to increased consumption per head.

This half-and-half split is interesting enough. But the split between the "rich" and the "poor" is even more interesting. Of the total increase in world fuel consumption from 5.5 billion to 23.2 billion tons c.e., i.e. an increase by 17.7 billion tons, the "rich" would account for nearly two-thirds and the "poor" for only a little over one-third. Over the whole thirty-four-year period, the world would use 425 billion tons of coal equivalent, with the "rich" using 321 billions or seventy-five per cent, and the "poor," 104 billions.

Now, does not this put a very interesting light on the total situation? These figures are not, of course, predictions: they are what might be called "exploratory calculations." I have assumed a very modest population growth on the part of the "rich"; and a population growth rate twice as high on the part of the "poor"; yet it is the "rich" and not the "poor" who do by far the greatest part of the damage—if "damage" it may be called. Even if the populations classified as "poor" grew only at the rate assumed for the "rich," the effect on total world fuel requirements would be hardly significant—a reduction of just over ten per cent. But if the "rich" decided—and I am not saying that this is likely—that their present *per capita* fuel consumption was really high enough and that they should not allow it to grow any further, considering that it is already fourteen times as high as that of the "poor"—now, that *would* make a difference: in spite of the assumed rise in the "rich" populations, it would cut total world fuel requirements in the year 2000 by over one-third.

The most important comment, however, is a question: Is it plausible to assume that world fuel consumption *could* grow to anything like 23,000 million tons c.e. a year by the year 2000, using 425,000 million tons c.e. during the thirty-four years in question? In the light of our present knowledge of fossil fuel reserves this is an implausible figure, even if we assume that one-quarter or one-third of the world total would come from nuclear fission.

It is clear that the "rich" are in the process of stripping the world of its once-for-all endowment of relatively cheap and simple fuels. It is their continuing economic growth which produces ever more exorbitant demands, with the result that the world's cheap and simple fuels could easily become dear and scarce long before the poor countries had acquired the wealth, education, industrial sophistication, and power of capital accumulation needed for the application of alternative fuels on any significant scale.

Exploratory calculations, of course, do not *prove* anything. A *proof* about the future is in any case impossible, and it has been sagely remarked that all predictions are unreliable, particularly those about the future. What is required is judgement, and exploratory calculations can at least help to inform our judgement. In any case, our calculations in a most important respect *understate* the magnitude of the problem. It is not realistic to treat the world as a unit. Fuel resources are very unevenly distributed, and any shortage of supplies, no matter how slight, would immediately divide the world into "haves" and "have-nots" along entirely novel lines. The specially favoured areas, such as the Middle East and North Africa, would attract envious attention on a scale scarcely imaginable today, while some high consumption areas, such as Western Europe and Japan, would move into the unenviable position of residual legatees. Here is a source of conflict if ever there was one.

As nothing can be *proved* about the future—not even about the

- *Area of productive land and ecosystems required to sustain the consumer lifestyle of the average North American with prevailing technology—the per capita ecological footprint: seven to nine hectares.*
- *Area of ecologically productive land and water per person on earth: two hectares.*
- *Number of earth-like planets that would be required in the year 2000, with prevailing technology, to support the entire human population sustainably at North American material standards: five.*
  —WILLIAM REES

relatively short-term future of the next thirty years—it is always possible to dismiss even the most threatening problems with the suggestion that something will turn up. There could be simply enormous and altogether unheard-of discoveries of new reserves of oil, natural gas, or even coal. And why should nuclear energy be confined to supplying one-quarter or one-third of total requirements? The problem can thus be shifted to another plane, but it refuses to go away. For the consumption of fuel on the indicated scale—assuming no insurmountable difficulties of fuel supply— would produce environmental hazards of an unprecedented kind.

Take nuclear energy. Some people say that the world's resources of relatively concentrated uranium are insufficient to sustain a really large nuclear programme—large enough to have a significant impact on the world fuel situation, where we have to reckon with thousands of millions, not simply with millions, of tons of coal equivalent. But assume that these people are wrong. Enough uranium will be found; it will be gathered together from the remotest corners of the earth, brought into the main centres of population, and made highly radioactive. It is hard to imagine a greater biological threat, not to mention the political danger that someone might use a tiny bit of this terrible substance for purposes not altogether peaceful.

On the other hand, if fantastic new discoveries of fossil fuels should make it unnecessary to force the pace of nuclear energy, there would be a problem of thermal pollution on quite a different scale from anything encountered hitherto.

Whatever the fuel, increases in fuel consumption by a factor of four and then five and then six . . . there is no plausible answer to the problem of pollution.

I have taken fuel merely as an example to illustrate a very simple thesis: that economic growth, which viewed from the point of view of economics, physics, chemistry, and technology, has no discernible limit, must necessarily run into decisive bottlenecks when viewed from the point of view of the environmental sciences. An attitude to life which seeks fulfillment in the single-minded pursuit of wealth—in short, materialism—does not fit into this world, because it contains within itself no limiting principle, while the environment in which it is placed is strictly limited. Already, the environment is trying to tell us that certain stresses are becoming excessive. As one problem is being "solved," ten new problems arise as a result of the first "solution." As Professor Barry Commoner emphasises, the new problems are not the consequences of incidental failure but of technological success.

Here again, however, many people will insist on discussing these matters solely in terms of optimism and pessimism, taking pride in their own optimism that "science will find a way out." They could be right only, I suggest, if there is a conscious and fundamental change in the *direction* of scientific effort. The developments of science and technology over the last hundred years have been such that the dangers have grown even faster than the opportunities. About this, I shall have more to say later.

Already, there is overwhelming evidence that the great self-balancing system of nature is becoming increasingly unbalanced in particular respects and at specific points. It would take us too far if I attempted to assemble the evidence here. The condition of Lake Erie, to which Professor Barry Commoner, among others, has drawn attention, should serve as a sufficient warning. Another decade or two, and all the inland water systems of the United States may be in a similar condition. In other words, the condition of unbalance may then no longer apply to specific points but have become generalised. The further this process is allowed to go, the more difficult it will be to reverse it, if indeed the point of no return has not been passed already.

We find, therefore, that the idea of unlimited economic growth, more and more until everybody is saturated with wealth, needs to be seriously questioned on at least two counts: the availability of basic resources and, alternatively or additionally, the capacity of the environment to cope with the degree of interference implied. So much about the physical-material aspect of the matter. Let us now turn to certain non-material aspects.

There can be no doubt that the idea of personal enrichment has a very strong appeal to human nature. Keynes, in the essay from which I have quoted already, advised us that the time was not yet for

With 10,000 people arriving every hour, and per-capita availability of resources and ecosystem services dropping by one-half to one-third over the next 50 years, no one can accurately predict when a limitation in a given resource or ecosystem service will affect commerce and society. Nevertheless, in the coming years and decades, it is clear that the value of natural capital will shift accordingly. And this inexorable shift, if recognized and accounted for in a timely way, will do much to change the scale, nature, and purpose of industrial society.
—PAUL HAWKEN

a "return to some of the most sure and certain principles of religion and traditional virtue—that avarice is a vice, that the exaction of usury is a misdemeanour, and the love of money is detestable."

Economic progress, he counselled, is obtainable only if we employ those powerful human drives of selfishness, which religion and traditional wisdom universally call upon us to resist. The modern economy is propelled by a frenzy of greed and indulges in an orgy of envy, and these are not accidental features but the very causes of its expansionist success. The question is whether such causes can be effective for long or whether they carry within themselves the seeds of destruction. If Keynes says that "foul is useful and fair is not," he propounds a statement of fact which may be true or false; or it may look true in the short run and turn out to be false in the longer run. Which is it?

I should think that there is now enough evidence to demonstrate that the statement is false in a very direct, practical sense. If human vices such as greed and envy are systematically cultivated, the inevitable result is nothing less than a collapse of intelligence. A man driven by greed or envy loses the power of seeing things as they really are, of seeing things in their roundness and wholeness, and his very successes become failures. If whole societies become infected by these vices, they may indeed achieve astonishing things but they become increasingly incapable of solving the most elementary problems of everyday existence. The Gross National Product may rise rapidly: as measured by statisticians but not as experienced by actual people, who find themselves oppressed by increasing frustration, alienation, insecurity, and so forth. After a while, even the Gross National Product refuses to rise any further, not because of scientific or technological failure, but because of a creeping paralysis of non-cooperation, as expressed in various types of escapism on the part, not only of the oppressed and exploited, but even of highly privileged groups.

One can go on for a long time deploring the irrationality and stupidity of men and women in high positions or low—"if only people would realise where their real interests lie!" But why do they not realise this? Either because their intelligence has been dimmed by greed and envy, or because in their heart of hearts they understand that their real interests lie somewhere quite different. There is a revolutionary saying that "Man shall not live by bread alone but by every word of God."

Here again, nothing can be "proved." But does it still look probable or plausible that the grave social diseases infecting many rich societies today are merely passing phenomena which an able government—if only we could get a really able government!—could eradicate by simply making faster use of science and technology or a more radical use of the penal system?

I suggest that the foundations of peace cannot be laid by universal prosperity, in the modern sense, because such prosperity, if attainable at all, is attainable only by cultivating such drives of human nature as greed and envy, which destroy intelligence, happiness, serenity, and thereby the peacefulness of man. It could well be that rich people treasure peace more highly than poor people, but only if they feel utterly secure—and this is a contradiction in terms. Their wealth depends on making inordinately large demands on limited world resources and thus puts them on an unavoidable collision course—not primarily with the poor (who are weak and defenceless) but with other rich people.

In short, we can say today that man is far too clever to be able to survive without wisdom. No one is really working for peace unless he is working primarily for the restoration of wisdom. The assertion that "foul is useful and fair is not" is the antithesis of wisdom. The hope that the pursuit of goodness and virtue can be postponed until we have attained universal prosperity and that by the single-minded pursuit of wealth, without bothering our heads about spiritual and moral questions, we could establish peace on earth, is an unrealistic, unscientific, and irrational hope. The exclusion of wisdom from economics, science, and technology was something which we could perhaps get away with for a little while, as long as we were relatively unsuccessful; but now that we have become very successful, the problem of spiritual and moral truth moves into the central position.

From an economic point of view, the central concept of wisdom is permanence. We must study the economics of permanence. Nothing makes economic sense unless its continuance for a long

Achieving sustainable community economic development means emphasizing sustainable employment and economic demand management (EDM). Sustainable employment includes: turning wastes into resources (e.g., recycling); improving efficiency with regard to energy and materials; converting to greater reliance on renewable energy sources; increasing community self-reliance (e.g., food and energy production); and sustainable management of natural resources (e.g., community forestry). EDM shifts our economic development emphasis from the traditional concern with increasing growth to reducing social dependence on economic growth.

—MARK ROSELAND

time can be projected without running into absurdities. There can be "growth" towards a limited objective, but there cannot be unlimited, generalised growth. It is more than likely, as Gandhi said, that "Earth provides enough to satisfy every man's need, but not for every man's greed." Permanence is incompatible with a predatory attitude which rejoices in the fact that "what were luxuries for our fathers have become necessities for us."

The cultivation and expansion of needs is the antithesis of wisdom. It is also the antithesis of freedom and peace. Every increase of needs tends to increase one's dependence on outside forces over which one cannot have control, and therefore increases existential fear. Only by a reduction of needs can one promote a genuine reduction in those tensions which are the ultimate causes of strife and war.

The economics of permanence implies a profound reorientation of science and technology, which have to open their doors to wisdom and, in fact, have to incorporate wisdom into their very structure. Scientific or technological "solutions" which poison the environment or degrade the social structure and man himself are of no benefit, no matter how brilliantly conceived or how great their superficial attraction. Ever-bigger machines, entailing ever-bigger concentrations of economic power and exerting ever-greater violence against the environment, do not represent progress: they are a denial of wisdom. Wisdom demands a new orientation of science and technology towards the organic, the gentle, the non-violent, the elegant and beautiful. Peace, as has often been said, is indivisible—how then could peace be built on a foundation of reckless science and violent technology? We must look for a revolution in technology to give us inventions and machines which reverse the destructive trends now threatening us all.

What is it that we really require from the scientists and technologists? I should answer: We need methods and equipment which are

—cheap enough so that they are accessible to virtually everyone;
—suitable for small-scale application; and
—compatible with man's need for creativity.

Out of these three characteristics is born non-violence and a relationship of man to nature which guarantees permanence. If only one of these three is neglected, things are bound to go wrong. Let us look at them one by one.

Methods and machines cheap enough to be accessible to virtually everyone—why should we assume that our scientists and technologists are unable to develop them? This was a primary concern of Gandhi: "I want the dumb millions of our land to be healthy and happy, and I want them to grow spiritually.... If we feel the need of machines, we certainly will have them. Every machine that helps every individual has a place," he said, "but there should be no place for machines that concentrate power in a few hands and turn the masses into mere machine minders, if indeed they do not make them unemployed."

Suppose it becomes the acknowledged purpose of inventors and engineers, observed Aldous Huxley, to provide ordinary people with the means of "doing profitable and intrinsically significant work, of helping men and women to achieve independence from bosses, so that they may become their own employers, or members of a self-governing, cooperative group working for subsistence and a local market...this differently orientated technological progress [would result in] a progressive decentralisation of population, of accessibility of land, of ownership of the means of production, of political and economic power." Other advantages, said Huxley, would be "a more humanly satisfying life for more people, a greater measure of genuine self-governing democracy and a blessed freedom from the silly or pernicious adult education provided by the mass producers of consumer goods through the medium of advertisements."[1]

If methods and machines are to be cheap enough to be generally accessible, this means that their cost must stand in some definable relationship to the level of incomes in the society in which they are to be used. I have myself come to the conclusion that the upper limit for the average amount of capital investment *per workplace* is probably given by the annual earnings of an able and ambitious industrial worker. That is to say, if such a man can normally earn, say $5,000 a year, the average cost of establishing his workplace should on no account be in excess of $5,000. If the cost is significantly

Schumacher argued that many small acts of erosion cannot be as bad as a big one. But China has the worst erosion from many small acts of land abuse over a longer period of history. Isn't the real issue how to harmonize the big, the mid, and the little for the benefit of the "globalocal" communities, and not put global and local in the ring as opponents?
—PETER WARSHALL

higher, the society in question is likely to run into serious troubles, such as an undue concentration of wealth and power among the privileged few; an increasing problem of "drop-outs" who cannot be integrated into society and constitute an ever-growing threat; "structural" unemployment; maldistribution of the population due to excessive urbanisation; and general frustration and alienation, with soaring crime rates, and so forth.

The second requirement is suitability for small-scale application. On the problem of "scale," Professor Leopold Kohr has written brilliantly and convincingly; its relevance to the economics of permanence is obvious. Small-scale operations, no matter how numerous, are always less likely to be harmful to the natural environment than large-scale ones, simply because their individual force is small in relation to the recuperative forces of nature. There is wisdom in smallness if only on account of the smallness and patchiness of human knowledge, which relies on experiment far more than on understanding. The greatest danger invariably arises from the ruthless application, on a vast scale, of partial knowledge such as we are currently witnessing in the application of nuclear energy, of the new chemistry in agriculture, of transportation technology, and countless other things.

Although even small communities are sometimes guilty of causing serious erosion, generally as a result of ignorance, this is trifling in comparison with the devastations caused by gigantic groups motivated by greed, envy, and the lust for power. It is, moreover, obvious that men organised in small units will take better care of *their* bit of land or other natural resources than anonymous companies or megalomanic governments which pretend to themselves that the whole universe is their legitimate quarry.

The third requirement is perhaps the most important of all—that methods and equipment should be such as to leave ample room for human creativity. Over the last hundred years no one has spoken more insistently and warningly on this subject than have the Roman pontiffs. What becomes of man if the process of production "takes away from work any hint of humanity, making of it a merely mechanical activity?" The worker himself is turned into a perversion of a free being.

"And so bodily labour [said Pius XI] which even after original sin was decreed by Providence for the good of man's body and soul, is in many instances changed into an instrument of perversion; for from the factory dead matter goes out improved, whereas men there are corrupted and degraded."

Again, the subject is so large that I cannot do more than touch upon it. Above anything else there is need for a proper philosophy of work which understands work not as that which it has indeed become, an inhuman chore as soon as possible to be abolished by automation, but as something "decreed by Providence for the good of man's body and soul." Next to the family, it is work and the relationships established by work that are the true foundations of society. If the foundations are unsound, how could society be sound? And if society is sick, how could it fail to be a danger to peace?

"War is a judgement," said Dorothy L. Sayers, "that overtakes societies when they have been living upon ideas that conflict too violently with the laws governing the universe.... Never think that wars are irrational catastrophes: they happen when wrong ways of thinking and living bring about intolerable situations."[2] Economically, our wrong living consists primarily in systematically cultivating greed and envy and thus building up a vast array of totally unwarrantable wants. It is the sin of greed that has delivered us over into the power of the machine. If greed were not the master of modern man—ably assisted by envy—how could it be that the frenzy of economism does not abate as higher "standards of living" are attained, and that it is precisely the richest societies which pursue their economic advantage with the greatest ruthlessness? How could we explain the almost universal refusal on the part of the rulers of the rich societies—whether organised along private enterprise or collectivist enterprise lines—to work towards *the humanisation of work?* It is only necessary to assert that something would reduce the "standard of living," and every debate is instantly closed. That soul-destroying, meaningless, mechanical, monotonous, moronic work is an insult to human nature which must necessarily and inevitably produce either escapism or aggression, and that no amount of "bread and circuses" can compensate for the damage done—these are facts which are neither denied nor acknowledged

Our garden proves that what we do with our lives is never absolute and that traditional thinking yields traditional and expected results. It also proves that though our actions may be small, the impact of our actions can reach far beyond us.

We began small, with land and dirt—work to be done and hands willing to do it. Sometime during their time working the earth, our participants—former prisoners—learn the reality of Schumacher's affirmation: "The difference between a man and a stone is little more than a deceptive appearance." They learn to care for another living thing. Then, as they watch these plants grow, they learn to care for themselves, and they grow.

And they grow other people. They bring their families and friends to our garden. They bring the food they ➨

but are met with an unbreakable conspiracy of silence—because to deny them would be too obviously absurd and to acknowledge them would condemn the central preoccupation of modern society as a crime against humanity.

The neglect, indeed the rejection, of wisdom has gone so far that most of our intellectuals have not even the faintest idea what the term could mean. As a result, they always tend to try and cure a disease by intensifying its causes. The disease having been caused by allowing cleverness to displace wisdom, no amount of clever research is likely to produce a cure. But what is wisdom? Where can it be found? Here we come to the crux of the matter: it can be read about in numerous publications but it can be *found* only inside oneself. To be able to find it, one has first to liberate oneself from such masters as greed and envy. The stillness following liberation—even if only momentary—produces the insights of wisdom which are obtainable in no other way.

They enable us to see the hollowness and fundamental unsatisfactoriness of a life devoted primarily to the pursuit of material ends, to the neglect of the spiritual. Such a life necessarily sets man against man and nation against nation, because man's needs are infinite and infinitude can be achieved only in the spiritual realm, never in the material. Man assuredly needs to rise above this humdrum "world"; wisdom shows him the way to do it; without wisdom, he is driven to build up a monster economy, which destroys the world, and to seek fantastic satisfactions, like landing a man on the moon. Instead of overcoming the "world" by moving towards saintliness, he tries to overcome it by gaining pre-eminence in wealth, power, science, or indeed any imaginable "sport."

These are the real causes of war, and it is chimerical to try to lay the foundations of peace without removing them first. It is doubly chimerical to build peace on economic foundations which, in turn, rest on the systematic cultivation of greed and envy, the very forces which drive men into conflict.

How could we even begin to disarm greed and envy? Perhaps by being much less greedy and envious ourselves; perhaps by resisting the temptation of letting our luxuries become needs; and perhaps by even scrutinising our needs to see if they cannot be simplified and reduced. If we do not have the strength to do any of this, could we perhaps stop applauding the type of economic "progress" which palpably lacks the basis of permanence and give what modest support we can to those who, unafraid of being denounced as cranks, work for non-violence: as conservationists, ecologists, protectors of wildlife, promoters of organic agriculture, distributists, cottage producers, and so forth? An ounce of practice is generally worth more than a ton of theory.

It will need many ounces, however, to lay the economic foundations of peace. Where can one find the strength to go on working against such obviously appalling odds? What is more: where can one find the strength to overcome the violence of greed, envy, hate, and lust within oneself?

I think Gandhi has given the answer: "There must be recognition of the existence of the soul apart from the body, and of its permanent nature, and this recognition must amount to a living faith; and, in the last resort, non-violence does not avail those who do not possess a living faith in the God of Love."

➡ *grow home to their families and communities. The disease of many communities and of many people, as Schumacher predicted, is metaphysical, which as our garden proves, is the beginning of a cure.*

—CATHERINE SNEED

CHAPTER 3

THE ROLE OF ECONOMICS

To say that our economic future is being determined by the economists would be an exaggeration; but that their influence, or in any case the influence of economists, is far-reaching can hardly be doubted. Economics plays a central role in shaping the activities of the modern world, inasmuch as it supplies the criteria of what is "economic" and what is "uneconomic," and there is no other set of criteria that exercises a greater influence over the actions of individuals and groups as well as over those of governments. It may be thought, therefore, that we should look to the economists for advice on how to overcome the dangers and difficulties in which the modern world finds itself, and how to achieve economic arrangements that vouchsafe peace and permanence.

How *does* economics relate to the problems discussed in the previous chapters? When the economist delivers a verdict that this or that activity is "economically sound" or "uneconomic," two important and closely related questions arise: First, what does this verdict mean? And, second, is the verdict conclusive in the sense that practical action can reasonably be based on it?

Going back into history we may recall that when there was talk about founding a professorship for political economy at Oxford 150 years ago, many people were by no means happy about the prospect. Edward Copleston, the great Provost of Oriel College, did not want to admit into the University's curriculum a science "so prone to usurp the rest"; even Henry Drummond of Albury Park, who endowed the professorship in 1825, felt it necessary to make it clear that he expected the University to keep the new study "in its proper place." The first professor, Nassau Senior, was certainly not to be kept in an *inferior* place. Immediately, in his inaugural lecture, he predicted that the new science "will rank in public estimation among the first of moral sciences in interest and in utility" and claimed that "the pursuit of wealth...is, to the mass of mankind, the great source of moral improvement." Not all economists, to be sure, have staked their claims quite so high. John Stuart Mill (1806–73) looked upon political economy "not as a thing by itself, but as a fragment of a greater whole; a branch of social philosophy, so interlinked with all the other branches that its conclusions, even in its own peculiar province, are only true conditionally, subject to interference and counteraction from causes not directly within its scope." And even Keynes, in contradiction to his own advice (already quoted) that "avarice and usury and precaution must be our gods for a little longer still," admonished us not to "overestimate the importance of the economic problem, or sacrifice to its supposed necessities other matters of greater and more permanent significance."

Such voices, however, are but seldom heard today. It is hardly an exaggeration to say that, with increasing affluence, economics has moved into the very centre of public concern, and economic performance, economic growth, economic expansion, and so forth have become the abiding interest, if not the obsession, of all modern societies. In the current vocabulary of condemnation there are few words as final and conclusive as the word "uneconomic." If an activity has been branded as uneconomic, its right to existence is not merely questioned but energetically denied. Anything that is found to be an impediment to economic growth is a shameful thing, and if people cling to it, they are thought of as either saboteurs or fools. Call a thing immoral or ugly, soul-destroying or a degradation of man, a peril to the peace of the world or to the well-being of future generations; as long as you have not shown it to be "uneconomic" you have not really questioned its right to exist, grow, and prosper.

But what does it *mean* when we say something is uneconomic? I am not asking what most people mean when they say this; because that is clear enough. They simply mean that it is like an

Schumacher argued that
profitability alone is not
an adequate measure of
whether something is
"economic" or not. A new
economics is needed that
takes into account not only
the profitability of a given
activity, but also its effect
upon people and the envi-
ronment, including the
resource base.

—GEORGE MᶜROBIE

illness: you are better off without it. The economist is supposed to be able to diagnose the illness and then, with luck and skill, remove it. Admittedly, economists often disagree among each other about the diagnosis and, even more frequently, about the cure; but that merely proves that the subject matter is uncommonly difficult and economists, like other humans, are fallible.

No, I am asking what *it* means, *what sort of meaning the method of economics actually produces*. And the answer to this question cannot be in doubt: something is uneconomic when it fails to earn an adequate profit in terms of money. The method of economics does not, and cannot, produce any other meaning. Numerous attempts have been made to obscure this fact, and they have caused a very great deal of confusion; but the fact remains. Society, or a group or an individual within society, may decide to hang on to an activity or asset for *non-economic reasons*—social, aesthetic, moral, or political—but this does in no way alter its *uneconomic* character. The judgement of economics, in other words, is an extremely *fragmentary* judgement; out of the large number of aspects which in real life have to be seen and judged together before a decision can be taken, economics supplies only one—whether a thing yields a money profit *to those who undertake it* or not.

Do not overlook the words "to those who undertake it." It is a great error to assume, for instance, that the methodology of economics is normally applied to determine whether an activity carried on by a group within society yields a profit to society as a whole. Even nationalised industries are not considered from this more comprehensive point of view. Every one of them is given a financial target—which is, in fact, an obligation—and is expected to pursue this target without regard to any damage it might be inflicting on other parts of the economy. In fact, the prevailing creed, held with equal fervour by all political parties, is that the common good will necessarily be maximised if everybody, every industry and trade, whether nationalised or not, strives to earn an acceptable "return" on the capital employed. Not even Adam Smith had a more implicit faith in the "hidden hand" to ensure that "what is good for General Motors is good for the United States."

However that may be, about the *fragmentary* nature of the judgements of economics there can be no doubt whatever. Even within the narrow compass of the economic calculus, these judgements are necessarily and *methodically* narrow. For one thing, they give vastly more weight to the short than to the long term, because in the long term, as Keynes put it with cheerful brutality, we are all dead. And then, second, they are based on a definition of cost which excludes all "free goods," that is to say, the entire God-given environment, except for those parts of it that have been privately appropriated. This means that an activity can be economic although it plays hell with the environment, and that a competing activity, if at some cost it protects and conserves the environment, will be uneconomic.

Economics, moreover, deals with goods in accordance with their market value and not in accordance with what they really are. The same rules and criteria are applied to primary goods, which man has to win from nature, and secondary goods, which presuppose the existence of primary goods and are manufactured from them. All goods are treated the same, because the point of view is fundamentally that of private profit-making, and this means that it is inherent in the methodology of economics to *ignore man's dependence on the natural world.*

Another way of stating this is to say that economics deals with goods and services from the point of view of the market, where willing buyer meets willing seller. The buyer is essentially a bargain hunter; he is not concerned with the origin of the goods or the conditions under which they have been produced. His sole concern is to obtain the best value for his money.

The market therefore represents only the surface of society and its significance relates to the momentary situation as it exists there and then. There is no probing into the depths of things, into the natural or social facts that lie behind them. In a sense, the market is the institutionalisation of individualism and non-responsibility. Neither buyer nor seller is responsible for anything but himself. It would be "uneconomic" for a wealthy seller to reduce his prices to poor customers merely because they are in need, or for a wealthy buyer to pay an extra price merely because the supplier is poor. Equally, it would be "uneconomic" for a buyer to give preference to

"Global economy" is the most sobering phrase for the future of the planet. It is like a super, free-ranging, buccaneer battleship using electronics as weapons. The only rule is "winner take all." It knows no boundaries or rules and roves land and sea making profits and destroying natural and human heritage heedlessly. It needs no windows to look out on the plant, animal, and human targets it is ravaging. Information comes through computer screens and destruction takes place with a tap on a keyboard. And what is this global economy delivering? Cheaper consumer products. But our heritage and future options are being sacrificed on the altar of "better shopping."

—ROBERT BATEMAN

home-produced goods if imported goods are cheaper. He does not, and is not expected to, accept responsibility for the country's balance of payments.

As regards the buyer's non-responsibility, there is, significantly, one exception: the buyer must be careful not to buy stolen goods. This is a rule against which neither ignorance nor innocence counts as a defence and which can produce extraordinarily unjust and annoying results. It is nevertheless required by the sanctity of private property, to which it testifies.

To be relieved of all responsibility except to oneself, means of course an enormous simplification of business. We can recognise that it is practical and need not be surprised that it is highly popular among businessmen. What may cause surprise is that it is also considered virtuous to make the maximum use of this freedom from responsibility. If a buyer refused a good bargain because he suspected that the cheapness of the goods in question stemmed from exploitation or other despicable practices (except theft), he would be open to the criticism of behaving "uneconomically," which is viewed as nothing less than a fall from grace. Economists and others are wont to treat such eccentric behaviour with derision if not indignation. The religion of economics has its own code of ethics, and the First Commandment is to behave "economically"—in any case when you are producing, selling, or buying. It is only when the bargain hunter has gone home and becomes a consumer that the First Commandment no longer applies: he is then encouraged to "enjoy himself" in any way he pleases. As far as the religion of economics is concerned, the consumer is extra-territorial. This strange and significant feature of the modern world warrants more discussion than it has yet received.

In the market place, for practical reasons, innumerable qualitative distinctions which are of vital importance for man and society are suppressed; they are not allowed to surface. Thus the reign of quantity celebrates its greatest triumphs in "The Market." Everything is equated with everything else. To equate things means to give them a price and thus to make them exchangeable. To the extent that economic thinking is based on the market, it takes the sacredness out of life, because there can be nothing sacred in something that has a price. Not surprisingly, therefore, if economic thinking pervades the whole of society, even simple non-economic values like beauty, health, or cleanliness can survive only if they prove to be "economic."

To press non-economic values into the framework of the economic calculus, economists use the method of cost/benefit analysis. This is generally thought to be an enlightened and progressive development, as it is at least an attempt to take account of costs and benefits which might otherwise be disregarded altogether. In fact, however, it is a procedure by which the higher is reduced to the level of the lower and the priceless is given a price. It can therefore never serve to clarify the situation and lead to an enlightened decision. All it can do is lead to self-deception or the deception of others; for to undertake to measure the immeasurable is absurd and constitutes but an elaborate method of moving from preconceived notions to foregone conclusions; all one has to do to obtain the desired results is to impute suitable values to the immeasurable costs and benefits. The logical absurdity, however, is not the greatest fault of the undertaking: what is worse, and destructive of civilisation, is the pretence that everything has a price or, in other words, that money is the highest of all values.

Economics operates legitimately and usefully within a "given" framework which lies altogether outside the economic calculus. We might say that economics does not stand on its own feet, or that it is a "derived" body of thought—derived from meta-economics. If the economist fails to study meta-economics, or, even worse, if he remains unaware of the fact that there are boundaries to the applicability of the economic calculus, he is likely to fall into a similar kind of error to that of certain medieval theologians who tried to settle questions of physics by means of biblical quotations. Every science is beneficial within its proper limits, but becomes evil and destructive as soon as it transgresses them.

The science of economics is "so prone to usurp the rest"—even more so today than it was 150 years ago, when Edward Copleston pointed to this danger—because it relates to certain very strong drives of human nature, such as envy and greed. All the greater is the duty of its experts, the economists, to understand and clarify its limitations, that is to say, to understand meta-economics.

What, then, is meta-economics? As economics deals with man

Money, for all its obvious advantages, introduces an element of abstraction into the economic process. This was less so in the past, when real goods were used as currency, to back currency, or denominate units of currency. Value was still understood in terms of the amount of labor applied to natural resources. When the Tibetan herdsman traded a brick of tea (once used as currency in Tibet) for his lamb, he had a picture of tea brewing in a bucket over a fire, and could imagine the days it took to cultivate the tea plant on a mountainside plantation and the hours of bending to gather the tiny new tea leaves. He could compare in his mind the value of a generalized brick of tea to that of the actual lamb in his arms.

At the end of the 20th century, money has become altogether abstracted from our daily experience. We talk of earning six percent interest, but have no ➡

➡ *picture of "what our money is doing tonight"—whether it is working to build wheelbarrows in Brazil, grow corn on chemically fertilized land in Iowa, or make shoes in a crowded factory in Thailand.*

—SUSAN WITT

in his environment, we may expect that meta-economics consists of two parts—one dealing with man and the other dealing with the environment. In other words, we may expect that economics must derive its aims and objectives from a study of man, and that it must derive at least a large part of its methodology from a study of nature.

In the next chapter, I shall attempt to show how the conclusions and prescriptions of economics change as the underlying picture of man and his purpose on earth changes. In this chapter, I confine myself to a discussion of the second part of meta-economics, i.e. the way in which a vital part of the methodology of economics has to be derived from a study of nature. As I have emphasised already, on the market all goods are treated the same, because the market is essentially an institution for unlimited bargain hunting, and this means that it is inherent in the methodology of modern economics, which is so largely market-oriented, to ignore man's dependence on the natural world. Professor E.H. Phelps Brown, in his Presidential Address to the Royal Economic Society on "The Underdevelopment of Economics," talked about "the smallness of the contribution that the most conspicuous developments of economics in the last quarter of a century have made to the solution of the most pressing problems of the times," and among these problems he lists "checking the adverse effects on the environment and the quality of life of industrialism, population growth and urbanism."

As a matter of fact, to talk of "the smallness of the contribution" is to employ an euphemism, as there is no contribution at all; on the contrary, it would not be unfair to say that economics, as currently constituted and practised, acts as a most effective barrier against the understanding of these problems, owing to its addiction to purely quantitative analysis and its timorous refusal to look into the real nature of things.

Economics deals with a virtually limitless variety of goods and services, produced and consumed by an equally limitless variety of people. It would obviously be impossible to develop any economic theory at all, unless one were prepared to disregard a vast array of qualitative distinctions. But it should be just as obvious that the total suppression of qualitative distinctions, while it makes theorising easy, at the same time makes it totally sterile. Most of the "conspicuous developments of economics in the last quarter of a century" (referred to by Professor Phelps Brown) are in the direction of quantification, at the expense of the understanding of qualitative differences. Indeed, one might say that economics has become increasingly intolerant of the latter, because they do not fit into its method and make demands on the practical understanding and the power of insight of economists, which they are unwilling or unable to fulfill. For example, having established by his purely quantitative methods that the Gross National Product of a country has risen by, say, five per cent, the economist-turned-econometrician is unwilling, and generally unable, to face the question of whether this is to be taken as a good thing or a bad thing. He would lose all his certainties if he even entertained such a question: growth of GNP must be a good thing, irrespective of what has grown and who, if anyone, has benefited. The idea that there could be pathological growth, unhealthy growth, disruptive or destructive growth is to him a perverse idea which must not be allowed to surface. A small minority of economists is at present beginning to question how much further "growth" will be possible, since infinite growth in a finite environment is an obvious impossibility; but even they cannot get away from the purely quantitative growth concept. Instead of insisting on *the primacy of qualitative distinctions,* they simply substitute non-growth for growth, that is to say, one emptiness for another.

It is of course true that quality is much more difficult to "handle" than quantity, just as the exercise of judgement is a higher function than the ability to count and calculate. Quantitative differences can be more easily grasped and certainly more easily defined than qualitative differences; their concreteness is beguiling and gives them the appearance of scientific precision, even when this precision has been purchased by the suppression of vital differences of quality. The great majority of economists are still pursuing the absurd ideal of making their "science" as scientific and precise as physics, as if there were no qualitative difference between mindless atoms and men made in the image of God.

The main subject matter of economics is "goods." Economists make some rudimentary distinctions between categories of goods

The growing local currency movement is providing a positive way to respond to the alienation from the natural world fostered by an expanding global marketplace, and to restore the possibility of regional economies based on social and ecological principles. In a simple barter economy, production methods are highly visible. The value of the carrots we offer in trade is directly related to our memories of hoeing in the garden, of building the compost pile, and of waiting for the rain after planting. And though our picture of the cordwood for which we are bartering is not as detailed, still we probably have seen our neighbor as he split and stacked the wood from the ash tree. Barter transactions link us inextricably to a particular place and time.
—SUSAN WITT

from the point of view of the *purchaser,* such as the distinction between consumers' goods and producers' goods; but there is virtually no attempt to take cognisance of what such goods actually are; for instance, whether they are man-made or God-given, whether they are freely reproducible or not. Once any goods, whatever their meta-economic character, have appeared on the market, they are treated the same, as objects for sale, and economics is primarily concerned with theorising on the bargain-hunting activities of the purchaser.

It is a fact, however, that there are fundamental and vital differences between various categories of "goods" which cannot be disregarded without losing touch with reality. The following might be called a minimum scheme of categorisation:

"Goods"

Primary		Secondary	
Non-renewable	Renewable	Manufactures	Services
(1)	(2)	(3)	(4)

There could hardly be a more important distinction, to start with, than that between primary and secondary goods, because the latter presuppose the availability of the former. An expansion of man's ability to bring forth secondary products is useless unless preceded by an expansion of his ability to win primary products from the earth, for man is not a producer but only a converter, and for every job of conversion he needs primary products. In particular, his power to convert depends on primary energy, which immediately points to the need for a vital distinction within the field of primary goods, that between non-renewable and renewable. As far as secondary goods are concerned, there is an obvious and basic distinction between manufactures and services. We thus arrive at a minimum of four categories, each of which is *essentially* different from each of the three others.

The market knows nothing of these distinctions. It provides a price tag for all goods and thereby enables us to pretend that they are all of equal significance. £5 worth of oil (category 1) equals £5 worth of wheat (category 2), which equals £5 worth of shoes (category 3) or £5 worth of hotel accommodation (category 4). The sole criterion to determine the relative importance of these different goods is the rate of profit that can be obtained by providing them. If categories 3 and 4 yield higher profits than categories 1 and 2, this is taken as a "signal" that it is "rational" to put additional resources into the former and withdraw resources from the latter.

I am not here concerned with discussing the reliability or rationality of the market mechanism, of what economists call the "invisible hand." This has endlessly been discussed, but invariably without attention to the *basic incommensurability* of the four categories detailed above. It has remained unnoticed, for instance—or if not unnoticed, it has never been taken seriously in the formulation of economic theory—that the concept of "cost" is essentially different as between renewable and non-renewable goods, as also between manufactures and services. In fact, without going into any further details, it can be said that economics, as currently constituted, fully applies only to manufactures (category 3), but it is being applied without discrimination to all goods and services, because an appreciation of the essential, qualitative differences between the four categories is entirely lacking.

These differences may be called meta-economic, inasmuch as they have to be recognised before economic analysis begins. Even more important is the recognition of the existence of "goods" which never appear on the market, because they cannot be, or have not been, privately appropriated, but are nonetheless an essential precondition of all human activity, such as air, water, the soil, and in fact the whole framework of living nature.

Until fairly recently the economists have felt entitled, with tolerably good reason, to treat the entire framework within which economic activity takes place as *given,* that is to say, as permanent and indestructible. It was no part of their job and, indeed, of their professional competence, to study the effects of economic activity upon the framework. Since there is now increasing evidence of environmental deterioration, particularly in living nature, the entire outlook and methodology of economics is being called into question. The study of economics is too narrow and too fragmentary to

Schumacher detested economic gimmicks such as input/output analysis, which the U.S. government is making strides to implement as a means of understanding the flow of money in the economy. At our Center for Maximum Potential Building Systems we have overlaid federal environmental data onto the financial model to trace environmental impacts throughout the life cycle of an industrial product. We also use Geographic Information System techniques to find where environmental problems exist, such as greenhouse gas emissions and airborne pollutants.

By admitting the complexities of what has become a very complicated economic system, we are developing a tool that begins to face the immensity of the problem. Schumacher might have said that such an attempt at such a scale can never be true due to the "patchiness of human knowledge"; and that smallness, in which many tiny ➡

➡ *experiments give us the feedback necessary to take the next step, is the only way to find a solution. So our approach takes a different stand, partially because the small-is-beautiful approach probably would never be listened to by the powers that be.*
—PLINY FISK

lead to valid insights, unless complemented and completed by a study of meta-economics.

The trouble about valuing means above ends—which, as confirmed by Keynes, is the attitude of modern economics—is that it destroys man's freedom and power to choose the ends he really favours; the development of means, as it were, dictates the choice of ends. Obvious examples are the pursuit of supersonic transport speeds and the immense efforts made to land men on the moon. The conception of these aims was not the result of any insight into real human needs and aspirations, which technology is meant to serve, but solely of the fact that the necessary technical means appeared to be available.

As we have seen, economics is a 'derived' science which accepts instructions from what I call meta-economics. In the following chapter, we shall explore what economic laws and what definitions of the concepts "economic" and "uneconomic" result, when the meta-economic basis of Western materialism is abandoned and the teaching of Buddhism is put in its place. The choice of Buddhism for this purpose is purely incidental; the teachings of Christianity, Islam, or Judaism could have been used just as well as those of any other of the great Eastern traditions.

CHAPTER 4

BUDDHIST ECONOMICS

"RIGHT LIVELIHOOD" is one of the requirements of the Buddha's Noble Eightfold Path. It is clear, therefore, that there must be such a thing as Buddhist economics.

Buddhist countries have often stated that they wish to remain faithful to their heritage. So Burma: "The New Burma sees no conflict between religious values and economic progress. Spiritual health and material well-being are not enemies: they are natural allies." Or: "We can blend successfully the religious and spiritual values of our heritage with the benefits of modern technology."[2] Or: "We Burmans have a sacred duty to conform both our dreams and our acts to our faith. This we shall ever do."[3]

All the same, such countries invariably assume that they can model their economic development plans in accordance with modern economics, and they call upon modern economists from so-called advanced countries to advise them, to formulate the policies to be pursued, and to construct the grand design for development, the Five-Year Plan or whatever it may be called. No one seems to think that a Buddhist way of life would call for Buddhist economics, just as the modern materialist way of life has brought forth modern economics.

Economists themselves, like most specialists, normally suffer from a kind of metaphysical blindness, assuming that theirs is a science of absolute and invariable truths, without any presuppositions. Some go as far as to claim that economic laws are as free from "metaphysics" or "values" as the law of gravitation. We need not, however, get involved in arguments of methodology. Instead, let us

Fritz spent all his free time in Burma studying Buddhism. He spent his weekends in a monastery and studied under Buddhist scholars. "I then began to ask myself," he said, "What would a Buddhist economics look like? And I concluded that it would be the exact opposite of our Western economics."

First, he argued, a Buddhist approach to economics would distinguish between misery, sufficiency, and surfeit. Economic growth would be good only to the point of sufficiency. Limitless growth and consumption would be disastrous. Secondly, a Buddhist economics would be based squarely on renewable resources: an economics of permanence. In contrast, Western economics is based on the ruthless exploitation of nonrenewable resources, and recognizes no limits to production and consumption—a nonsustainable system.

—GEORGE McROBIE

When Schumacher was an economist working for the British government, he was sent to Burma to advise the people and their government on how to develop economically using technologic, scientific, advanced techniques of "progress." After a few months he realized that the Burmese did not need this Western style of development and technological agriculture. They had their own perfectly good economic system, which he called "Buddhist economics."

When he returned to Great Britain, he wrote the essay, "Buddhist Economics," and gave it to his fellow economists in government. They said: "Mr. Schumacher, economics is all very well, but what does Buddhism have to do with it?" Schumacher replied: "Economics without Buddhism, i.e. without spiritual, human, and ecological values, is like sex without love."

—SATISH KUMAR

take some fundamentals and see what they look like when viewed by a modern economist and a Buddhist economist.

There is universal agreement that a fundamental source of wealth is human labour. Now, the modern economist has been brought up to consider "labour" or work as little more than a necessary evil. From the point of view of the employer, it is in any case simply an item of cost, to be reduced to a minimum if it cannot be eliminated altogether, say, by automation. From the point of view of the workman, it is a "disutility"; to work is to make a sacrifice of one's leisure and comfort, and wages are a kind of compensation for the sacrifice. Hence the ideal from the point of view of the employer is to have output without employees, and the ideal from the point of view of the employee is to have income without employment.

The consequences of these attitudes both in theory and in practice are, of course, extremely far-reaching. If the ideal with regard to work is to get rid of it, every method that "reduces the work load" is a good thing. The most potent method, short of automation, is the so-called "division of labour" and the classical example is the pin factory eulogised in Adam Smith's *Wealth of Nations*.[4] Here it is not a matter of ordinary specialisation, which mankind has practised from time immemorial, but of dividing up every complete process of production into minute parts, so that the final product can be produced at great speed without anyone having had to contribute more than a totally insignificant and, in most cases, unskilled movement of his limbs.

The Buddhist point of view takes the function of work to be at least threefold: to give a man a chance to utilise and develop his faculties; to enable him to overcome his ego-centredness by joining with other people in a common task; and to bring forth the goods and services needed for a becoming existence. Again, the consequences that flow from this view are endless. To organise work in such a manner that it becomes meaningless, boring, stultifying, or nerve-racking for the worker would be little short of criminal; it would indicate a greater concern with goods than with people, an evil lack of compassion and a soul-destroying degree of attachment to the most primitive side of this worldly existence. Equally, to strive for leisure as an alternative to work would be considered a complete misunderstanding of one of the basic truths of human existence, namely that work and leisure are complementary parts of the same living process and cannot be separated without destroying the joy of work and the bliss of leisure.

From the Buddhist point of view, there are therefore two types of mechanisation which must be clearly distinguished: one that enhances a man's skill and power and one that turns the work of man over to a mechanical slave, leaving man in a position of having to serve the slave. How to tell the one from the other? "The craftsman himself," says Ananda Coomaraswamy, a man equally competent to talk about the modern West as the ancient East, "can always, if allowed to, draw the delicate distinction between the machine and the tool. The carpet loom is a tool, a contrivance for holding warp threads at a stretch for the pile to be woven round them by the craftsmen's fingers; but the power loom is a machine, and its significance as a destroyer of culture lies in the fact that it does the essentially human part of the work."[5] It is clear, therefore, that Buddhist economics must be very different from the economics of modern materialism, since the Buddhist sees the essence of civilisation not in a multiplication of wants but in the purification of human character. Character, at the same time, is formed primarily by a man's work. And work, properly conducted in conditions of human dignity and freedom, blesses those who do it and equally their products. The Indian philosopher and economist J.C. Kumarappa sums the matter up as follows:

> If the nature of the work is properly appreciated and applied, it will stand in the same relation to the higher faculties as food is to the physical body. It nourishes and enlivens the higher man and urges him to produce the best he is capable of. It directs his free will along the proper course and disciplines the animal in him into progressive channels. It furnishes an excellent background for man to display his scale of values and develop his personality.[6]

If a man has no chance of obtaining work he is in a desperate position, not simply because he lacks an income but because he lacks this nourishing and enlivening factor of disciplined work

By focusing on a foreign country such as Burma, Schumacher gave us the nonthreatening means to look for and question the root values of our own lives and Western culture. He helped us seek a root intention that would bring us back into harmony with the cosmos and give new direction to our lives. Out of this has arisen new economics, new sciences, new patterns of living and learning—in total, the transformation of all aspects of our lives, which is bringing into being a vibrant new culture within the shell of the old.
—TOM BENDER

*One issue about which Fritz
and I agreed to disagree was
the role of women in society.
Schumacher was a product
of his European culture and
era. I was just emerging into
my own feminist awareness.
We both admired the loving,
caring, sharing role that
women had so faithfully
played through most of
human history. However,
Schumacher, like many of
our male colleagues at that
time, still believed that only
women could nurture chil-
dren and the local commu-
nity. These beliefs, of course,
are no longer tenable today
—especially as we learn that
gender-equity is essential if
we are to redirect our societies in more peaceful,
sustainable paths.
  Yet Fritz encouraged my
determination to account for
the "Love Economy"—50
percent of all useful products
and services in even industrial
societies which are unpaid
and largely produced by ➠*

which nothing can replace. A modern economist may engage in
highly sophisticated calculations on whether full employment
"pays" or whether it might be more "economic" to run an economy
at less than full employment so as to ensure a greater mobility of
labour, a better stability of wages, and so forth. His fundamental
criterion of success is simply the total quantity of goods produced
during a given period of time. "If the marginal urgency of goods is
low," says Professor Galbraith in *The Affluent Society,* "then so is the
urgency of employing the last man or the last million men in the
labour force."[7] And again: "If…we can afford some unemployment in the interest of stability—a proposition, incidentally, of im-
peccably conservative antecedents—then we can afford to give
those who are unemployed the goods that enable them to sustain
their accustomed standard of living."

From a Buddhist point of view, this is standing the truth on its
head by considering goods as more important than people and consumption as more important than creative activity. It means shifting the emphasis from the worker to the product of work, that is,
from the human to the subhuman, a surrender to the forces of evil.
The very start of Buddhist economic planning would be a planning
for full employment, and the primary purpose of this would in fact
be employment for everyone who needs an "outside" job: it would
not be the maximisation of employment nor the maximisation of
production. Women, on the whole, do not need an "outside" job,
and the large-scale employment of women in offices or factories
would be considered a sign of serious economic failure. In particular, to let mothers of young children work in factories while the children run wild would be as uneconomic in the eyes of a Buddhist
economist as the employment of a skilled worker as a soldier in the
eyes of a modern economist.

While the materialist is mainly interested in goods, the Buddhist is mainly interested in liberation. But Buddhism is "The
Middle Way" and therefore in no way antagonistic to physical well-
being. It is not wealth that stands in the way of liberation but the attachment to wealth; not the enjoyment of pleasurable things but
the craving for them. The keynote of Buddhist economics, therefore, is simplicity and non-violence. From an economist's point of

view, the marvel of the Buddhist way of life is the utter rationality of its pattern—amazingly small means leading to extraordinarily satisfactory results.

For the modern economist this is very difficult to understand. He is used to measuring the "standard of living" by the amount of annual consumption, assuming all the time that a man who consumes more is "better off" than a man who consumes less. A Buddhist economist would consider this approach excessively irrational: since consumption is merely a means to human well-being, the aim should be to obtain the maximum of well-being with the minimum of consumption. Thus, if the purpose of clothing is a certain amount of temperature comfort and an attractive appearance, the task is to attain this purpose with the smallest possible effort, that is, with the smallest annual destruction of cloth and with the help of designs that involve the smallest possible input of toil. The less toil there is, the more time and strength is left for artistic creativity. It would be highly uneconomic, for instance, to go in for complicated tailoring, like the modern West, when a much more beautiful effect can be achieved by the skillful draping of uncut material. It would be the height of folly to make material so that it should wear out quickly and the height of barbarity to make anything ugly, shabby, or mean. What has just been said about clothing applies equally to all other human requirements. The ownership and the consumption of goods is a means to an end, and Buddhist economics is the systematic study of how to attain given ends with the minimum means.

Modern economics, on the other hand, considers consumption to be the sole end and purpose of all economic activity, taking the factors of production—land, labour, and capital—as the means. The former, in short, tries to maximise human satisfactions by the optimal pattern of consumption, while the latter tries to maximise consumption by the optimal pattern of productive effort. It is easy to see that the effort needed to sustain a way of life which seeks to attain the optimal pattern of consumption is likely to be much smaller than the effort needed to sustain a drive for maximum consumption. We need not be surprised, therefore, that the pressure and strain of living is very much less in, say, Burma than it is in the

➤ *women. They include volunteering, caring for the young, old and sick, household management, do-it-yourself housing, food-growing, and community service. Traditional economics scorns such loving work as "uneconomic," while only self-interested maximizing of one's own advantage is recognized as economically rational. Such theories are based on fear of scarcity and survival, which is the economics of reptilian brains. Today we learn from the United Nations Human Development Index that this unpaid work is estimated at $16 trillion, which is missing from the gross domestic product of all countries.*
—HAZEL HENDERSON

United States, in spite of the fact that the amount of labour-saving machinery used in the former country is only a minute fraction of the amount used in the latter.

Simplicity and non-violence are obviously closely related. The optimal pattern of consumption, producing a high degree of human satisfaction by means of a relatively low rate of consumption, allows people to live without great pressure and strain and to fulfill the primary injunction of Buddhist teaching: "Cease to do evil; try to do good." As physical resources are everywhere limited, people satisfying their needs by means of a modest use of resources are obviously less likely to be at each other's throats than people depending upon a high rate of use. Equally, people who live in highly self-sufficient local communities are less likely to get involved in large-scale violence than people whose existence depends on worldwide systems of trade.

From the point of view of Buddhist economics, therefore, production from local resources for local needs is the most rational way of economic life, while dependence on imports from afar and the consequent need to produce for export to unknown and distant peoples is highly uneconomic and justifiable only in exceptional cases and on a small scale. Just as the modern economist would admit that a high rate of consumption of transport services between a man's home and his place of work signifies a misfortune and not a high standard of life, so the Buddhist economist would hold that to satisfy human wants from faraway sources rather than from sources nearby signifies failure rather than success. The former tends to take statistics showing an increase in the number of ton/miles per head of the population carried by a country's transport system as proof of economic progress, while to the latter—the Buddhist economist—the same statistics would indicate a highly undesirable deterioration in the *pattern* of consumption.

Another striking difference between modern economics and Buddhist economics arises over the use of natural resources. Bertrand de Jouvenel, the eminent French political philosopher, has characterised "Western man" in words which may be taken as a fair description of the modern economist:

He tends to count nothing as an expenditure, other than human effort; he does not seem to mind how much mineral matter he wastes and, far worse, how much living matter he destroys. He does not seem to realise at all that human life is a dependent part of an ecosystem of many different forms of life. As the world is ruled from towns where men are cut off from any form of life other than human, the feeling of belonging to an ecosystem is not revived. This results in a harsh and improvident treatment of things upon which we ultimately depend, such as water and trees.[8]

The teaching of the Buddha, on the other hand, enjoins a reverent and non-violent attitude not only to all sentient beings but also, with great emphasis, to trees. Every follower of the Buddha ought to plant a tree every few years and look after it until it is safely established, and the Buddhist economist can demonstrate without difficulty that the universal observation of this rule would result in a high rate of genuine economic development independent of any foreign aid. Much of the economic decay of southeast Asia (as of many other parts of the world) is undoubtedly due to a heedless and shameful neglect of trees.

Modern economics does not distinguish between renewable and non-renewable materials, as its very method is to equalise and quantify everything by means of a money price. Thus, taking various alternative fuels, like coal, oil, wood, or water-power: the only difference between them recognised by modern economics is relative cost per equivalent unit. The cheapest is automatically the one to be preferred, as to do otherwise would be irrational and "uneconomic." From a Buddhist point of view, of course, this will not do; the essential difference between non-renewable fuels like coal and oil on the one hand and renewable fuels like wood and water-power on the other cannot be simply overlooked. Non-renewable goods must be used only if they are indispensable, and then only with the greatest care and the most meticulous concern for conservation. To use them heedlessly or extravagantly is an act of violence, and while complete non-violence may not be attainable on this earth, there is

Buddhist economics is very relevant today, and more and more people are catching on. They are learning that by consuming less, they can live happier and more satisfied, productive lives. A 1995 Merck Foundation survey indicates that 28 percent of Americans have dropped out of the high-paying rat-race jobs in big cities and accepted lower salaries to live in smaller towns for an increase in quality of life. As well, more people are concerned about clean air, better education, and cultural opportunities than the strength of the stockmarket and the gross national product. They want quality-of-life equations. The Calvert-Henderson Quality of Life Indicators, for example, measure the state of 12 important aspects of quality of life, including: culture, recreation, environment, health, education, shelter, public safety, energy efficiency, and the military; and expand data on employment incomes and wealth, and the poverty gap and unpaid work.

—HAZEL HENDERSON

First written in 1966, these words have been contemptuously ignored by mainstream economists ever since. The roaring, oil-fueled engine of production and consumption that propels the world's economy has drowned out Schumacher's warning. But the global oil supply will almost certainly peak between 2005–2015, and then rapidly decline. The complex, unstable engine will slow and disintegrate as it runs out of fuel. Who will the economists blame for the collapse? Everyone but themselves.

—DAVID EHRENFELD

nonetheless an ineluctable duty on man to aim at the ideal of non-violence in all he does.

Just as a modern European economist would not consider it a great economic achievement if all European art treasures were sold to America at attractive prices, so the Buddhist economist would insist that a population basing its economic life on non-renewable fuels is living parasitically, on capital instead of income. Such a way of life could have no permanence and could therefore be justified only as a purely temporary expedient. As the world's resources of non-renewable fuels—coal, oil, and natural gas—are exceedingly unevenly distributed over the globe and undoubtedly limited in quantity, it is clear that their exploitation at an ever-increasing rate is an act of violence against nature which must almost inevitably lead to violence between men.

This fact alone might give food for thought even to those people in Buddhist countries who care nothing for the religious and spiritual values of their heritage and ardently desire to embrace the materialism of modern economics at the fastest possible speed. Before they dismiss Buddhist economics as nothing better than a nostalgic dream, they might wish to consider whether the path of economic development outlined by modern economics is likely to lead them to places where they really want to be. Towards the end of his courageous book *The Challenge of Man's Future,* Professor Harrison Brown of the California Institute of Technology gives the following appraisal:

> Thus we see that, just as industrial society is fundamentally unstable and subject to reversion to agrarian existence, so within it the conditions which offer individual freedom are unstable in their ability to avoid the conditions which impose rigid organisation and totalitarian control. Indeed, when we examine all of the foreseeable difficulties which threaten the survival of industrial civilisation, it is difficult to see how the achievement of stability and the maintenance of individual liberty can be made compatible.[9]

Even if this were dismissed as a long-term view there is the immediate question of whether "modernisation," as currently practised without regard to religious and spiritual values, is actually producing agreeable results. As far as the masses are concerned, the results appear to be disastrous—a collapse of the rural economy, a rising tide of unemployment in town and country, and the growth of a city proletariat without nourishment for either body or soul.

It is in the light of both immediate experience and long-term prospects that the study of Buddhist economics could be recommended even to those who believe that economic growth is more important than any spiritual or religious values. For it is not a question of choosing between "modern growth" and "traditional stagnation." It is a question of finding the right path of development, the Middle Way between materialist heedlessness and traditionalist immobility, in short, of finding "Right Livelihood."

It is interesting to note the slow and quiet ways that deep and powerful groundswells of change such as Buddhist economics wend their way into our consciousness. Schumacher's monastic experiences in Burma occurred in 1955. Thirteen years later they came into focus in a 1968 issue of Resurgence. *It took another six years for* Small is Beautiful *to be published with that core essay; then another 25 years to the present, during which time it has begun to have a deep effect on our culture.*

—TOM BENDER

CHAPTER 5

A QUESTION OF SIZE

I WAS BROUGHT UP on an interpretation of history which suggested that in the beginning was the family; then families got together and formed tribes; then a number of tribes formed a nation; then a number of nations formed a "Union" or "United States" of this or that; and that, finally, we could look forward to a single World Government. Ever since I heard this plausible story I have taken a special interest in the process, but could not help noticing that the opposite seemed to be happening: a proliferation of nation-states. The United Nations Organisation started some twenty-five years ago with some sixty members; now there are more than twice as many, and the number is still growing. In my youth, this process of proliferation was called "Balkanisation" and was thought to be a very bad thing. Although everybody said it was bad, it has now been going on merrily for over fifty years, in most parts of the world. Large units tend to break up into smaller units. This phenomenon, so mockingly the opposite of what I had been taught, whether we approve of it or not, should at least not pass unnoticed.

Second, I was brought up on the theory that in order to be prosperous a country had to be big—the bigger the better. This also seemed quite plausible. Look at what Churchill called "the pumpernickel principalities" of Germany before Bismarck; and then look at the Bismarckian Reich. Is it not true that the great prosperity of Germany became possible only through this unification? All the same, the German-speaking Swiss and the German-speaking Austrians, who did not join, did just as well economically, and if we make a list of all the most prosperous countries in the world, we find that most of them are very small; whereas a list of all the biggest countries in the world shows most of them to be very poor indeed. Here again, there is food for thought.

And third, I was brought up on the theory of the "economies of scale"—that with industries and firms, just as with nations, there is an irresistible trend, dictated by modern technology, for units to become ever bigger. Now, it is quite true that today there are more large organisations and probably also bigger organisations than ever before in history; but the number of small units is also growing and certainly not declining in countries like Britain and the United States, and many of these small units are highly prosperous and provide society with most of the really fruitful new developments. Again, it is not altogether easy to reconcile theory and practice, and the situation as regards this whole issue of size is certainly puzzling to anyone brought up on these three concurrent theories.

Even today, we are generally told that gigantic organisations are inescapably necessary; but when we look closely we can notice that as soon as great size has been created there is often a strenuous attempt to attain smallness within bigness. The great achievement of Mr. Sloan of General Motors was to structure this gigantic firm in such a manner that it became, in fact, a federation of fairly reasonably sized firms. In the British National Coal Board, one of the biggest firms of Western Europe, something very similar was attempted under the chairmanship of Lord Robens; strenuous efforts were made to evolve a structure which would maintain the unity of one big organisation and at the same time create the "climate" or feeling of there being a federation of numerous "quasi-firms." The monolith was transformed into a well-coordinated assembly of lively, semi-autonomous units, each with its own drive and sense of achievement. While many theoreticians—who may not be too closely in touch with real life—are still engaging in the idolatry of large size, with practical people in the actual world there is a tremendous longing and striving to profit, if at all possible, from the convenience, humanity, and manageability of smallness. This, also, is a tendency which anyone can easily observe for himself.

Let us now approach our subject from another angle and ask what is actually *needed*. In the affairs of men, there always appears

In 1998, more than 5000 corporate mergers with a combined value of more than $2 trillion took place in the United States. Federal agencies approved virtually every merger application, even when their own studies empirically verified the "convenience, humanity, and manageability of smallness."

Consider the case of banks. In 1996, two Federal Reserve economists found no improved efficiencies when bank assets grow beyond $200 million, a size larger than 80 percent of the 12,000 banks operating in the United States. Other studies provided evidence that small banks serve their communities better. Small banks make over 80 percent of all commercial loans to very small business borrowers, concluded a 1996 Federal Research study. Fees for checking accounts and other basic services were on average 15 percent higher at large, multi-state banks than at small, community banks, concluded a 1997 study by the U.S. Public Interest Research Group.

—DAVID MORRIS

Wastewater treatment is among the industries today where "What's the right size for the job?" is starting to be asked, and in time, will yield profound changes. A recent study in Adelaide, South Australia found that sewage treatment plants are probably orders of magnitude larger than their economic optimum, for the same basic reasons that electric power plants in the 1970s and 1980s became so oversized: designers focused on presumed economies of scale in the plant itself while ignoring the spiraling cost of the sewage-collection network.

Sewering a larger area to serve a larger treatment plant rapidly becomes very costly, not only because the area served rises as the square of its radius, but also because an increasing amount of that area must be traversed without a yield in revenue. In addition, downhill flow in longer sewers ➡

to be a need for at least two things simultaneously, which, on the face of it, seem to be incompatible and to exclude one another. We always need both freedom and order. We need the freedom of lots and lots of small, autonomous units, and, at the same time, the orderliness of large-scale, possibly global, unity and coordination. When it comes to action, we obviously need small units, because action is a highly personal affair, and one cannot be in touch with more than a very limited number of persons at any one time. But when it comes to the world of ideas, to principles or to ethics, to the indivisibility of peace and also of ecology, we need to recognise the unity of mankind and base our actions upon this recognition. Or to put it differently, it is true that all men are brothers, but it is also true that in our active personal relationships we can, in fact, be brothers to only a few of them, and we are called upon to show more brotherliness to them than we could possibly show to the whole of mankind. We all know people who freely talk about the brotherhood of man while treating their neighbours as enemies, just as we also know people who have, in fact, excellent relations with all their neighbours while harbouring, at the same time, appalling prejudices about all human groups outside their particular circle.

What I wish to emphasise is the *duality* of the human requirement when it comes to the question of size: there is no *single* answer. For his different purposes man needs many different structures, both small ones and large ones, some exclusive and some comprehensive. Yet people find it most difficult to keep two seemingly opposite necessities of truth in their minds at the same time. They always tend to clamour for a final solution, as if in actual life there could ever be a final solution other than death. For constructive work, the principal task is always the restoration of some kind of balance. Today, we suffer from an almost universal idolatry of giantism. It is therefore necessary to insist on the virtues of smallness—where this applies. (If there were a prevailing idolatry of smallness, irrespective of subject or purpose, one would have to try and exercise influence in the opposite direction.)

The question of scale might be put in another way: what is needed in all these matters is to discriminate, to get things sorted out. For every activity there is a certain appropriate scale, and the more active and intimate the activity, the smaller the number of people that can take part, the greater is the number of such relationship arrangements that need to be established. Take teaching: one listens to all sorts of extraordinary debates about the superiority of the teaching machine over some other forms of teaching. Well, let us discriminate: what are we trying to teach? It then becomes immediately apparent that certain things can only be taught in a very intimate circle, whereas other things can obviously be taught en masse, via the air, via television, via teaching machines, and so on.

What scale is appropriate? It depends on what we are trying to do. The question of scale is extremely crucial today, in political, social, and economic affairs just as in almost everything else. What, for instance, is the appropriate size of a city? And also, one might ask, what is the appropriate size of a country? Now these are serious and difficult questions. It is not possible to programme a computer and get the answer. The really serious matters of life cannot be calculated. We cannot directly calculate what is right; but we jolly well know what is wrong! We can recognise right and wrong at the extremes, although we cannot normally judge them finely enough to say: "This ought to be five per cent more"; or "that ought to be five per cent less."

Take the question of size of a city. While one cannot judge these things with precision, I think it is fairly safe to say that the upper limit of what is desirable for the size of a city is probably something of the order of half a million inhabitants. It is quite clear that above such a size nothing is added to the virtue of the city. In places like London, or Tokyo, or New York, the millions do not add to the city's real value but merely create *enormous* problems and produce human degradation. So probably the order of magnitude of 500,000 inhabitants could be looked upon as the upper limit. The question of the lower limit of a real city is much more difficult to judge. The finest cities in history have been very small by twentieth-century standards. The instruments and institutions of city culture depend, no doubt, on a certain accumulation of wealth. But how much wealth has to be accumulated depends on the type of culture pursued. Philosophy, the arts, and religion cost very, very little money. Other types of what claims to be "high culture"—space research or

➡ *requires frequent pumping stations to lift the sewage back up to reasonable pipe-burial depths. The whole system turns out to become cheaper if the area served is hundreds or thousands of times smaller than normally assumed. Further, newer technologies of choice may be nontoxic, biological systems and innovative methods of sanitation, such as Swedish separating toilets that eliminate sewage at the source, treating human waste as a resource to recycle for soil nutrients.*
—AMORY LOVINS

Within a few years the majority of humankind will be living in cities. According to the United Nations, the world's urban population is expected to grow by about 50 percent to almost three billion in the 1990s. By 2025, about 5.1 billion people will reside in cities, an increase of 70 percent in the first quarter of the century. This means that in the next 27 years, the urban population alone is expected to grow by the equivalent of the total human population in the 1930s! Most of this growth will occur in the Third World. By 2015, 23 of the 27 cities expected to reach 10 million will be in developing countries, as will 36–39 of the 44 cities of between 5 and 10 million inhabitants.

Many analysts see global urbanization as evidence of humanity's increasing independence from nature. This is a perceptual error. Urbanization blinds the modern eye to ecological reality by ➡

ultra-modern physics—cost a lot of money, but are somewhat remote from the real needs of men.

I raise the question of the proper size of cities both for its own sake but also because it is, to my mind, the most relevant point when we come to consider the size of nations.

The idolatry of giantism that I have talked about is possibly one of the causes and certainly one of the effects of modern technology, particularly in matters of transport and communications. A highly developed transport and communications system has one immensely powerful effect: it makes people *footloose*.

Millions of people start moving about, deserting the rural areas and the smaller towns to follow the city lights, to go to the big city, causing a pathological growth. Take the country in which all this is perhaps most exemplified—the United States. Sociologists are studying the problem of "megalopolis." The word "metropolis" is no longer big enough; hence "megalopolis." They freely talk about the polarisation of the population of the United States into three immense megalopolitan areas: one extending from Boston to Washington, a continuous built-up area, with sixty million people; one around Chicago, another sixty million; and one on the West Coast, from San Francisco to San Diego, again a continuous built-up area with sixty million people; the rest of the country being left practically empty; deserted provincial towns, and the land cultivated with vast tractors, combine harvesters, and immense amounts of chemicals.

If this is somebody's conception of the future of the United States, it is hardly a future worth having. But whether we like it or not, this is the result of people having become footloose; it is the result of that marvellous mobility of labour which economists treasure above all else.

Everything in this world has to have a *structure*, otherwise it is chaos. Before the advent of mass transport and mass communications, the structure was simply there, because people were relatively immobile. People who wanted to move did so; witness the flood of saints from Ireland moving all over Europe. There were communications, there was mobility, but no footlooseness. Now, a great deal of structure has collapsed, and a country is like a big cargo ship in which the load is in no way secured. It tilts, and all the load slips over, and the ship founders.

One of the chief elements of structure for the whole of mankind is of course *the state*. And one of the chief elements or instruments of structuralisation (if I may use that term), is *frontiers,* national frontiers. Now previously, before this technological intervention, the relevance of frontiers was almost exclusively political and dynastic; frontiers were delimitations of political power, determining how many people you could raise for war. Economists fought against such frontiers becoming economic barriers—hence the ideology of free trade. But, then, people and things were not footloose; transport was expensive enough so that movements, both of people and of goods, were never more than marginal. Trade in the pre-industrial era was not a trade in essentials, but a trade in precious stones, precious metals, luxury goods, spices and—unhappily—slaves. The basic requirements of life had of course to be indigenously produced. And the movement of populations, except in periods of disaster, was confined to persons who had a very special reason to move, such as the Irish saints or the scholars of the University of Paris.

But now everything and everybody has become mobile. All structures are threatened, and all structures are *vulnerable* to an extent that they have never been before.

Economics, which Lord Keynes had hoped would settle down as a modest occupation similar to dentistry, suddenly becomes the most important subject of all. Economic policies absorb almost the entire attention of government, and at the same time become ever more impotent. The simplest things, which only fifty years ago one could do without difficulty, cannot get done any more. The richer a society, the more impossible it becomes to do worthwhile things without immediate pay-off. Economics has become such a thraldom that it absorbs almost the whole of foreign policy. People say, "Ah yes, we don't like to go with these people, but we depend on them economically so we must humour them." It tends to absorb the whole of ethics and to take precedence over all other human considerations. Now, quite clearly, this is a pathological development, which has, of course, many roots, but one of its clearly visible

➡ *separating people both spatially and psychologically from the ecosystems that (still) support them. The fact remains that cities require ever greater quantities of food, resource commodities, and energy—all often shipped great distances— to sustain the increasingly consumer lifestyles of their inhabitants.*
—WILLIAM REES

Deputation to the Standing
Committee on General
Government conducting
hearings on the City of
Toronto Act, Bill 103 to
amalgamate six munici-
palities into one large city:

*I oppose amalgamation of
Toronto, North York, Etobi-
coke, Scarborough, York and
East York for many of the
same reasons others oppose
it, but will use my ten
minutes to emphasize that
cities do not thrive from
central planning—including
megacity planning.*

*A city of social and
economic vitality contains
and nourishes details and
differences in mind-boggling
quantities. Respect for details
and differences is of the
essence. For instance, a small
town can be economically
pretty much all of a piece—
that is, flourishing or
declining as a unit. But in a
city some places are apt to be
in social or economic trouble
at the same time other parts
are prospering or main-
taining an even keel.* ➡

roots lies in the great achievements of modern technology in terms
of transport and communications.

While people, with an easy-going kind of logic, believe that fast
transport and instantaneous communications open up a new dimension of freedom (which they do in some rather trivial respects),
they overlook the fact that these achievements also tend to destroy
freedom, by making everything extremely vulnerable and extremely insecure, unless conscious policies are developed and conscious action is taken to mitigate the destructive effects of these
technological developments.

Now, these destructive effects are obviously most severe in *large*
countries, because, as we have seen, frontiers produce "structure,"
and it is a much bigger decision for someone to cross a frontier, to
uproot himself from his native land and try and put down roots in
another land, than to move within the frontiers of his country. The
factor of footlooseness is, therefore, the more serious, the bigger
the country. Its destructive effects can be traced both in the rich and
in the poor countries. In the rich countries such as the United
States of America, it produces, as already mentioned, "megalopolis." It also produces a rapidly increasing and ever more intractable
problem of "drop-outs," of people, who, having become footloose,
cannot find a place anywhere in society. Directly connected to this,
it produces an appalling problem of crime, alienation, stress, social
breakdown, right down to the level of the family. In the poor countries, again most severely in the largest ones, it produces mass migration into cities, mass unemployment, and, as vitality is drained
out of the rural areas, the threat of famine. The result is a "dual society" without any inner cohesion, subject to a maximum of political instability.

As an illustration, let me take the case of Peru. The capital city,
Lima, situated on the Pacific coast, had a population of 175,000 in
the early 1920s, just fifty years ago. Its population is now approaching three million. The once beautiful Spanish city is now infested
by slums, surrounded by misery-belts that are crawling up the An-
des. But this is not all. *People are arriving from the rural areas at the
rate of a thousand a day*—and *nobody knows what to do with them*. The
social or psychological structure of life in the hinterland has col-

lapsed; people have become footloose and arrive in the capital city to squat on some empty land (against the police who come to beat them out) to build their mud hovels and look for a job. *And nobody knows what to do with them.* Nobody knows how to stop the drift.

Imagine that in 1864 Bismarck had annexed the whole of Denmark instead of only a small part of it, and that nothing had happened since. The Danes would be an ethnic minority in Germany, perhaps struggling to maintain their language by becoming bilingual, the official language of course being German. Only by thoroughly Germanising themselves could they avoid becoming second-class citizens. There would be an irresistible drift of the most ambitious and enterprising Danes, thoroughly Germanised, to the mainland in the south, and what then would be the status of Copenhagen? That of a remote provincial city. Or imagine Belgium as part of France. What would be the status of Brussels? Again, that of an unimportant provincial city. I don't have to enlarge on it. Imagine now that Denmark a part of Germany, and Belgium a part of France, suddenly wanted independence. There would be endless, heated arguments that these "non-countries" could not be economically viable, that their desire for independence was, to quote a famous political commentator, "adolescent emotionalism, political naïvety, phoney economics, and sheer bare-faced opportunism."

How can one talk about the economics of small independent countries? How can one discuss a problem that is a non-problem? There is no such thing as the viability of states or of nations, there is only a problem of viability of people: people, actual persons like you and me, are viable when they can stand on their own feet and earn their keep. You do not make non-viable people viable by putting large numbers of them into one huge community, and you do not make viable people non-viable by splitting a large community into a number of smaller, more intimate, more coherent and more manageable groups. All this is perfectly obvious and there is absolutely nothing to argue about. Some people ask: "What happens when a country, composed of one rich province and several poor ones, falls apart because the rich province secedes?" Most probably the answer is: "Nothing very much happens." The rich will continue to be rich and the poor will continue to be poor. "But if, before secession,

➡ *Thus a city's government ought to be flexible enough to respond to radically different needs and opportunities at the same given time. For example, last year at the initiative of the mayor and council, the City of Toronto introduced a new planning philosophy into two small specific downtown areas in serious trouble. Not incidentally, the change was made with patience and complete democratic procedures and safeguards....*

Megacity bureaucracies do not employ this sort of pinpointed awareness and responsiveness. They can't, because their jurisdictions are too big and complex. I would judge that the City of Toronto is probably close to the limit at which true flexible responsiveness of the kind mentioned is feasible.
—JANE JACOBS

This raises a new complication for those interested in optimal city size and efficient settlement patterns. In an era of accelerating global change, how economically and socially secure is a city of 10 million—indeed any city—if distant sources of food, water, energy, or other critical resources are threatened by climate change, increasing resource competition, dwindling supplies, or civil/international strife? Do development patterns that increase inter-regional dependence on vulnerable resource flows make ecological or geopolitical sense?

—WILLIAM REES

the rich province had subsidised the poor, what happens then?" Well then, of course, the subsidy might stop. But the rich rarely subsidise the poor; more often they exploit them. They may not do so directly so much as through the terms of trade. They may obscure the situation a little by a certain redistribution of tax revenue or small-scale charity but the last thing they want to do is secede from the poor.

The normal case is quite different, namely that the poor provinces wish to separate from the rich, and that the rich want to hold on because they know that exploitation of the poor within one's own frontiers is infinitely easier than exploitation of the poor beyond them. Now if a poor province wishes to secede at the risk of losing some subsidies, what attitude should one take?

Not that we have to decide this, but what should we think about it? Is it not a wish to be applauded and respected? Do we not *want* people to stand on their own feet, as free and self-reliant men? So again this is a "non-problem." I would assert therefore that there is no problem of viability, as all experience shows. If a country wishes to export all over the world, and import from all over the world, it has never been held that it had to annex the whole world in order to do so.

What about the absolute necessity of having a large internal market? This again is an optical illusion if the meaning of "large" is conceived in terms of political boundaries. Needless to say, a prosperous market is better than a poor one, but whether that market is outside the political boundaries or inside, makes on the whole very little difference. I am not aware, for instance, that Germany, in order to export a large number of Volkswagens to the United States, a very prosperous market, could only do so after annexing the United States. But it does make a lot of difference if a poor community or province finds itself politically tied to or ruled by a rich community or province. Why? Because, in a mobile, footloose society the law of disequilibrium is infinitely stronger than the so-called law of equilibrium. Nothing succeeds like success, and nothing stagnates like stagnation. The successful province drains the life out of the unsuccessful, and without protection against the strong, the weak have no chance; either they remain weak or they must migrate and join the strong; they cannot effectively help themselves.

A most important problem in the second half of the twentieth century is the geographical distribution of population, the question of "regionalism." But regionalism, not in the sense of combining a lot of states into free-trade systems, but in the opposite sense of developing all the regions within each country. This, in fact, is the most important subject on the agenda of all the larger countries today. And a lot of the nationalism of small nations today, and the desire for self-government and so-called independence, is simply a logical and rational response to the need for regional development. In the poor countries in particular there is no hope for the poor unless there is successful regional development, a development effort outside the capital city covering all the rural areas wherever people happen to be.

If this effort is not brought forth, their only choice is either to remain in their miserable condition where they are, or to migrate into the big city where their condition will be even more miserable. It is a strange phenomenon indeed that the conventional wisdom of present-day economics can do nothing to help the poor.

Invariably it proves that only such policies are viable as have in fact the result of making those already rich and powerful, richer and more powerful. It proves that industrial development only pays if it is as near as possible to the capital city or another very large town, and not in the rural areas. It proves that large projects are invariably more economic than small ones, and it proves that capital-intensive projects are invariably to be preferred as against labour-intensive ones. The economic calculus, as applied by present-day economics, forces the industrialist to eliminate the human factor because machines do not make mistakes, which people do. Hence the enormous effort at automation and the drive for ever-larger units. This means that those who have nothing to sell but their labour remain in the weakest possible bargaining position. The conventional wisdom of what is now taught as economics by-passes the poor, the very people for whom development is really needed. The economics of giantism and automation is a left-over of nine-

We should recognize that pulling a thousand people away from sure subsistence in a land-based economy into an urban context where they compete for a hundred new jobs is not a net gain in employment: 900 people have, in effect, become unemployed.
—HELENA
NORBERG-HODGE

Fritz's deceptively simple but prophetic questions about scale are gaining force. Decades later, they are turning out to lie at the core not only of commercial competitive advantage, but also of appropriate technology and right livelihood—issues on which the future of the world depends. The next industrial revolution that is now emerging—a capitalism that behaves according to the proper value of natural and human capital—will at last recognize the modest economist E.F. Schumacher as among its seers, inspirations, and saviors.

—AMORY LOVINS

teenth-century conditions and nineteenth-century thinking and it is totally incapable of solving any of the real problems of today. An entirely new system of thought is needed, a system based on attention to people, and not primarily attention to goods—(the goods will look after themselves!). It could be summed up in the phrase, "production by the masses, rather than mass production." What was impossible, however, in the nineteenth century, is possible now. And what was in fact—if not necessarily at least understandably—neglected in the nineteenth century is unbelievably urgent now. That is, the conscious utilisation of our enormous technological and scientific potential for the fight against misery and human degradation—a fight in intimate contact with actual people, with individuals, families, small groups, rather than states and other anonymous abstractions. And this presupposes a political and organisational structure that can provide this intimacy.

What is the meaning of democracy, freedom, human dignity, standard of living, self-realisation, fulfillment? Is it a matter of goods, or of people? Of course it is a matter of people. But people can be themselves only in small comprehensible groups. Therefore we must learn to think in terms of an articulated structure that can cope with a multiplicity of small-scale units. If economic thinking cannot grasp this it is useless. If it cannot get beyond its vast abstractions, the national income, the rate of growth, capital/output ratio, input-output analysis, labour mobility, capital accumulation; if it cannot get beyond all this and make contact with the human realities of poverty, frustration, alienation, despair, breakdown, crime, escapism, stress, congestion, ugliness, and spiritual death, then let us scrap economics and start afresh.

Are there not indeed enough "signs of the times" to indicate that a new start is needed?

PART II

RESOURCES

CHAPTER 6

THE GREATEST RESOURCE—
EDUCATION

THROUGHOUT HISTORY and in virtually every part of the earth men have lived and multiplied, and have created some form of culture. Always and everywhere they have found their means of subsistence and something to spare. Civilisations have been built up, have flourished, and, in most cases, have declined and perished. This is not the place to discuss why they have perished; but we can say: there must have been some failure of resources. In most instances new civilisations have arisen, on the same ground, which would be quite incomprehensible if it had been simply the *material* resources that had given out before. How could such resources have reconstituted themselves?

All history—as well as all current experience—points to the fact that it is man, not nature, who provides the primary resource: that the key factor of all economic development comes out of the mind of man. Suddenly, there is an outburst of daring, initiative, invention, constructive activity, not in one field alone, but in many fields all at once. No one may be able to say where it came from in the first place; but we can see how it maintains and even strengthens itself: through various kinds of schools, in other words, through education. In a very real sense, therefore, we can say that education is the most vital of all resources.

If Western civilisation is in a state of permanent crisis, it is not far-fetched to suggest that there may be something wrong with its education. No civilisation, I am sure, has ever devoted more energy and resources to organised education, and if we believe in nothing else, we certainly believe that education is, or should be, the key to everything. In fact, the belief in education is so strong that we treat

Most people now associate Schumacher's name with problems of economics and the scale of technology, not with education. But the most incandescent pages in the book have to do with education because there he probed the origins of the crisis. All of the rest he regarded as symptoms arising from a disorder in our basic convictions propagated by formal education.

—DAVID ORR

it as the residual legatee of all our problems. If the nuclear age brings new dangers; if the advance of genetic engineering opens the doors to new abuses; if commercialism brings new temptations—the answer must be more and better education. The modern way of life is becoming ever more complex: this means that everybody must become more highly educated. "By 1984," it was said recently, "it will be desirable that the most ordinary of men is not embarrassed by the use of a logarithm table, the elementary concepts of the calculus, and by the definitions and uses of such words as electron, coulomb, and volt. He should further have become able not only to handle a pen, pencil, and ruler but also a magnetic tape, valve, and transistor. The improvement of communications between individuals and groups depends on it." Most of all, it appears, the international situation calls for prodigious educational efforts. The classical statement on this point was delivered by Sir Charles (now Lord) Snow in his "Rede Lecture" some years ago: "To say that we must educate ourselves or perish, is a little more melodramatic than the facts warrant. To say, we have to educate ourselves or watch a steep decline in our lifetime, is about right." According to Lord Snow, the Russians are apparently doing much better than anyone else and will "have a clear edge," "unless and until the Americans and we educate ourselves both sensibly and imaginatively."

Lord Snow, it will be recalled, talked about "The Two Cultures and the Scientific Revolution" and expressed his concern that "the intellectual life of the whole of Western society is increasingly being split into two polar groups.... At one pole we have the literary intellectuals...at the other the scientists." He deplores the "gulf of mutual incomprehension" between these two groups and wants it bridged. It is quite clear how he thinks this "bridging" operation is to be done; the aims of his educational policy would be, first, to get as many "alpha-plus scientists as the country can throw up"; second, to train "a much larger stratum of alpha professionals" to do the supporting research, high-class design, and development; third, to train "thousands upon thousands" of other scientists and engineers; and finally, to train "politicians, administrators, an entire community, who know enough science to have a sense of what the scientists are talking about." If this fourth and last group can at least be educated enough to "have a sense" of what the real people, the scientists and engineers, are talking about, so Lord Snow seems to suggest, the gulf of mutual incomprehension between the "Two Cultures" may be bridged.

These ideas on education, which are by no means unrepresentative of our times, leave one with the uncomfortable feeling that ordinary people, including politicians, administrators, and so forth, are really not much use; they have failed to make the grade: but, at least, they should be educated enough to have a sense of what is going on, and to know what the scientists mean when they talk—to quote Lord Snow's example—about the Second Law of Thermodynamics. It is an uncomfortable feeling, because the scientists never tire of telling us that the fruits of their labours are "neutral": whether they enrich humanity or destroy it depends on how they are used. And who is to decide how they are used? There is nothing in the training of scientists and engineers to enable them to take such decisions, or else, what becomes of the neutrality of science?

If so much reliance is today being placed in the power of education to enable ordinary people to cope with the problems thrown up by scientific and technological progress, then there must be something more to education than Lord Snow suggests. Science and engineering produce "know-how"; but "know-how" is nothing by itself; it is a means without an end, a mere potentiality, an unfinished sentence. "Know-how" is no more a culture than a piano is music. Can education help us to finish the sentence, to turn the potentiality into a reality to the benefit of man?

To do so, the task of education would be, first and foremost, the transmission of ideas of value, of what to do with our lives. There is no doubt also the need to transmit know-how but this must take second place, for it is obviously somewhat foolhardy to put great powers into the hands of people without making sure that they have a reasonable idea of what to do with them. At present, there can be little doubt that the whole of mankind is in mortal danger, not because we are short of scientific and technological know-how, but because we tend to use it destructively, without wisdom. More education can help us only if it produces more wisdom.

In fewer than 25 pages Schumacher described the heart of the modern predicament. It is not, in his view, simply the problem of overcoming the gulf between scientists and everybody else, as C.P. Snow put it in Two Cultures. *It is rather a far deeper problem in which know-how has preceded know-why because our central convictions have been thrown into disorder.*
—DAVID ORR

The essence of education, I suggested, is the transmission of values, but values do not help us to pick our way through life unless they have become our own, a part, so to say, of our mental make-up. This means that they are more than mere formulae or dogmatic assertions: that we think and feel with them, that they are the very instruments through which we look at, interpret, and experience the world. When we think, we do not just think: we think with ideas. Our mind is not a blank, a *tabula rasa*. When we begin to think we can do so only because our mind is already filled with all sorts of ideas *with which* to think. All through our youth and adolescence, before the conscious and critical mind begins to act as a sort of censor and guardian at the threshold, ideas seep into our mind, vast hosts and multitudes of them. These years are, one might say, our Dark Ages during which we are nothing but inheritors; it is only in later years that we can gradually learn to sort out our inheritance.

First of all, there is language. Each word is an idea. If the language which seeps into us during our Dark Ages is English, our mind is thereby furnished by a set of ideas which is significantly different from the set represented by Chinese, Russian, German, or even American. Next to words, there are the rules of putting them together: grammar, another bundle of ideas, the study of which has fascinated some modern philosophers to such an extent that they thought they could reduce the whole of philosophy to a study of grammar.

All philosophers—and others—have always paid a great deal of attention to ideas *seen as the result of thought and observation;* but in modern times all too little attention has been paid to the study of the ideas which form the very instruments by which thought and observation proceed. On the basis of experience and conscious thought small ideas may easily be dislodged, but when it comes to bigger, more universal, or more subtle ideas it may not be so easy to change them. Indeed, it is often difficult to become aware of them, as they are the instruments and not the results of our thinking— just as you can see what is outside you, but cannot easily see that with which you see, the eye itself. And even when one has become aware of them it is often impossible to judge them on the basis of ordinary experience.

We often notice the existence of more or less fixed ideas in other people's minds—ideas *with which* they think without being aware of doing so. We then call them prejudices, which is logically quite correct because they have merely seeped into the mind and are in no way the result of a judgement. But the word "prejudice" is generally applied to ideas that are patently erroneous and recognisable as such by anyone except the prejudiced man. Most of the ideas with which we think are not of that kind at all. To some of them, like those incorporated in words and grammar, the notions of truth or error cannot even be applied; others are quite definitely not prejudices but the result of a judgement; others again are tacit assumptions or presuppositions which may be very difficult to recognise.

I say, therefore, that we think *with* or *through* ideas and that what we call thinking is generally the application of pre-existing ideas to a given situation or set of facts. When we think about, say, the political situation we apply to that situation our political ideas, more or less systematically, and attempt to make that situation "intelligible" to ourselves by means of these ideas. Similarly everywhere else. Some of the ideas are ideas of value, that is to say, we evaluate the situation in the light of our value-ideas.

The way in which we experience and interpret the world obviously depends very much indeed on the kind of ideas that fill our minds. If they are mainly small, weak, superficial, and incoherent, life will appear insipid, uninteresting, petty, and chaotic. It is difficult to bear the resultant feeling of emptiness, and the vacuum of our minds may only too easily be filled by some big, fantastic notion—political or otherwise—which suddenly seems to illumine everything and to give meaning and purpose to our existence. It needs no emphasis that herein lies one of the great dangers of our time.

When people ask for education they normally mean something more than mere training, something more than mere knowledge of facts, and something more than a mere diversion. Maybe they cannot themselves formulate precisely what they are looking for; but I think what they are really looking for is ideas that would make the world, and their own lives, intelligible to them. When a thing is intelligible you have a sense of participation; when a thing is unintelligible you have a sense of estrangement. "Well, I don't know," you hear people say, as an impotent protest against the un-intelligibility of the world as they meet it. If the mind cannot bring to the world a set—or, shall we say, a tool-box—of powerful ideas, the world must appear to it as a chaos, a mass of unrelated phe-nomena, of meaningless events. Such a man is like a person in a strange land without any signs of civilisation, without maps or sign-posts or indicators of any kind. Nothing has any meaning to him; nothing can hold his vital interest; he has no means of making any-thing intelligible to himself.

All traditional philosophy is an attempt to create an orderly sys-tem of ideas by which to live and to interpret the world. "Philosophy as the Greeks conceived it," writes Professor Kuhn, "is one single effort of the human mind to interpret the system of signs and so to relate man to the world as a comprehensive order within which a place is assigned to him." The classical-Christian culture of the late Middle Ages supplied man with a very complete and astonishingly coherent interpretation of signs, i.e. a system of vital ideas giving a most detailed picture of man, the universe, and man's place in the universe. This system, however, has been shattered and frag-mented, and the result is bewilderment and estrangement, never more dramatically put than by Kierkegaard in the middle of last century:

> One sticks one's finger into the soil to tell by the smell in what land one is: I stick my finger into existence—it smells of nothing. Where am I? Who am I? How came I here? What is this thing called the world? What does this world mean? Who is it that has lured me into this thing and now leaves me there?...How did I come into the world? Why was I not even consulted...but was thrust into the ranks as though I had been bought of a kidnapper, a dealer in souls? How did I obtain an interest in this big enterprise they call reality? Why should I have an interest in it? Is it not a voluntary concern? And if I am compelled to take part in it, where is the direc-tor?...Whither shall I turn with my complaint?

Perhaps there is not even a director. Bertrand Russell said that the whole universe is simply "the outcome of accidental collocations of atoms" and claimed that the scientific theories leading to this conclusion "if not quite beyond dispute, are yet so nearly certain, that no philosophy that rejects them can hope to stand.... Only on the firm foundation of unyielding despair can the soul's habitation henceforth be safely built." Sir Fred Hoyle, the astronomer, talks of "the truly dreadful situation in which we find ourselves. Here we are in this wholly fantastic universe with scarcely a clue as to whether our existence has any real significance."

Estrangement breeds loneliness and despair, the "encounter with nothingness," cynicism, empty gestures of defiance, as we can see in the greater part of existentialist philosophy and general literature today. Or it suddenly turns—as I have mentioned before—into the ardent adoption of a fanatical teaching which, by a monstrous simplification of reality, pretends to answer all questions. So, what is the cause of estrangement? Never has science been more triumphant; never has man's power over his environment been more complete nor his progress faster. It cannot be a lack of know-how that causes the despair not only of religious thinkers like Kierkegaard but also of leading mathematicians and scientists like Russell and Hoyle. We know how to do many things, but do we know *what* to do? Ortega y Gasset put it succinctly: "We cannot live on the human level without ideas. Upon them depends what we do. Living is nothing more or less than doing one thing instead of another." What, then, is education? It is the transmission of ideas which enable man to choose between one thing and another, or, to quote Ortega again, "to live a life which is something above meaningless tragedy or inward disgrace."

How could, for instance, a knowledge of the Second Law of Thermodynamics help us in this? Lord Snow tells us that when educated people deplore the "illiteracy of scientists" he sometimes asks "How many of them could describe the Second Law of Thermodynamics?" The response, he reports, is usually cold and negative. "Yet," he says, "I was asking something which is about the

Despair is the result of intellect, not of heart. "The great ideas of the 19th century may fill our minds in one way or another, but our hearts do not believe in them all the same." Schumacher's remedy was not to discard specialization in education, but to go deeper into the metaphysical assumptions underlying modern knowledge and to reconnect knowledge with a "center constituted by our most basic convictions."

The role of education in this process was to produce "whole men" who "will not be in doubt about his basic convictions." But caught between heart and intellect we are "saved from despair, but landed in confusion." For Schumacher, the way out of this impasse was to recover the awareness that there are higher and lower levels of knowledge. The lower level deals with what he termed "convergent" problems that are solvable through logic or scientific research. "Divergent" problems, on the ➡

scientific equivalent of: Have you read a work of Shakespeare's?" Such a statement challenges the entire basis of our civilisation. What matters is the tool-box of ideas with which, by which, through which, we experience and interpret the world. The Second Law of Thermodynamics is nothing more than a working hypothesis suitable for various types of scientific research. On the other hand—a work by Shakespeare: teeming with the most vital ideas about the *inner* development of man, showing the whole grandeur and misery of human existence. How could these two things be equivalent? What do I miss, as a human being, if I have never heard of the Second Law of Thermodynamics? The answer is: Nothing.[1] And what do I miss by not knowing Shakespeare? Unless I get my understanding from another source, I simply miss my life. Shall we tell our children that one thing is as good as another—here a bit of knowledge of physics, and there a bit of knowledge of literature? If we do so, the sins of the fathers will be visited upon the children unto the third and fourth generation, because that normally is the time it takes from the birth of an idea to its full maturity when it fills the minds of a new generation and makes them think *by it*.

Science cannot produce ideas by which we could live. Even the greatest ideas of science are nothing more than working hypotheses, useful for purposes of special research but completely inapplicable to the conduct of our lives or the interpretation of the world. If, therefore, a man seeks education because he feels estranged and bewildered, because his life seems to him empty and meaningless, he cannot get what he is seeking by studying any of the natural sciences, i.e. by acquiring "know-how." That study has its own value which I am not inclined to belittle, it tells him a great deal about how things work in nature or in engineering: but it tells him nothing about the meaning of life and can in no way cure his estrangement and secret despair.

Where, then, shall he turn? Maybe, in spite of all that he hears about the scientific revolution and ours being an age of science, he turns to the so-called humanities. Here indeed he can find, if he is lucky, great and vital ideas to fill his mind, ideas with which to think and through which to make the world, society, and his own life intelligible. Let us see what are the main ideas he is likely to find today. I cannot attempt to make a complete list; so I shall confine myself to the enumeration of six leading ideas, all stemming from the nineteenth century, which still dominate, as far as I can see, the minds of "educated" people today.

1. There is the idea of evolution—that higher forms continually develop out of lower forms, as a kind of natural and automatic process. The last hundred years or so have seen the systematic application of this idea to all aspects of reality without exception.
2. There is the idea of competition, natural selection, and the survival of the fittest, which purports to explain the natural and automatic process of evolution and development.
3. There is the idea that all the higher manifestations of human life, such as religion, philosophy, art, etc.—what Marx calls "the phantasmagorias in the brains of men"—are nothing but "necessary supplements of the material life process," a superstructure erected to disguise and promote economic interests, the whole of human history being the history of class struggles.
4. In competition, one might think, with the Marxist interpretation of all higher manifestations of human life, there is, fourthly, the Freudian interpretation which reduces them to the dark stirrings of a subconscious mind and explains them mainly as the results of unfulfilled incest-wishes during childhood and early adolescence.
5. There is the general idea of relativism, denying all absolutes, dissolving all norms and standards, leading to the total undermining of the idea of truth in pragmatism, and affecting even mathematics, which has been defined by Bertrand Russell as "the subject in which we never know what we are talking about, or whether what we say is true."
6. Finally there is the triumphant idea of positivism, that valid knowledge can be attained only through the methods of the natural sciences and hence that no knowledge is genuine unless it is based on generally observable facts. Positivism, in other words, is solely interested in "know-how" and de-

nies the possibility of objective knowledge about meaning and purpose of any kind.

No one, I think, will be disposed to deny the sweep and power of these six "large" ideas. They are not the result of any narrow empiricism. No amount of factual enquiry could have verified any one of them. They represent tremendous leaps of the imagination into the unknown and unknowable. Of course, the leap is taken from a small platform of observed fact. These ideas could not have lodged themselves as firmly in men's minds, as they have done, if they did not contain important elements of truth. But their essential character is their claim of universality. Evolution takes everything into its stride, not only material phenomena from *nebulae* to *homo sapiens* but also all mental phenomena, such as religion or language. Competition, natural selection, and the survival of the fittest are not presented as one set of observations among others, but as universal laws. Marx does not say that some parts of history are made up of class struggles; no, "scientific materialism," not very scientifically, extends this partial observation to nothing less than the whole of "the history of all hitherto existing society." Freud, again, is not content to report a number of clinical observations but offers a universal theory of human motivation, asserting, for instance, that all religion is nothing but an obsessional neurosis. Relativism and positivism, of course, are purely metaphysical doctrines, with the peculiar and ironical distinction that they deny the validity of all metaphysics, including themselves.

What do these six "large" ideas have in common, besides their non-empirical, metaphysical nature? They all assert that what had previously been taken to be something of a higher order is really "nothing but" a more subtle manifestation of the "lower"—unless, indeed, the very distinction between higher and lower is denied. Thus man, like the rest of the universe, is really nothing but an accidental collocation of atoms. The difference between a man and a stone is little more than a deceptive appearance. Man's highest cultural achievements are nothing but disguised economic greed or the outflow of sexual frustrations. In any case, it is meaningless to say that man should aim at the "higher" rather than the "lower" because no intelligible meaning can be attached to purely subjective notions like "higher" or "lower," while the word "should" is just a sign of authoritarian megalomania.

The ideas of the fathers in the nineteenth century have been visited on the third and fourth generations living in the second half of the twentieth century. To their originators, these ideas were simply the result of their intellectual processes. In the third and fourth generations, they have become the very tools and instruments through which the world is being experienced and interpreted. Those that bring forth new ideas are seldom ruled by them. But their ideas obtain power over men's lives in the third and fourth generations when they have become a part of that great mass of ideas, including language, which seeps into a person's mind during his "Dark Ages."

These nineteenth-century ideas are firmly lodged in the minds of practically everybody in the Western world today, whether educated or uneducated. In the uneducated mind they are still rather muddled and nebulous, too weak to make the world intelligible. Hence the longing for education, that is to say, for something that will lead us out of the dark wood of our muddled ignorance into the light of understanding.

I have said that a purely scientific education cannot do this for us because it deals only with ideas of know-how, whereas we need to understand why things are as they are and what we are to do with our lives. What we learn by studying a particular science is in any case too specific and specialised for our wider purposes. So we turn to the humanities to obtain a clear view of the large and vital ideas of our age. Even in the humanities we may get bogged down in a mass of specialised scholarship, furnishing our minds with lots of small ideas just as unsuitable as the ideas which we might pick up from the natural sciences. But we may also be more fortunate (if fortunate it is) and find a teacher who will "clear our minds," clarify the ideas—the "large" and universal ideas already existent in our minds—and thus make the world intelligible for us.

Such a process would indeed deserve to be called "education." And what do we get from it today? A view of the world, as a wasteland in which there is no meaning or purpose, in which man's consciousness is an unfortunate cosmic accident, in which anguish and despair are the only final realities. If by means of a real education man manages to climb to what Ortega calls "the Height of Our Times" or "the Height of the Ideas of our Times," he finds himself in an abyss of nothingness. He may feel like echoing Byron:

> *Sorrow is knowledge; they who know the most*
> *Must mourn the deepest o'er the fatal truth,*
> *The Tree of Knowledge is not that of Life.*

In other words, even a humanistic education lifting us to the height of the ideas of our time cannot "deliver the goods," because what men are quite legitimately looking for is life more abundant, and not sorrow.

What has happened? How is such a thing possible?

The leading ideas of the nineteenth century, which claimed to do away with metaphysics, are themselves a bad, vicious, life-destroying type of metaphysics. We are suffering from them as from a fatal disease. It is not true that knowledge is sorrow. But poisonous errors bring unlimited sorrow in the third and fourth generation. The errors are not in science but in the philosophy put forward in the name of science. As Etienne Gilson put it more than twenty years ago:

Such a development was by no means inevitable, but the progressive growth of natural science had made it more and more probable. The growing interest taken by men in the practical results of science was in itself both natural and legitimate, but it helped them to forget that science is knowledge, and practical results but its by-products.... Before their unexpected success in finding conclusive explanations of the material world, men had begun either to despise all disciplines in which such demonstrations could not be found, or to rebuild those disciplines after the pattern of the physical sciences. As a consequence, metaphysics and ethics had to be either ignored or, at least, replaced by new positive sciences; in either case, they would be eliminated. A very dangerous move indeed, which accounts for the perilous position in which Western culture has now found itself.

It is not even true that metaphysics and ethics would be eliminated. On the contrary, all we got was bad metaphysics and appalling ethics.

Historians know that metaphysical errors can lead to death. R.G. Collingwood wrote:

> The Patristic diagnosis of the decay of Greco-Roman civilisation ascribes that event to a metaphysical disease.... It was not barbarian attacks that destroyed the Greco-Roman world.... The cause was a metaphysical cause. The "pagan" world was failing to keep alive its own fundamental convictions, they [the patristic writers] said, because owing to faults in metaphysical analysis it had become confused as to what these convictions were.... If metaphysics had been a mere luxury of the intellect, this would not have mattered.

This passage can be applied, without change, to present-day civilisation. We have become confused as to what our convictions really are. The great ideas of the nineteenth century may fill our minds in one way or another, but our hearts do not believe in them all the same. Mind and heart are at war with one another, not, as is commonly asserted, reason and faith. Our reason has become beclouded by an extraordinary, blind, and unreasonable faith in a set of fantastic and life-destroying ideas inherited from the nineteenth century. It is the foremost task of our reason to recover a truer faith than that.

Education cannot help us as long as it accords no place to metaphysics. Whether the subjects taught are subjects of science or of the humanities, if the teaching does not lead to a clarification of metaphysics, that is to say, of our fundamental convictions, it cannot educate a man and, consequently, cannot be of real value to society.

It is often asserted that education is breaking down because of

over-specialisation. But this is only a partial and misleading diagnosis. Specialisation is not in itself a faulty principle of education.
What would be the alternative—an amateurish smattering of all
major subjects? Or a lengthy *studium generale* in which men are
forced to spend their time sniffing at subjects which they do not
wish to pursue, while they are being kept away from what they want
to learn? This cannot be the right answer, since it can only lead to
the type of intellectual man whom Cardinal Newman castigated—
"an intellectual man, as the world now conceives of him,...one
who is full of 'views' on all subjects of philosophy, on all matters of
the day." Such "viewiness" is a sign of ignorance rather than knowledge. "Shall I teach you the meaning of knowledge?" said Con-
fucius. "When you know a thing to recognise that you know it,
and when you do not, to know that you do not know—that is
knowledge."

What is at fault is not specialisation, but the lack of depth with
which the subjects are usually presented, and the absence of metaphysical awareness. The sciences are being taught without any
awareness of the presuppositions of science, of the meaning and
significance of scientific laws, and of the place occupied by the natural sciences within the whole cosmos of human thought. The result is that the presuppositions of science are normally mistaken
for its findings. Economics is being taught without any awareness
of the view of human nature that underlies present-day economic
theory. In fact, many economists are themselves unaware of the
fact that such a view is implicit in their teaching and that nearly all
their theories would have to change if that view changed. How
could there be a rational teaching of politics without pressing all
questions back to their metaphysical roots? Political thinking must
necessarily become confused and end in "double-talk" if there is a
continued refusal to admit the serious study of the metaphysical
and ethical problems involved. The confusion is already so great
that it is legitimate to doubt the educational value of studying many
of the so-called humanistic subjects. I say "so-called" because a subject that does not make explicit its view of human nature can hardly
be called humanistic.

All subjects, no matter how specialised, are connected with a centre; they are like rays emanating from a sun. The centre is constituted by our most basic convictions, by those ideas which really have the power to move us. In other words, the centre consists of metaphysics and ethics, of ideas that—whether we like it or not—transcend the world of facts. Because they transcend the world of facts, they cannot be proved or disproved by ordinary scientific method. But that does not mean that they are purely "subjective" or "relative" or mere arbitrary conventions. They must be true to reality, although they transcend the world of facts—an apparent paradox to our positivistic thinkers. If they are not true to reality, the adherence to such a set of ideas must inevitably lead to disaster.

Education can help us only if it produces "whole men." The truly educated man is not a man who knows a bit of everything, not even the man who knows all the details of all subjects (if such a thing were possible): the "whole man," in fact, may have little detailed knowledge of facts and theories, he may treasure the *Encyclopaedia Britannica* because "she knows and he needn't," *but he will be truly in touch with the centre.* He will not be in doubt about his basic convictions, about his view on the meaning and purpose of his life. He may not be able to explain these matters in words, but the conduct of his life will show a certain sureness of touch which stems from his inner clarity.

I shall try to explain a little bit further what is meant by "centre." All human activity is a striving after something thought of as good. This is not more than a tautology, but it helps us to ask the right question: "Good for whom?" Good for the striving person. So, unless that person has sorted out and coordinated his manifold urges, impulses, and desires, his strivings are likely to be confused, contradictory, self-defeating, and possibly highly destructive. The "centre," obviously, is the place where he has to create for himself an orderly system of ideas about himself and the world, which can regulate the direction of his various strivings. If he has never given any thought to this (because he is always too busy with more important things, or he is proud to think "humbly" of himself as an agnostic), the centre will not by any means be empty: it will be filled with all those vital ideas which, in one way or another, have seeped into his

Revitalizing local economies means rethinking education—examining the connection between ever greater specialization and increasing dependence on an ever larger economic arena. Today, modern education is training children around the world for the centralized global economy. Essentially the same curriculum is taught in every environment, no matter what the cultural tradition or local resources.

Promoting regional and local adaptation in the schools would be an essential part of the revitalization of local economies. Training in locally-adapted agriculture, architecture, artisan production, and appropriate technologies suited to the specifics of climate and local resources would further a real decentralization of production for basic needs. Rather than educating the young for ever greater specialization in a competitive, "jobless growth" economy, children would be equipped for ➡

→ diverse economic systems that depended primarily, but not exclusively, on local resources. This, of course, would not mean that information about the rest of the world would be excluded. On the contrary, knowledge about other cultures and cultural exchange programs would be an important part of the educational process.
—HELENA
NORBERG-HODGE

mind during his Dark Ages. I have tried to show what these ideas are likely to be today: a total denial of meaning and purpose of human existence on earth, leading to the total despair of anyone who really believes in them. Fortunately, as I said, the heart is often more intelligent than the mind and refuses to accept these ideas in their full weight. So the man is saved from despair, but landed in confusion. His fundamental convictions are confused; hence his actions, too, are confused and uncertain. If he would only allow the light of consciousness to fall on the centre and face the question of his fundamental convictions, he could create order where there is disorder. That would "educate" him, in the sense of leading him out of the darkness of his metaphysical confusion.

I do not think, however, that this can be successfully done unless he quite consciously accepts—even if only provisionally—a number of metaphysical ideas which are almost directly opposite to the ideas (stemming from the nineteenth century) that have lodged in his mind. I shall mention three examples.

While the nineteenth-century ideas deny or obliterate the hierarchy of levels in the universe, the notion of an hierarchical order is an indispensable instrument of understanding. Without the recognition of "Levels of Being" or "Grades of Significance" we cannot make the world intelligible to ourselves nor have we the slightest possibility to define our own position, the position of man, in the scheme of the universe. It is only when we can see the world as a ladder, and when we can see man's position on the ladder, that we can recognise a meaningful task for man's life on earth. Maybe it is man's task—or simply, if you like, man's happiness—to attain a higher degree of realisation of his potentialities, a higher level of being or "grade of significance" than that which comes to him "naturally": we cannot even study this possibility except by recognising the existence of a hierarchical structure. To the extent that we interpret the world through the great, vital ideas of the nineteenth century, we are blind to these differences of level, because we have been blinded.

As soon, however, as we accept the existence of "levels of being," we can readily understand, for instance, why the methods of physical science cannot be applied to the study of politics or economics, or why the findings of physics—as Einstein recognised—have no philosophical implications.

If we accept the Aristotelian division of metaphysics into ontology and epistemology, the proposition that there are levels of being is an ontological proposition; I now add an epistemological one: the nature of our thinking is such that we cannot help thinking in opposites.

It is easy enough to see that all through our lives we are faced with the task of reconciling opposites which, in logical thought, cannot be reconciled. The typical problems of life are insoluble on the level of being on which we normally find ourselves. How can one reconcile the demands of freedom and discipline in education? Countless mothers and teachers, in fact, do it, but no one can write down a solution. They do it by bringing into the situation a force that belongs to a higher level where opposites are transcended—the power of love.

G.N.M. Tyrell has put forward the terms "divergent" and "convergent" to distinguish problems which cannot be solved by logical reasoning from those that can. Life is being kept going by divergent problems which have to be "lived" and are solved only in death. Convergent problems on the other hand are man's most useful invention; they do not, as such, exist in reality, but are created by a process of abstraction. When they have been solved, the solution can be written down and passed on to others, who can apply it without needing to reproduce the mental effort necessary to find it. If this were the case with human relations—in family life, economics, politics, education, and so forth—well, I am at a loss how to finish the sentence. There would be no more human relations but only mechanical reactions; life would be a living death. Divergent problems, as it were, force man to strain himself to a level above himself; they demand, and thus provoke the supply of, forces from a higher level, thus bringing love, beauty, goodness, and truth into our lives. It is only with the help of these higher forces that the opposites can be reconciled in the living situation.

The physical sciences and mathematics are concerned exclusively with convergent problems. That is why they can progress cumulatively, and each new generation can begin just where their forbears left off. The price, however, is a heavy one. Dealing exclusively with convergent problems does not lead into life but away from it.

> Up to the age of thirty, or beyond it [wrote Charles Darwin in his autobiography], poetry of many kinds...gave me great pleasure, and even as a schoolboy I took intense delight in Shakespeare, especially in the historical plays. I have also said that formerly pictures gave me considerable, and music very great, delight. But now for many years I cannot endure to read a line of poetry: I have tried lately to read Shakespeare, and found it so intolerably dull that it nauseated me. I have also lost almost any taste for pictures or music.... My mind seems to have become a kind of machine for grinding general laws out of large collections of fact, but why this would have caused the atrophy of that part of the brain alone, on which the higher tastes depend, I cannot conceive.... The loss of these talents is a loss of happiness, and may possibly be injurious to the intellect, and more probably to the moral character, by enfeebling the emotional part of our nature.[2]

This impoverishment, so movingly described by Darwin, will overwhelm our entire civilisation if we permit the current tendencies to continue which Gilson calls "the extension of positive science to social facts." All divergent problems can be turned into convergent problems by a process of "reduction." The result, however, is the loss of all higher forces to ennoble human life, and the degradation not only of the emotional part of our nature, but also, as Darwin sensed, of our intellect and moral character. The signs are everywhere visible today.

The true problems of living—in politics, economics, education, marriage, etc.—are always problems of overcoming or reconciling opposites. They are divergent problems and have no solution in the ordinary sense of the word. They demand of man not merely the employment of his reasoning powers but the commitment of his whole personality. Naturally, spurious solutions, by way of a clever formula, are always being put forward; but they never work for long, because they invariably neglect one of the two opposites and thus lose the very quality of human life. In economics, the solution offered may provide for freedom but not for planning, or vice versa. In industrial organisation, it may provide for discipline but not for workers' participation in management, or vice versa. In politics, it might provide for leadership without democracy or, again, for democracy without leadership.

To have to grapple with divergent problems tends to be exhausting, worrying, and wearisome. Hence people try to avoid it and to run away from it. A busy executive who has been dealing with divergent problems all day long will read a detective story or solve a crossword puzzle on his journey home. He has been using his brain all day; why does he go on using it? The answer is that the detective story and the crossword puzzle present convergent problems, and *that* is the relaxation. They require a bit of brainwork, even difficult brainwork, but they do not call for this straining and stretching to a higher level which is the specific challenge of a divergent problem, a problem in which irreconcilable opposites have to be reconciled. It is only the latter that are the real stuff of life.

Finally, I turn to a third class of notions, which really belong to metaphysics, although they are normally considered separately: ethics.

The most powerful ideas of the nineteenth century, as we have seen, have denied or at least obscured the whole concept of "levels of being" and the idea that some things are higher than others. This, of course, has meant the destruction of ethics, which is based on the distinction of good and evil, claiming that good is higher than evil. Again, the sins of the fathers are being visited on the third and fourth generations who now find themselves growing up without moral instruction of any kind. The men who conceived the idea that "morality is bunk" did so with a mind well-stocked with moral ideas. But the minds of the third and fourth generations are no longer well-stocked with such ideas: they are well-stocked with ideas conceived in the nineteenth century, namely, that "morality is bunk," that everything that appears to be "higher" is really nothing but something quite mean and vulgar.

Schumacher's view of education and research, if adopted, would invert our present priorities that are mostly focused on convergent problems of one sort or another. He would have us restore core values to education to clarify our central convictions. If we failed to do this, "education, far from ranking as man's greatest resource, will then be an agent of destruction." A quarter of a century later, we still have not found our bearings. It is not implausible that education, in the larger perspective, is indeed an agent of destruction. We still train far more young people to be technicians in service to that great scam called the global economy than we educate whole persons capable of building the kind of decent and human-scaled world he described.
—DAVID ORR

Our society and educational system teaches us that solutions lie in progress—better and faster technology and more machines. When we as a society fail, so often we place blame on these machines and on technology. But the crisis, as Schumacher warned us, is not what is wrong with machines, but what is wrong with us. Schumacher identified the root of what is wrong with us: a failure of thinking, of values, and ultimately, of education. The solution, too, Schumacher foretold, lies in us. We are our own impetus for progress. Progress lies not first in the teaching of how to make or build, or the knowledge of simple facts, but in how to live.

—CATHERINE SNEED

The resulting confusion is indescribable. What is the *Leitbild*, as the Germans say, the guiding image, in accordance with which young people could try to form and educate themselves? There is none, or rather there is such a muddle and mess of images that no sensible guidance issues from them. The intellectuals, whose function it would be to get these things sorted out, spend their time proclaiming that everything is relative—or something to the same effect. Or they deal with ethical matters in terms of the most unabashed cynicism.

I shall give an example already alluded to above. It is significant because it comes from one of the most influential men of our time, the late Lord Keynes. "For at least another hundred years," he wrote, "we must pretend to ourselves and to every one that fair is foul and foul is fair; for foul is useful and fair is not. Avarice and usury and precaution must be our gods for a little longer still."

When great and brilliant men talk like this, we cannot be surprised if there arises a certain confusion between fair and foul, which leads to double talk as long as things are quiet, and to crime when they get a bit more lively. That avarice, usury, and precaution (i.e. economic security) should be our gods was merely a bright idea for Keynes; he surely had nobler gods. But ideas are the most powerful things on earth, and it is hardly an exaggeration to say that by now the gods he recommended have been enthroned.

In ethics, as in so many other fields, we have recklessly and wilfully abandoned our great classical-Christian heritage. We have even degraded the very words without which ethical discourse cannot carry on, words like "virtue," "love," "temperance." As a result, we are totally ignorant, totally uneducated in the subject that, of all conceivable subjects, is the most important. We have no ideas to think with and therefore are only too ready to believe that ethics is a field where thinking does no good. Who knows anything today of the Seven Deadly Sins or of the Four Cardinal Virtues? Who could even name them? And if these venerable, old ideas are thought not to be worth bothering about, what new ideas have taken their place?

What is to take the place of the soul and life-destroying metaphysics inherited from the nineteenth century? The task of our generation, I have no doubt, is one of metaphysical reconstruction. It is not as if we have to invent anything new; at the same time, it is not good enough merely to revert to the old formulations. Our task—and the task of all education—is to understand the present world, the world in which we live and make our choices.

The problems of education are merely reflections of the deepest problems of our age. They cannot be solved by organisation, administration, or the expenditure of money, even though the importance of all these is not denied. We are suffering from a metaphysical disease, and the cure must therefore be metaphysical. Education which fails to clarify our central convictions is mere training or indulgence. For it is our central convictions that are in disorder, and, as long as the present anti-metaphysical temper persists, the disorder will grow worse. Education, far from ranking as man's greatest resource, will then be an agent of destruction, in accordance with the principle *corruptio optimi pessima*.

CHAPTER 7

THE PROPER USE OF LAND

Among material resources, the greatest, unquestionably, is the land. Study how a society uses its land, and you can come to pretty reliable conclusions as to what its future will be.

The land carries the topsoil, and the topsoil carries an immense variety of living beings including man. In 1955, Tom Dale and Vernon Gill Carter, both highly experienced ecologists, published a book called *Topsoil and Civilisation*. I cannot do better, for the purposes of this chapter, than quote some of their opening paragraphs:

> Civilised man was nearly always able to become master of his environment temporarily. His chief troubles came from his delusions that his temporary mastership was permanent. He thought of himself as "master of the world," while failing to understand fully the laws of nature.
>
> Man, whether civilised or savage, is a child of nature—he is not the master of nature. He must conform his actions to certain natural laws if he is to maintain his dominance over his environment. When he tries to circumvent the laws of nature, he usually destroys the natural environment that sustains him. And when his environment deteriorates rapidly, his civilisation declines.
>
> One man has given a brief outline of history by saying that "civilised man has marched across the face of the earth and left a desert in his footprints." This statement may be somewhat of an exaggeration, but it is not without foundation. Civilised man has despoiled most of the lands on which

he has lived for long. This is the main reason why his progressive civilisations have moved from place to place. It has been the chief cause for the decline of his civilisations in older settled regions. It has been the dominant factor in determining all trends of history.

The writers of history have seldom noted the importance of land use. They seem not to have recognised that the destinies of most of man's empires and civilisations were determined largely by the way the land was used. While recognising the influence of environment on history, they fail to note that man usually changed or despoiled his environment.

How did civilised man despoil this favourable environment? He did it mainly by depleting or destroying the natural resources. He cut down or burned most of the usable timber from forested hillsides and valleys. He overgrazed and denuded the grasslands that fed his livestock. He killed most of the wildlife and much of the fish and other water life. He permitted erosion to rob his farm land of its productive topsoil. He allowed eroded soil to clog the streams and fill his reservoirs, irrigation canals, and harbours with silt. In many cases, he used and wasted most of the easily mined metals or other needed minerals. Then his civilisation declined amidst the despoliation of his own creation or he moved to new land. There have been from ten to thirty different civilisations that have followed this road to ruin (the number depending on who classifies the civilisations).[1]

It takes almost 50 years to grow a forest for an Indian, and the logging companies can cut it down in a few years. That is what we are fighting. But the struggle is not solely about forest preservation and biodiversity. It is also about cultural preservation. Although clearcut once at the turn of the century, White Earth has recovered. Its biodiversity is cherished— cherished for what it provides the people and because each plant is alive, has spirit and value on its own. Simply stated, we cannot be a forest culture without a forest.
—WINONA LADUKE

The "ecological problem," it seems, is not as new as it is frequently made out to be. Yet there are two decisive differences: the earth is now much more densely populated than it was in earlier times and there are, generally speaking, no new lands to move to; and the rate of change has enormously accelerated, particularly during the last quarter of a century.

All the same, it is still the dominant belief today that, whatever may have happened with earlier civilisations, our own modern, Western civilisation has emancipated itself from dependence upon nature. A representative voice is that of Eugene Rabinowitch, editor-in-chief of the *Bulletin of Atomic Scientists*.

> The only animals [he says (in *The Times* of 29 April 1972)] whose disappearance may threaten the biological viability of man on earth are the bacteria normally inhabiting our bodies. For the rest there is no convincing proof that mankind could not survive even as the only animal species on earth! If economical ways could be developed for synthesising food from inorganic raw materials—which is likely to happen sooner or later—man may even be able to become independent of plants, on which he now depends as sources of his food....
>
> I personally—and, I suspect, a vast majority of mankind—would shudder at the idea [of a habitat without animals and plants]. But millions of inhabitants of "city jungles" of New York, Chicago, London or Tokyo have grown up and spent their whole lives in a practically "azoic" habitat (leaving out rats, mice, cockroaches and other such obnoxious species) and have survived.

Eugene Rabinowitch obviously considers the above a "rationally justifiable" statement. He deplores that "many rationally unjustifiable things have been written in recent years—some by very reputable scientists—about the sacredness of natural ecological systems, their inherent stability and the danger of human interference with them."

What is "rational" and what is "sacred"? Is man the master of nature or its child? If it becomes "economical" to synthesise food from inorganic materials—"which is likely to happen sooner or later"—if we become independent of plants, the connection between topsoil and civilisation will be broken. Or will it? These questions suggest that "The Proper Use of Land" poses, not a technical nor an economic, but primarily a metaphysical problem. The problem obviously belongs to a higher level of rational thinking than that represented by the last two quotations.

There are always some things which we do for their own sakes, and there are other things which we do for some other purpose. One of the most important tasks for any society is to distinguish between ends and means-to-ends, and to have some sort of cohesive view and agreement about this. Is the land merely a means of production or is it something more, something that is an end in itself? And when I say "land," I include the creatures upon it.

Anything we do just for the sake of doing it does not lend itself to utilitarian calculation. For instance, most of us try to keep ourselves reasonably clean. Why? Simply for hygienic reasons? No, the hygienic aspect is secondary; we recognise cleanliness as a value in itself. We do not calculate its value; the economic calculus simply does not come in. It could be argued that to wash is uneconomic: it costs time and money and produces nothing—except cleanliness. There are many activities which are totally uneconomic, but they are carried on for their own sakes. The economists have an easy way of dealing with them: they divide all human activities between "production" and "consumption." Anything we do under the heading of "production" is subject to the economic calculus, and anything we do under the heading of "consumption" is not. But real life is very refractory to such classifications, because man-as-producer and man-as-consumer is in fact the same man, who is always producing and consuming *at the same time*. Even a worker in his factory consumes certain "amenities," commonly referred to as "working conditions," and when insufficient "amenities" are provided he cannot—or refuses to—carry on. And even the man who consumes water and soap may be said to be producing cleanliness.

We produce in order to be able to afford certain amenities and comforts as "consumers." If, however, somebody demanded these same amenities and comforts while he was engaged in "production," he would be told that this would be uneconomic, that it would be inefficient, and that society could not afford such inefficiency. In other words, everything depends on whether it is done by man-as-producer or by man-as-consumer. If man-as-producer travels first-class or uses a luxurious car, this is called a waste of money; but if the same man in his other incarnation of man-as-consumer does the same, this is called a sign of a high standard of life.

Nowhere is this dichotomy more noticeable than in connection with the use of the land. The farmer is considered simply as a producer who must cut his costs and raise his efficiency by every possible device, even if he thereby destroys—for man-as-consumer—the health of the soil and the beauty of the landscape, and even if the end effect is the depopulation of the land and the overcrowding of cities. There are large-scale farmers, horticulturists, food manufacturers, and fruit growers today who would never think of consuming any of their own products. "Luckily," they say, "we have enough money to be able to afford to buy products which have been organically grown, without the use of poisons." When they are asked why they themselves do not adhere to organic methods and avoid the use of poisonous substances, they reply that they could not afford to do so. What man-as-producer can afford is one thing; what man-as-consumer can afford is quite another thing. But since the two are the same man, the question of what man—or society—can really afford gives rise to endless confusion.

There is no escape from this confusion as long as the land and the creatures upon it are looked upon as *nothing but* "factors of production." They are, of course, factors of production, that is to say, means-to-ends, but this is their secondary, not their primary, nature. Before everything else, they are ends-in-themselves; they are meta-economic, and it is therefore rationally justifiable to say, as a statement of fact, that they are in a certain sense sacred. Man has not made them, and it is irrational for him to treat things that he has not made and cannot make and cannot recreate once he has spoilt them, in the same manner and spirit as he is entitled to treat things of his own making.

The higher animals have an economic value because of their utility; but they have a meta-economic value in themselves. If I have a car, a man-made thing, I might quite legitimately argue that the best way to use it is never to bother about maintenance and simply run it to ruin. I may indeed have calculated that this is the most economical method of use. If the calculation is correct, nobody can criticise me for acting accordingly, for there is nothing sacred about a man-made thing like a car. But if I have an animal—be it only a calf or a hen—a living, sensitive creature, am I allowed to treat it as nothing but a utility? Am I allowed to run it to ruin?

It is no use trying to answer such questions scientifically. They are metaphysical, not scientific, questions. It is a metaphysical error, likely to produce the gravest practical consequences, to equate "car" and "animal" on account of their utility, while failing to recognise the most fundamental difference between them, that of "level of being." An irreligious age looks with amused contempt upon the hallowed statements by which religion helped our forbears to appreciate metaphysical truths. "And the Lord God took man and put him in the Garden of Eden"—not to be idle, but "to dress it and keep it." "And he also gave man dominion over the fish in the sea and the fowl in the air, and over every living being that moves upon the earth." When he had made "the beast of the earth after his kind, and cattle after their kind, and everything that creepeth upon the earth after his kind," he saw that it was "good." But when he saw everything he had made, the entire biosphere, as we say today, "behold, it was *very* good." Man, the highest of his creatures, was given "dominion," not the right to tyrannise, to ruin and exterminate. It is no use talking about the dignity of man without accepting that *noblesse oblige*. For man to put himself into a wrongful relationship with animals, and particularly those long domesticated by him, has always, in all traditions, been considered a horrible and infinitely dangerous thing to do. There have been no sages or holy men in our or in anybody else's history who were cruel to animals or who looked upon them as *nothing but* utilities, and innumerable are the legends and stories which link sanctity as well as happiness with a loving kindness towards lower creation.

It is interesting to note that modern man is being told, in the name of science, that he is really *nothing but* a naked ape or even an accidental collocation of atoms. "Now we can define man," says Professor Joshua Lederberg. "Genotypically at least, he is six feet of a particular molecular sequence of carbon, hydrogen, oxygen, nitrogen and phosphorous atoms." As modern man thinks so "humbly" of himself, he thinks even more "humbly" of the animals which serve his needs: and treats them as if they were machines.

Agriculture, Schumacher argued, must learn from nature and work with nature, and learn also how to protect the wider environment and all that lives within it. This requires a shift from industrialized chemical farming to organic husbandry. The mass production of throwaway products based on fossil energy, capital, and chemical intensive forms of production, whether in manufacture or agriculture, is no longer possible or acceptable. This view would be consistent with most interpretations of deep ecology.
—GEORGE MᶜROBIE

Other, less sophisticated—or is it less depraved?—people take a different attitude. As H. Fielding Hall reported from Burma:

> To him [the Burmese] men are men, and animals are animals, and men are far the higher. But he does not deduce from this that man's superiority gives him permission to ill-treat or kill animals. It is just the reverse. It is because man is so much higher than the animal that he can and must observe towards animals the very greatest care, feel for them the very greatest compassion, be good to them in every way he can. The Burmese's motto should be *noblesse oblige*. He knows the meaning, if he knows not the words.[3]

In Proverbs we read that the just man takes care of his beast, but the heart of the wicked is merciless, and St. Thomas Aquinas wrote: "It is evident that if a man practises a compassionate affection for animals, he is all the more disposed to feel compassion for his fellowmen." No one ever raised the question of whether they could *afford* to live in accordance with these convictions. At the level of values, of ends-in-themselves, there is no question of "affording."

What applies to the animals upon the land applies equally, and without any suspicion of sentimentality, to the land itself. Although ignorance and greed have again and again destroyed the fertility of the soil to such an extent that whole civilisations foundered, there have been no traditional teachings which failed to recognise the meta-economic value and significance of "the generous earth." And where these teachings were heeded, not only agriculture but also all other factors of civilisation achieved health and wholeness. Conversely, where people imagined that they could not "afford" to care for the soil and work with nature, instead of against it, the resultant sickness of the soil has invariably imparted sickness to all the other factors of civilisation.

In our time, the main danger to the soil, and therewith not only to agriculture but to civilisation as a whole, stems from the townsman's determination to apply to agriculture the principles of industry. No more typical representative of this tendency could be found than Dr. Sicco L. Mansholt, who, as Vice-President of the European

Economic Community, launched the Mansholt Plan for European Agriculture. He believes that the farmers are "a group that has still not grasped the rapid changes in society." Most of them ought to get out of farming and become industrial labourers in the cities, because "factory workers, men on building sites and those in administrative jobs—have a five-day week and two weeks' annual holiday already. Soon they may have a four-day week and four weeks' holiday per year. And the farmer: *he is condemned to working a seven-day week because the five-day cow has not been invented, and he gets no holiday at all.*"[4] The Mansholt Plan, accordingly, is designed to achieve, as quickly as humanely possible, the amalgamation of many small family farms into large agricultural units operated as if they were factories, and the maximum rate of reduction in the community's agricultural population. Aid is to be given "which would enable the older as well as the younger farmers to leave agriculture."[5]

In the discussion of the Mansholt Plan, agriculture is generally referred to as one of Europe's "industries." The question arises of whether agriculture is, in fact, an industry, or whether it might be something *essentially* different. Not surprisingly, as this is a meta-physical—or meta-economic—question, it is never raised by economists.

Now, the fundamental "principle" of agriculture is that it deals with life, that is to say, with living substances. Its products are the results of processes of life and its means of production is the living soil. A cubic centimetre of fertile soil contains billions of living organisms, the full exploration of which is far beyond the capacities of man. The fundamental "principle" of modern industry, on the other hand, is that it deals with man-devised processes which work reliably only when applied to man-devised, non-living materials. The ideal of industry is the elimination of living substances. Man-made materials are preferable to natural materials, because we can make them to measure and apply perfect quality control. Man-made machines work more reliably and more predictably than do such living substances as men. The ideal of industry is to eliminate the living factor, even including the human factor, and to turn the productive process over to machines. As Alfred North Whitehead defined life as "an offensive directed against the repetitious mecha-

Inanimate things can be perfectly controlled and made to measure for standardized mass production. Biotechnology is an attempt to use a living substance as if it were inanimate, that is, a controlled input with clearly defined functions. But one of the objections to genetically modified organisms is that they may not behave as perfectly controllable inputs: their consequences for people and the environment are still unknown. This is apart from the power that genetically modified organisms can give multinationals over the lives of poor farmers in developing countries and everywhere else.

—GEORGE MᶜROBIE

nism of the universe," so we may define modern industry as "an offensive against the unpredictability, unpunctuality, general waywardness and cussedness of living nature, including man."

In other words, there can be no doubt that the fundamental "principles" of agriculture and of industry, far from being compatible with each other, are in opposition. Real life consists of the tensions produced by the incompatibility of opposites, each of which is needed, and just as life would be meaningless without death, so agriculture would be meaningless without industry. It remains true, however, that agriculture is primary, whereas industry is secondary, which means that human life can continue without industry, whereas it cannot continue without agriculture. Human life at the level of civilisation, however, demands the *balance* of the two principles, and this balance is ineluctably destroyed when people fail to appreciate the *essential* difference between agriculture and industry—a difference as great as that between life and death—and attempt to treat agriculture as just another industry.

The argument is, of course, a familiar one. It was put succinctly by a group of internationally recognised experts in *A Future for European Agriculture*:

> Different parts of the world possess widely differing advantages for the production of particular products, depending on differences in climate, the quality of the soil and the cost of labour. All countries would gain from a division of labour which enabled them to concentrate production on their most highly productive agricultural operations. This would result both in higher income for agriculture and lower costs for the entire economy, particularly for industry. No fundamental justification can be found for agricultural protectionism.[6]

If this were so it would be totally incomprehensible that agricultural protectionism, throughout history, has been the rule rather than the exception. Why are most countries, most of the time, unwilling to gain these splendid rewards from so simple a prescription? Precisely because there is more involved in "agricultural operations" than the production of incomes and the lowering of costs: what is involved is the whole relationship between man and nature, the whole life-style of a society, the health, happiness, and harmony of man, as well as the beauty of his habitat. If all these things are left out of the experts' considerations, man himself is left out—even if our experts try to bring him in, as it were, after the event, by pleading that the community should pay for the "social consequences" of their policies. The Mansholt Plan, say the experts, "represents a bold initiative. It is based on the acceptance of a fundamental principle: agricultural income can only be maintained if the reduction in the agricultural population is accelerated, and if farms rapidly reach an economically viable size." Or again: "Agriculture, in Europe at least, is essentially directed towards food-production.... It is well known that the demand for food increases relatively slowly with increases in real income. This causes the total incomes earned in agriculture to rise more slowly in comparison with the incomes earned in industry; to maintain the same rate of growth of incomes per head is only possible if there is an adequate rate of decline in the numbers engaged in agriculture."...[8] "The conclusions seem inescapable: under circumstances which are normal in other advanced countries, the community would be able to satisfy its own needs with only one-third as many farmers as now."[9]

No serious exception can be taken to these statements if we adopt—as the experts have adopted—the metaphysical position of the crudest materialism, for which money costs and money incomes are the ultimate criteria and determinants of human action, *and the living world has no significance beyond that of a quarry for exploitation.*

On a wider view, however, the land is seen as a priceless asset which it is man's task and happiness "to dress and to keep." We can say that man's management of the land must be primarily orientated towards three goals—health, beauty, and permanence. The fourth goal—the only one accepted by the experts—productivity, will then be attained almost as a by-product. The crude materialist view sees agriculture as "essentially directed towards food-production." A wider view sees agriculture as having to fulfill at least three tasks:

There is no way to affix a price for a way of life. And that, perhaps more than anything else, encapsulates the struggle of the White Earth Anishinaabeg people with the U.S. government, logging companies, and wild rice tycoons. For a hundred years, native people have been saying that their way of life—their land, trees, and very future—cannot be quantified and is not for sale. For that same amount of time, government and industry accountants have been picking away, trying to come up with a formula to compensate Indians. There seems to be no meeting of minds, nor will there be in the next generations.
—WINONA LADUKE

—to keep man in touch with living nature, of which he is
and remains a highly vulnerable part;

—to humanise and ennoble man's wider habitat; and

—to bring forth the foodstuffs and other materials which are
needed for a becoming life.

I do not believe that a civilisation which recognises only the third of
these tasks, and which pursues it with such ruthlessness and violence that the other two tasks are not merely neglected but systematically counteracted, has any chance of long-term survival.

Today, we take pride in the fact that the proportion of people engaged in agriculture has fallen to very low levels and continues to
fall. Great Britain produces some sixty per cent of its food requirements while only three per cent of its working population are working on farms. In the United States, there were still twenty-seven per
cent of the nation's workers in agriculture at the end of World War
I, and fourteen per cent at the end of World War II; the estimate for
1971 shows only 4.4 per cent. These declines in the proportion of
workers engaged in agriculture are generally associated with a massive flight from the land and a burgeoning of cities. At the same
time, however, to quote Lewis Herber:

> Metropolitan life is breaking down, psychologically, eco-
> nomically and biologically. Millions of people have acknowl-
> edged this breakdown by voting with their feet, they have
> picked up their belongings and left. If they have not been
> able to sever their connections with the metropolis, at least
> they have tried. As a social symptom the effort is signifi-
> cant.[10]

In the vast modern towns, says Mr. Herber, the urban dweller is
more isolated than his ancestors were in the countryside: "The city
man in a modern metropolis has reached a degree of anonymity,
social atomisation and spiritual isolation that is virtually unprecedented in human history."

So what does he do? He tries to get into the suburbs and becomes a
commuter. Because rural culture has broken down, the rural peo-

ple are fleeing from the land; and because metropolitan life is breaking down, urban people are fleeing from the cities. "Nobody," according to Dr. Mansholt, "can afford the luxury of not acting economically,"[12] with the result that everywhere life tends to become intolerable for anyone except the very rich.

I agree with Mr. Herber's assertion that "reconciliation of man with the natural world is no longer merely desirable, it has become a necessity." And this cannot be achieved by tourism, sightseeing, or other leisure-time activities, but only by changing the structure of agriculture in a direction exactly opposite to that proposed by Dr. Mansholt and supported by the experts quoted above: instead of searching for means to accelerate the drift out of agriculture, we should be searching for policies to reconstruct rural culture, to open the land for the gainful occupation to larger numbers of people, whether it be on a full-time or a part-time basis, and to orientate all our actions on the land towards the threefold ideal of health, beauty, and permanence.

The social structure of agriculture, which has been produced by—and is generally held to obtain its justification from—large-scale mechanisation and heavy chemicalisation, makes it impossible to keep man in real touch with living nature; in fact, it supports all the most dangerous modern tendencies of violence, alienation, and environmental destruction. Health, beauty, and permanence are hardly even respectable subjects for discussion, and this is yet another example of the disregard of human values—and this means a disregard of man—which inevitably results from the idolatry of economism.

If "beauty is the splendour of truth," agriculture cannot fulfill its second task, which is to humanise and ennoble man's wider habitat, unless it clings faithfully and assiduously to the truths revealed by nature's living processes. One of them is the law of return; another is diversification—as against any kind of monoculture; another is decentralisation, so that some use can be found for even quite inferior resources which it would never be rational to transport over long distances. Here again, both the trend of things and the advice of the experts is in the exactly opposite direction—towards the industrialisation and depersonalisation of agriculture, towards concentration, specialisation, and any kind of material waste

In later writings Schumacher elaborated this rather short-hand statement: the task is to work with nature to find ways of improving soil fertility and maximizing genetic variety of plants and animals in contrast to the industrial agriculture approach of attempting to subdue and control nature by chemicals, factory farming, and biotechnology—all forms of violence. This non-violent approach of collaborating with nature and respecting all forms of life is perfectly consistent with the approach of deep ecology.
—GEORGE McROBIE

Trees are not just a vast array of species that adorn the globe, providing food, shelter, warmth, and protection for all kinds of animals and birds. They are the absolutely irreplacable anchors of the soils and processors of the air upon which all of the earth's life-support systems depend. They are vastly more important to the successful continuance of the planet earth than any other species—than, say, the human.

Planting a tree makes a statement: Against the tree destroyers, the rampant developers, the exploiters, the humans-above-all chauvinists; For the protectors, the deep ecologists and bioregionals, the equality of species, and the living earth herself. What's more, the act of planting a tree is often a group or communal event. It brings together people in a concrete action with specific and visible effects, providing an occasion to labor in service to some higher idea, and talk about its effects and impacts.

—KIRKPATRICK SALE

that promises to save labour. As a result, the wider human habitat, far from being humanised and ennobled by man's agricultural activities, becomes standardised to dreariness or even degraded to ugliness.

All this is being done because man-as-producer cannot afford "the luxury of not acting economically," and therefore cannot produce the very necessary "luxuries"—like health, beauty, and permanence—which man-as-consumer desires more than anything else. It would cost too much; and the richer we become, the less we can "afford." The aforementioned experts calculate that the "burden" of agricultural support within the Community of the Six amounts to "nearly three per cent of Gross National Product," an amount they consider "far from negligible." With an annual growth rate of over three percent of Gross National Product, one might have thought that such a "burden" could be carried without difficulty; but the experts point out that "national resources are largely committed to personal consumption, investment and public services.... By using so large a proportion of resources to prop up declining enterprises, whether in agriculture or in industry, the Community foregoes the opportunity to undertake...necessary improvements"[13] in these other fields.

Nothing could be clearer. If agriculture does not pay, it is just a "declining enterprise." Why prop it up? There are no "necessary improvements" as regards the land, but only as regards farmers' incomes, and these can be made if there are fewer farmers. This is the philosophy of the townsman, alienated from living nature, who promotes his own scale of priorities by arguing in economic terms that we cannot "afford" any other. In fact, any society can afford to look after its land and keep it healthy and beautiful in perpetuity. There are no technical difficulties and there is no lack of relevant knowledge. There is no need to consult economic experts when the question is one of priorities. We know too much about ecology today to have any excuse for the many abuses that are currently going on in the management of the land, in the management of animals, in food storage, food processing, and in heedless urbanisation. If we permit them, this is not due to poverty, as if we could not afford to stop them; it is due to the fact that, as a society, we have no firm basis of belief in any meta-economic values, and when there is no such belief the economic calculus takes over. This is quite inevitable. How could it be otherwise? Nature, it has been said, abhors a vacuum, and when the available "spiritual space" is not filled by some higher motivation, then it will necessarily be filled by something lower—by the small, mean, calculating attitude to life which is rationalised in the economic calculus.

I have no doubt that a callous attitude to the land and to the animals thereon is connected with, and symptomatic of, a great many other attitudes, such as those producing a fanaticism of rapid change and a fascination with novelties—technical, organisational, chemical, biological, and so forth—which insists on their application long before their long-term consequences are even remotely understood. In the simple question of how we treat the land, next to people our most precious resource, our entire way of life is involved, and before our policies with regard to the land will really be changed, there will have to be a great deal of philosophical, not to say religious, change. It is not a question of what we can afford but of what we choose to spend our money on. If we could return to a generous recognition of meta-economic values, our landscapes would become healthy and beautiful again and our people would regain the dignity of man, who knows himself as higher than the animal but never forgets that *noblesse oblige.*

CHAPTER 8

RESOURCES FOR INDUSTRY

THE MOST STRIKING THING about modern industry is that it requires so much and accomplishes so little. Modern industry seems to be inefficient to a degree that surpasses one's ordinary powers of imagination. Its inefficiency therefore remains unnoticed.

Industrially, the most advanced country today is undoubtedly the United States of America. With a population of about 207 million, it contains 5.6 per cent of mankind; with only about fifty-seven people per square mile—as against a world average of over seventy—and being situated wholly within the northern temperate zone, it ranks as one of the great sparsely populated areas of the world. It has been calculated that if the entire world population were put into the United States, its density of population would then be just about that of England now. This may be thought to be an "unfair" comparison; but even if we take the United Kingdom as a whole, we find a population density that is more than ten times that of the United States (which means that the United States could accommodate more than half the present world population before it attained a density equal to that of the United Kingdom now), and there are many other industrialised countries where densities are even higher. Taking the whole of Europe, exclusive of the U.S.S.R., we find a population density of 242.7 persons per square mile, or $4^1/_4$ times that of the United States. It cannot be said, therefore, that—relatively speaking—the United States is disadvantaged by having too many people and too little space.

Nor could it be said that the territory of the United States was poorly endowed with natural resources. On the contrary, in all human history no large territory has ever been opened up which has more excellent and wonderful resources and, although much has been exploited and ruined since, this still remains true today.

All the same, the industrial system of the United States cannot subsist on internal resources alone and has therefore had to extend its tentacles right around the globe to ensure its raw material supplies. For the 5.6 per cent of the world population which live in the United States require something of the order of forty per cent of the world's primary resources to keep going. Whenever estimates are produced which relate to the next ten, twenty, or thirty years, the message that emerges is one of ever-increasing dependence of the United States economy on raw material and fuel supplies from outside the country. The National Petroleum Council, for instance, calculates that by 1985 the United States will have to cover fifty-seven per cent of its total oil requirements from imports, which would then greatly exceed—at 800 million tons—the total oil imports which Western Europe and Japan currently obtain from the Middle East and Africa.

An industrial system which uses forty per cent of the world's primary resources to supply less than six per cent of the world's population could be called efficient only if it obtained strikingly successful results in terms of human happiness, well-being, culture, peace, and harmony. I do not need to dwell on the fact that the American system fails to do this, or that there are not the slightest prospects that it could do so *if only* it achieved a higher rate of growth of production, associated, as it must be, with an ever-greater call upon the world's finite resources. Professor Walter Heller, former Chairman of the U.S. President's Council of Economic Advisers, no doubt reflected the opinion of most modern economists when he expressed this view:

> We need expansion to fulfill our nation's aspirations. In a fully employed, high-growth economy you have a better chance to free public and private resources to fight the battle of land, air, water and noise pollution than in a low-growth economy.

We have become the quintessential opposite of what Schumacher had hoped. We are now run by greed, a false economic system, and the exploitation of the unknowing individual as we plummet headlong into environmental catastrophe. Tolerance levels of environmental contaminants are a laughingstock, with only a small percent of the total toxic release being reported in the United States. Under the North American Free Trade Agreement, big business has proliferated low-paying, assembly-line jobs throughout the U.S.–Mexican border and parts of Central America, polluting the environment and undermining indigenous technologies. And natural capital is so exploited that 20 to 30 percent of our biodiversity may be gone in the next 25 years, spelling irretrievable loss for those higher on the food chain.

—PLINY FISK

The mainstream view of the environment today is sharply different from what it was when Schumacher wrote Small is Beautiful. At that time, environmental problems were almost universally regarded as minor, technical, soluble, and politically uncontentious. They were considered by-products of economic growth and social progress that would be duly solved by further applications of growth and progress. Today, throughout the industrialized world, governments and parties of both left and right now acknowledge that environmental problems are indeed very serious, requiring solutions that are not merely technical, and may not be available at all without significant social and economic change.

—MARK ROSELAND

"I cannot conceive," he says, "a successful economy without growth." But if the United States' economy cannot conceivably be successful without further rapid growth, and if that growth depends on being able to draw ever-increasing resources from the rest of the world, what about the other 94.4 per cent of mankind which are so far "behind" America?

If a high-growth economy is needed to fight the battle against pollution, which itself appears to be the result of high growth, what hope is there of ever breaking out of this extraordinary circle? In any case, the question needs to be asked whether the earth's resources are likely to be adequate for the further development of an industrial system that consumes so much and accomplishes so little.

More and more voices are being heard today which claim that they are not. Perhaps the most prominent among these voices is that of a study group at the Massachusetts Institute of Technology which produces *The Limits to Growth*, a report for the Club of Rome's project on the predicament of mankind. The report contains, among other material, an interesting table which shows the known global reserves; the number of years known global reserves will last at current global consumption rates; the number of years known global reserves will last with consumption continuing to grow exponentially; and the number of years they could meet growing consumption if they were five times larger than they are currently known to be: all this for nineteen non-renewable natural resources of vital importance to industrial societies. Of particular interest is the last column of the table which shows "U.S. Consumption as % of World Total." The figures are as follows:

Aluminum	42%	Molybdenum	40%
Chromium	19%	Natural Gas	63%
Coal	44%	Nickel	38%
Cobalt	32%	Petroleum	33%
Copper	33%	Platinum Group	31%
Gold	26%	Silver	26%
Iron	28%	Tin	24%
Lead	25%	Tungsten	22%
Manganese	14%	Zinc	26%
Mercury	24%		

In only one or two of these commodities is U.S. production sufficient to cover U.S. consumption. Having calculated when, under certain assumptions, each of these commodities will be exhausted, the authors give their general conclusion, cautiously, as follows:

> Given present resource consumption rates and the projected increase in these rates, the great majority of the currently important non-renewable resources will be extremely costly 100 years from now.

In fact, they do not believe that very much time is left before modern industry, "heavily dependent on a network of international agreements with the producing countries for the supply of raw materials," might be faced with crises of unheard-of proportions.

> Added to the difficult economic question of the fate of various industries as resource after resource becomes prohibitively expensive is the imponderable political question of the relationships between producer and consumer nations as the remaining resources become concentrated in more limited geographical areas. Recent nationalisation of South American mines and successful Middle Eastern pressures to raise oil prices suggest that the political question may arise long before the ultimate economic one.

It was perhaps useful, but hardly essential, for the MIT group to make so many elaborate and hypothetical calculations. In the end, the group's conclusions derive from its assumptions, and it does not require more than a simple act of insight to realise that infinite growth of material consumption in a finite world is an impossibility. Nor does it require the study of large numbers of commodities, of trends, feedback loops, system dynamics, and so forth, to come to the conclusion *that time is short*. Maybe it was useful to employ a computer for obtaining results which any intelligent person can reach with the help of a few calculations on the back of an envelope, because the modern world believes in computers and masses of facts, and it abhors simplicity. But it is always dangerous and normally self-defeating to try and cast out devils by Beelzebub, the prince of the devils.

For the modern industrial system is not gravely threatened by possible scarcities and high prices of most of the materials to which the MIT study devotes such ponderous attention. Who could say how much of these commodities there might be in the crust of the earth; how much will be extracted, by ever more ingenious methods, before it is meaningful to talk of global exhaustion; how much might be won from the oceans; and how much might be recycled? Necessity is indeed the mother of invention, and the inventiveness of industry, marvellously supported by modern science, is unlikely to be easily defeated on these fronts.

It would have been better for the furtherance of insight if the MIT team had concentrated its analysis on the one material factor the availability of which is the precondition of all others and *which cannot be recycled*—energy.

I have already alluded to the energy problem in some of the earlier chapters. It is impossible to get away from it. It is impossible to overemphasise its centrality. It might be said that energy is for the mechanical world what consciousness is for the human world. If energy fails, everything fails.

As long as there is enough primary energy—at tolerable prices—there is no reason to believe that bottlenecks in any other primary materials cannot be either broken or circumvented. On the other hand, a shortage of primary energy would mean that the demand for most other primary products would be so curtailed that a question of shortage with regard to them would be unlikely to arise.

Although these basic facts are perfectly obvious, they are not yet sufficiently appreciated. There is still a tendency, supported by the excessively *quantitative* orientation of modern economics, to treat the energy supply problem as just one problem alongside countless others—as indeed was done by the MIT team. The quantitative orientation is so bereft of qualitative understanding that even the quality of "orders of magnitude" ceases to be appreciated. And this, in fact, is one of the main causes of the lack of realism with which the energy supply prospects of modern industrial society are generally discussed. It is said, for instance, that "coal is on the way out and will be replaced by oil," and when it is pointed out that this would mean the speedy exhaustion of all proved and expected (i.e. yet-to-be-discovered) oil reserves, it is blandly asserted that "we are rapidly moving into the nuclear age," so that there is no need to worry about anything, least of all about the conservation of fossil fuel resources. Countless are the learned studies, produced by national and international agencies, committees, research institutes, and so forth, which purport to demonstrate, with a vast array of subtle calculation, that the demand for Western European coal is declining and will continue to decline so quickly that the only problem is how to get rid of coal miners fast enough. Instead of looking at the total situation, which has been and still is highly predictable, the authors of these studies almost invariably look at innumerable constituent parts of the total situation, none of which is separately predictable, since the parts cannot be understood unless the whole is understood.

To give only one example, an elaborate study by the European Coal and Steel Community, undertaken in 1960–61, provided precise quantitative answers to virtually every question anyone might have wished to ask about fuel and energy in the Common Market countries up to 1975. I had occasion to review this report shortly after publication, and it may not be out of place to quote a few passages from this review:[1]

> It may seem astonishing enough that anyone should be able to predict the development of miners' wages and productivity in his own country fifteen years ahead: it is even more astonishing to find him predicting the prices and transatlantic freight rates of American coal. A certain quality of U.S. coal, we are told, will cost "about $14.50 per ton" free North Sea port in 1970, and "a little more," in 1975. "About $14.50," the report says, should be taken as meaning "anything between $13.75 and $15.25," a margin of uncertainty of $1.50 or ± five per cent.

From a resource point of view, the main threat in nonsustainable development is not so much that we are running out of non-renewables (for instance fossil fuels or heavy metals). The main threat is that the productivity of our renewable resource base (vital ecosystems) is declining. The main problem is that waste molecules from the use of nonrenewables have negative effects on our renewable resource base through climate change, acid rain, eutrophy, toxic metals, etc. This perspective is often lost in the debate, but it is the perspective of The Natural Step.

—KARL-HENRIK ROBÈRT

(In fact, the c.i.f.* price of U.S. coal in European ports rose to between $24 and $25 per ton for new contracts concluded in October 1970!)

Similarly, the price of fuel oil will be something of the order of $17–$19 per ton, while estimates of various kinds are given for natural gas and nuclear energy. Being in the possession of these (and many other) "facts," the authors find it an easy matter to calculate how much of the Community's coal production will be competitive in 1970, and the answer is "about 125 million, i.e. a little over half the present production."

It is fashionable today to assume that any figures about the future are better than none. To produce figures about the unknown, the current method is to make a guess about something or other—called an "assumption"—and to derive an estimate from it by subtle calculation. The estimate is then presented as the result of scientific reasoning, something far superior to mere guesswork. This is a pernicious practice which can only lead to the most colossal planning errors, because it offers a bogus answer where, in fact, an entrepreneurial judgment is required.

The study here under review employs a vast array of arbitrary assumptions, which are then, as it were, put into a calculating machine to produce a "scientific" result. It would have been cheaper, and indeed more honest, simply to assume the result.

As it happened, the "pernicious practice" did maximise the planning errors; the capacity of the Western European coal industry was virtually cut down to half its former size, not only in the Community but in Britain as well. Between 1960 and 1970 the dependence on fuel imports of the European Community grew from thirty per cent to over sixty per cent and that of the United Kingdom, from twenty-five per cent to forty-four per cent. Although it was perfectly *possible* to foresee the total situation that would have to be met during the 1970s and thereafter, the governments of West-

---

*Carriage, insurance, freight, i.e. price on delivery.

ern Europe, supported by the great majority of economists, deliberately destroyed nearly half of their coal industries, as if coal was *nothing but* one of innumerable marketable commodities, to be produced as long as it was profitable to do so and to be scrapped as soon as production ceased to be profitable. The question of what was to take the place of indigenous coal supplies *in the long term* was answered by assurances that there would be abundant supplies of other fuels at low prices "for the foreseeable future," these assurances being based on nothing other than wishful thinking.

It is not as if there was—or is now—a lack of information, or that the policy-makers happened to have overlooked important facts. No, there was perfectly adequate knowledge of the current situation and there were perfectly reasonable and realistic estimates of future trends. But the policy-makers were incapable of drawing correct conclusions from what they knew to be true. The arguments of those who pointed to the likelihood of severe energy shortages in the foreseeable future were not taken up and refuted by counter-arguments but simply derided or ignored. It did not require a great deal of insight to realise that, whatever the long-term future of nuclear energy might be, the fate of world industry during the remainder of this century would be determined primarily by oil. What could be said about oil prospects a decade or so ago? I quote from a lecture delivered in April 1961.

> To say anything about the long-term prospects of crude oil availability is made invidious by the fact that some thirty or fifty years ago somebody may have predicted that oil supplies would give out quite soon, and, look at it, they didn't. A surprising number of people seem to imagine that by pointing to erroneous predictions made by somebody or other a long time ago they have somehow established that oil will never give out no matter how fast is the growth of the annual take. With regard to future oil supplies, as with regard to atomic energy, many people manage to assume a position of limitless optimism, quite impervious to reason.

I prefer to base myself on information coming from the oil people themselves. They are not saying that oil will

The Bruntland Commission affirmed that our economies can dematerialize, and indeed are doing that today. In many countries there is a shift in the gross national product from the component of goods to the component of services. The cutting edge of this shift is in Europe, although a few United States companies are making headway, such as Interface Carpet, one of the largest carpet companies in the world.

After reading Paul Hawken's book, The Ecology of Commerce, Ray Anderson realized he didn't need to sell carpets; what people wanted was the services of carpeting. He decided to provide customers with continuously new carpeting by recycling soiled carpet squares. The company became more profitable—its big customers (hotels, airports, etc.) like offering fresh, clean carpeting. His goal now is to not use one more drop of virgin oil by the year 2002. Many European companies are following a similar path by taking back old TV sets, faxes, and computers and reconditioning them for re-sale.
—HAZEL HENDERSON

shortly give out; on the contrary, they are saying that very much more oil is still to be found than has been found to date and that the world's oil reserves, recoverable at a reasonable cost, may well amount to something of the order of 200,000 million tons, that is about 200 times the current annual take. We know that the so-called "proved" oil reserves stand at present at about 40,000 million tons, and we certainly do not fall into the elementary error of thinking that that is all the oil there is likely to be. No, we are quite happy to believe that the almost unimaginably large amount of a further 160,000 million tons of oil will be discovered during the next few decades. Why almost unimaginable? Because, for instance, the great recent discovery of large oil deposits in the Sahara (which has induced many people to believe that the future prospects of oil have been fundamentally changed thereby) would hardly affect this figure one way or another. Present opinion of the experts appears to be that the Saharan oil fields may ultimately yield as much as 1,000 million tons. This is an impressive figure when held, let us say, against the present annual oil requirements of France; but it is quite insignificant as a contribution to the 160,000 million tons which we assume will be discovered in the foreseeable future. That is why I said "almost unimaginable," because 160 such discoveries as that of Saharan oil are indeed difficult to imagine. All the same, let us assume that they can be made and will be made.

It looks therefore as if proved oil reserves should be enough for forty years and total oil reserves for 200 years— at the current rate of consumption. Unfortunately, however, the rate of consumption is not stable but has a long history of growth at a rate of six or seven per cent a year. Indeed, if this growth stopped from now on, there could be no question of oil displacing coal; and everybody appears to be quite confident that the growth of oil—we are speaking on a world scale—will continue at the established rate. Industrialisation is spreading right across the world and is being carried forward mainly by the power of oil. Does anybody assume that this process would suddenly cease? If not, it might be worth our while to consider, purely arithmetically, how long it could continue.

What I propose to make now is not a prediction but simply an exploratory calculation or, as the engineers might call it, a feasibility study. A growth rate of seven per cent means doubling in ten years. In 1970, therefore, world oil consumption might be at the rate of 2,000 million tons per annum. [In the event, it amounted to 2,273 million tons.] The amount taken during the decade would be roughly 15,000 million tons. To maintain proved reserves at 40,000 million tons new provings during the decade would have to amount to about 15,000 million tons. Proved reserves, which are at present forty times annual take, would then be only twenty times, the annual take having doubled. There would be nothing inherently absurd or impossible in such a development. Ten years, however, is a very short time when we are dealing with problems of fuel supply. So let us look at the following ten years leading up to about 1980. If oil consumption continued to grow at roughly seven per cent per annum, it would rise to about 4,000 million tons a year in 1980. The total take during this second decade would be roughly 30,000 million tons. If the "life" of proved reserves were to be maintained at twenty years—and few people would care to engage in big investments without being able to look to at least twenty years for writing them off—it would not suffice merely to replace the take of 30,000 million tons; it would be necessary to end up with proved reserves at 80,000 million tons (twenty times 4,000). New discoveries during that second decade would therefore have to amount to not less than 70,000 million tons. Such a figure, I suggest, already looks pretty fantastic. What is more, by that time we would have used up about 45,000 million tons out of our original 200,000 million tons total. The remaining 155,000 million tons, discovered and not-yet-discovered, would allow a continuation of the 1980 rate of consumption for less than forty years. No further arithmetical demonstration is needed to

What Schumacher missed is that petroleum may be replaceable by renewables such as hydrogen fuel cells, and that water is probably more limiting than oil in any economic model. Water is the future natural capital of most import and does not appear in his book.

—PETER WARSHALL

make us realise that a continuation of rapid *growth* beyond 1980 would then be virtually impossible.

This, then, is the result of our "feasibility study": if there is any truth at all in the estimates of total oil reserves which have been published by the leading oil geologists, there can be no doubt that the oil industry will be able to sustain its established rate of growth for another ten years; there is considerable doubt whether it will be able to do so for twenty years; and there is almost a certainty that it will not be able to continue rapid growth beyond 1980. In that year, or rather around that time, world oil consumption would be greater than ever before and proved oil reserves, in absolute amount, would also be the highest ever. There is no suggestion that the world would have reached the end of its oil resources; but it would have reached the end of oil growth. As a matter of interest, I might add that this very point appears to have been reached already today with natural gas in the United States. It has reached its all-time high; but the relation of current take to remaining reserves is such that it may now be impossible for it to grow any further.

As far as Britain is concerned—a highly industrialised country with a high rate of oil consumption but without indigenous supplies—the oil crisis will come, not when all the world's oil is exhausted, but when world oil supplies cease to expand. If this point is reached, as our exploratory calculation would suggest that it might, in about twenty years' time, when industrialisation will have spread right across the globe and the underdeveloped countries have had their appetite for a higher standard of living thoroughly whetted, although still finding themselves in dire poverty, what else could be the result but an intense struggle for oil supplies, even a violent struggle, in which any country with large needs and negligible indigenous supplies will find itself in a very weak position.

You can elaborate the exploratory calculation if you wish, varying the basic assumptions by as much as fifty per cent; you will find that the results do not become significantly different. If you wish to be very optimistic, you may find that the point of maximum growth may not be reached by 1980 but a few years later. What does it matter? We, or our children, will merely be a few years older.

All this means that the National Coal Board has one overriding task and responsibility, being the trustees of the nation's coal reserves: to be able to supply plenty of coal when the world-wide scramble for oil comes. This would not be possible if it permitted the industry, or a substantial part of the industry, to be liquidated because of the present glut and cheapness of oil, a glut which is due to all sorts of temporary causes....

What, then, will be the position of coal in, say, 1980? All indications are that the demand for coal in this country will then be larger than it is now. There will still be plenty of oil, but not necessarily enough to meet all requirements. There may be a world-wide scramble for oil, reflected possibly in greatly enhanced oil prices. We must all hope that the National Coal Board will be able to steer the industry safely through the difficult years that lie ahead, maintaining as well as possible its power to produce efficiently something of the order of 200 million tons of coal a year. Even if from time to time it may look as if less coal and more imported oil were cheaper or more convenient for certain users or for the economy as a whole, it is the longer-term prospect that must rule national fuel policy. And this longer-term prospect must be seen against such world-wide developments as population growth and industrialisation. The indications are that by the 1980s we shall have a world population at least one-third bigger than now and a level of world industrial production at least two-and-a-half times as high as today, with fuel use more than doubled. To permit a doubling of total fuel consumption it will be necessary to increase oil fourfold; to double hydroelectricity; to maintain natural gas production at least at the present level; to obtain a substantial (though still modest) contribution from nuclear energy, and to get roughly twenty per cent more coal than now. No doubt,

The industrial revolution in the 19th century and the explosion of human numbers and cultural artifacts in the 20th have all been fired by fossil fuels. Society's dependence on abundant cheap energy is now complete—each citizen of the industrial world has the energy equivalent of 200 slaves. But industrial civilization is like a rocket, accelerating giddily even as its fuel runs out. The question for the 21st century is whether available substitutes can even soften the inevitable crash.

—WILLIAM REES

many things will happen during the next twenty years which we cannot foresee today. Some may increase the need for coal and some may decrease it. Policy cannot be based on the unforeseen or unforeseeable. If we base present policy on what can be foreseen at present, it will be a policy of conservation for the coal industry, not of liquidation....

These warnings, and many others uttered throughout the 1960s, did not merely remain unheeded but were treated with derision and contempt—until the general fuel supplies scare of 1970. Every new discovery of oil, or of natural gas, whether in the Sahara, in the Netherlands, in the North Sea, or in Alaska, was hailed as a major event which "fundamentally changed all future prospects," as if the type of analysis given above had not already *assumed* that enormous new discoveries would be made every year. The main criticism that can today be made of the exploratory calculations of 1961 is that all the figures are slightly understated. Events have moved even faster than I expected ten or twelve years ago.

Even today, soothsayers are still at work suggesting that there is no problem. During the 1960s, it was the oil companies who were the main dispensers of bland assurances, although the figures they provided totally disproved their case. Now, after nearly half the capacity and much more than half the workable reserves of the Western European coal industries have been destroyed, they have changed their tune. It used to be said that OPEC—the Organisation of Petroleum Exporting Countries—would never amount to anything, because Arabs could never agree with each other, let alone with non-Arabs; today it is clear that OPEC is the greatest cartel-monopoly the world has ever seen. It used to be said that the oil exporting countries *depended* on the oil importing countries just as much as the latter depended on the former; today it is clear that this is based on nothing but wishful thinking, because the need of the oil consumers is so great and their demand so inelastic that the oil exporting countries, acting in unison, can in fact raise their revenues by the simple device of curtailing output. There are still people who say that if oil prices rose too much (whatever that may mean) oil would price itself out of the market; but it is perfectly obvious that there is no ready substitute for oil to take its place on a quantitatively significant scale, so that oil, in fact, cannot price itself out of the market.

The oil producing countries, meanwhile, are beginning to realise that money alone cannot build new sources of livelihood for their populations. To build them needs, in addition to money, immense efforts and a great deal of time. Oil is a "wasting asset," and the faster it is allowed to waste, the shorter is the time available for the development of a new basis of economic existence. The conclusions are obvious: it is in the real longer-term interest of *both* the oil exporting *and* the oil importing countries that the "life-span" of oil should be prolonged as much as possible. The former need time to develop alternative sources of livelihood and the latter need time to adjust their oil-dependent economies to a situation—which is absolutely certain to arise within the lifetime of most people living today—when oil will be scarce and very dear. The greatest danger to both is a continuation of rapid growth in oil production and consumption throughout the world. Catastrophic developments on the oil front could be avoided only if the *basic harmony of the long-term interests of both groups of countries* came to be fully realised and concerted action were taken to stabilise and gradually reduce the annual flow of oil into consumption.

As far as the oil importing countries are concerned, the problem is obviously most serious for Western Europe and Japan. These two areas are in danger of becoming the "residuary legatees" for oil imports. No elaborate computer studies are required to establish this stark fact. Until quite recently, Western Europe lived in the comfortable illusion that "we are entering the age of limitless, cheap energy" and famous scientists, among others, gave it as their considered opinion that in future "energy will be a drug on the market." The British White Paper on Fuel Policy, issued in November 1967, proclaimed that:

> The discovery of natural gas in the North Sea is a major event in the evolution of Britain's energy supplies. It follows closely upon the coming of age of nuclear power as a potential major source of energy. Together, these two develop-

ments will lead to fundamental changes in the pattern of energy demand and supply in the coming years.

Five years later, all that needs to be said is that Britain is more dependent on imported oil than ever before. A report presented to the Secretary of State for the Environment in February 1972, introduces its chapter on energy with the words:

> There is deep-seated unease revealed by the evidence sent to us about the future energy resources, both for this country and for the world as a whole. Assessments vary about the length of time that will elapse before fossil fuels are exhausted, but it is increasingly recognised that their life is limited and satisfactory alternatives must be found. The huge incipient needs of developing countries, the increases in population, the rate at which some sources of energy are being used up without much apparent thought of the consequences, the belief that future resources will be available only at ever-increasing economic cost and the hazards which nuclear power may bring in its train are all factors which contribute to the growing concern.

It is a pity that the "growing concern" did not show itself in the 1960s, during which nearly half the British coal industry was abandoned as "uneconomic"—and, once abandoned, it is virtually lost for ever—and it is astonishing that, despite "growing concern," there is continuing pressure from highly influential quarters to go on with pit closures for "economic" reasons.

CHAPTER 9

NUCLEAR ENERGY—
SALVATION OR DAMNATION?

Т
HE MAIN CAUSE of the complacency—now gradually diminishing—about future energy supplies was undoubtedly the
emergence of nuclear energy, which, people felt, had arrived just in
time. Little did they bother to inquire precisely *what* it was that
had arrived. It was new, it was astonishing, it was progress, and
promises were freely given that it would be cheap. Since a new
source of energy would be needed sooner or later, why not have it at
once?

The following statement was made six years ago. At the time, it
seemed highly unorthodox.

> The religion of economics promotes an idolatry of rapid
> change, unaffected by the elementary truism that a change
> which is not an unquestionable improvement is a doubtful
> blessing. The burden of proof is placed on those who take
> the "ecological viewpoint": unless *they* can produce evidence
> of marked injury to man, the change will proceed. Common
> sense, on the contrary, would suggest that the burden of
> proof should lie on the man who wants to introduce a
> change; *he* has to demonstrate that there *cannot* be any dam-
> aging consequences. But this would take too much time,
> and would therefore be uneconomic. Ecology, indeed, ought
> to be a compulsory subject for all economists, whether pro-
> fessionals or laymen, as this might serve to restore at least a
> modicum of balance. For ecology holds "that an environ-
> mental setting developed over millions of years must be con-

sidered to have some merit. Anything so complicated as a planet, inhabited by more than a million and a half species of plants and animals, all of them living together in a more or less balanced equilibrium in which they continuously use and re-use the same molecules of the soil and air, cannot be improved by aimless and uninformed tinkering. All changes in a complex mechanism involve some risk and should be undertaken only after careful study of all the facts available. Changes should be made on a small scale first so as to provide a test before they are widely applied. When information is incomplete, changes should stay close to the natural processes which have in their favour the indisputable evidence of having supported life for a very long time.[1]

The argument, six years ago, proceeded as follows:

Of all the changes introduced by man into the household of nature, large-scale nuclear fission is undoubtedly the most dangerous and profound. As a result, ionising radiation has become the most serious agent of pollution of the environment and the greatest threat to man's survival on earth. The attention of the layman, not surprisingly, has been captured by the atom bomb, although there is at least a chance that it may never be used again. The danger to humanity created by the so-called peaceful uses of atomic energy may be much greater. There could indeed be no clearer example of the prevailing dictatorship of economics. Whether to build conventional power stations, based on coal or oil, or nuclear stations, is being decided on economic grounds, with perhaps a small element of regard for the "social consequences" that might arise from an over-speedy curtailment of the coal industry. But that nuclear fission represents an incredible, incomparable, and unique hazard for human life does not enter any calculation and is never mentioned. People whose business it is to judge hazards, the insurance companies, are reluctant to insure nuclear power stations anywhere in the world for third party risk, with the result that special legislation has had to be passed whereby the State accepts big liabilities.[2] Yet, insured or not, the hazard remains, and such is the thraldom of the religion of economics that the only question that appears to interest either governments or the public is whether "it pays."

It is not as if there were any lack of authoritative voices to warn us. The effects of alpha, beta, and gamma rays on living tissues are perfectly well known: the radiation particles are like bullets tearing into an organism, and the damage they do depends primarily on the dosage and the type of cells they hit.[3] As long ago as 1927, the American biologist H.J. Muller published his famous paper on genetic mutations produced by X-ray bombardment,[4] and since the early 1930s the genetic hazard of exposure has been recognised also by non-geneticists.[5] It is clear that here is a hazard with a hitherto un-experienced "dimension," endangering not only those who might be directly affected by this radiation but their offspring as well.

A new "dimension" is given also by the fact that while man now can—and does—create radioactive elements, there is nothing he can do to reduce their radioactivity once he has created them. No chemical reaction, no physical interference, only the passage of time reduces the intensity of radiation once it has been set going. Carbon-14 has a half-life of 5,900 years, which means that it takes nearly 6,000 years for its radioactivity to decline to one-half of what it was before. The half-life of strontium-90 is twenty-eight years. But whatever the length of the half-life, some radiation continues almost indefinitely, and there is nothing that can be done about it, except to try and put the radioactive substance into a safe place.

But what is a safe place, let us say, for the enormous amounts of radioactive waste products created by nuclear reactors? No place on earth can be shown to be safe. It was thought at one time that these wastes could safely be dumped into the deepest parts of the oceans, on the assumption that no life could subsist at such depths.[6] But this has since been disproved by Soviet deep-sea exploration. Wherever there is life, radioactive substances are absorbed into the biological cycle. Within hours of depositing these materials in water, the great bulk of them can be found in living organisms. Plankton, algae, and many sea animals have the power of concentrating these substances by a factor of 1,000 and in some cases even a million. As one organism feeds on another, the radioactive materials climb up the ladder of life and find their way back to man.[7]

No international agreement has yet been reached on waste disposal. The conference of the International Atomic Energy Organisation at Monaco, in November 1959, ended in disagreement, mainly on account of the violent objections raised by the majority of countries against the American and British practice of disposal into the oceans.[8] "High-level" wastes continue to be dumped into the sea, while quantities of so-called "intermediate" and "low-level" wastes are discharged into rivers or directly into the ground. An U.S. Atomic Energy Commission report observes laconically that the liquid wastes "work their way slowly into ground water, leaving all or part [*sic!*] of their radioactivity held either chemically or physically in the soil."[9]

The most massive wastes are, of course, the nuclear reactors themselves after they have become unserviceable. There is a lot of discussion on the trivial economic question of whether they will last for twenty, twenty-five, or thirty years. No one discusses the humanly vital point that they cannot be dismantled and cannot be shifted but have to be left standing where they are, probably for centuries, perhaps for thousands of years, an active menace to all life, silently leaking radioactivity into air, water, and soil. No one has considered the number and location of these satanic mills which will relentlessly accumulate. Earthquakes, of course, are not supposed to happen, nor wars, nor civil disturbances, nor riots like those that infested American cities. Disused nuclear power stations will stand as unsightly monuments to unquiet man's assumption that nothing but tranquillity, from now on, stretches before him, or else—that the future counts as nothing compared with the slightest economic gain now.

Meanwhile, a number of authorities are engaged in defining "maximum permissible concentrations" (MPCs) and "maximum permissible levels" (MPLs) for various radioactive elements. The MPC purports to define the quantity of a given radioactive substance that the human body can be allowed to accumulate. But it is known that any accumulation produces biological damage. "Since we don't know that these effects can be completely recovered from," observes the U.S. Naval Radiological Laboratory, "we have to fall back on an arbitrary decision about how much we will put up with; i.e. what is 'acceptable' or 'permissible'—not a scientific finding, but an administrative decision." We can hardly be surprised when men of outstanding intelligence and integrity, such as Albert

Schweitzer, refuse to accept such administrative decisions with equanimity: "Who has given them the right to do this? Who is even entitled to give such a permission?" The history of these decisions is, to say the least, disquieting. The British Medical Research Council noted some twelve years ago that:

> The maximum permissible level of strontium-90 in the human skeleton, accepted by the International Commission on Radiological Protection, corresponds to 1000 micro-microcuries per gramme of calcium (= 1000 S.U.). But this is the maximum permissible level for adults in special occupations and is not suitable for application to the population as a whole or to the children with their greater sensitivity to radiation.[12]

A little later, the MPC for strontium-90, as far as the general population was concerned, was reduced by ninety per cent, and then by another third, to sixty-seven S.U. Meanwhile, the MPC for workers in nuclear plants was raised to 2000 S.U.

We must be careful, however, not to get lost in the jungle of controversy that has grown up in this field. The point is that very serious hazards have already been created by the "peaceful uses of atomic energy," affecting not merely the people alive today but all future generations, although so far nuclear energy is being used only on a statistically insignificant scale. The real development is yet to come, on a scale which few people are capable of imagining. If this is really going to happen, there will be a continuous traffic in radioactive substances from the "hot" chemical plants to the nuclear stations and back again; from the stations to waste-processing plants; and from there to disposal sites. A serious accident, whether during transport or production, can cause a major catastrophe; and the radiation levels throughout the world will rise relentlessly from generation to generation. Unless all living geneticists are in error, there will be an equally relentless, though no doubt somewhat delayed, increase in the number of harmful mutations. K.Z. Morgan, of the Oak Ridge Laboratory, emphasises that the damage can be very subtle, a deterioration of all kinds of organic qualities, such as

Nuclear power ultimately collapsed in America and most of the world. Citizens by the millions judged radiation too dangerous and reactors and their operators too imperfect, and they demanded and won greater measures to reduce the likelihood and consequences of reactor accidents. This proved to be a supremely costly endeavor, one which, by the time of the Three Mile Island accident, was already making reactor power unmarketable.

This outcome may lack moral finality, but it would have pleased Schumacher to see the market price of nuclear power brought somewhat in line with its enormous social costs— a defeat for "economics" that became a triumph for humankind.
—CHARLES KOMANOFF

mobility, fertility, and the efficiency of sensory organs. "If a small dose has any effect at all at any stage of the life cycle of an organism, then chronic radiation at this level can be more damaging than a single massive dose.... Finally, stress and changes in mutation rates may be produced even when there is no immediately obvious effect on survival of irradiated individuals."[14]

Leading geneticists have given their warnings that everything possible should be done to avoid any increases in mutation rates;[15] leading medical men have insisted that the future of nuclear energy must depend primarily on researches into radiation biology which are as yet still totally incomplete;[16] leading physicists have suggested that "measures much less heroic than building...nuclear reactors" should be tried to solve the problem of future energy supplies—a problem which is in no way acute at present;[17] and leading students of strategic and political problems, at the same time, have warned us that there is really no hope of preventing the proliferation of the atom bomb, if there is a spread of plutonium capacity, such as was "spectacularly launched by President Eisenhower in his 'atoms for peace proposals' of 8 December 1953."[18]

Yet all these weighty opinions play no part in the debate on whether we should go immediately for a large "second nuclear programme" or stick a bit longer to the conventional fuels which, whatever may be said for or against them, do not involve us in entirely novel and admittedly incalculable risks. None of them are even mentioned: the whole argument, which may virtually affect the very future of the human race, is conducted exclusively in terms of immediate advantage, as if two rag and bone merchants were trying to agree on a quantity discount.

What, after all, is the fouling of air with smoke compared with the pollution of air, water, and soil with ionising radiation? Not that I wish in any way to belittle the evils of conventional air and water pollution; but we must recognise "dimensional differences" when we encounter them: radioactive pollution is an evil of an incomparably greater "dimension" than anything mankind has known before. One might even ask: what is the point of insisting on clean air, if the air is laden with radioactive particles? And even if the air could be protected, what is the point of it, if soil and water are being poisoned?

Even an economist might well ask: what is the point of economic progress, a so-called higher standard of living, when the earth, the only earth we have, is being contaminated by substances which may cause malformations in our children or grandchildren? Have we learned nothing from the thalidomide tragedy? Can we deal with matters of such a basic character by means of bland assurances or official admonitions that "in the absence of proof that [this or that innovation] is in any way deleterious, it would be the height of irresponsibility to raise a public alarm"?[19] Can we deal with them simply on the basis of a short-term profitability calculation?

> It might be though [wrote Leonard Beaton] that all the resources of those who fear the spread of nuclear weapons would have been devoted to heading off these developments for as long as possible. The United States, the Soviet Union and Britain might be expected to have spent large sums of money trying to prove that conventional fuels, for example, had been underrated as a source of power.... In fact...the efforts which have followed must stand as one of the most inexplicable political fantasies in history. Only a social psychologist could hope to explain why the possessors of the most terrible weapons in history have sought to spread the necessary industry to produce them.... Fortunately...power reactors are still fairly scarce.[20]

In fact, a prominent American nuclear physicist, A.W. Weinberg, has given some sort of explanation: "There is," he says, "an understandable drive on the part of men of good will to build up the positive aspects of nuclear energy simply because the negative aspects are so distressing." But he also adds the warning that "there are very compelling personal reasons why atomic scientists sound optimistic when writing about their impact on world affairs. Each of us must justify to himself his preoccupation with instruments of nuclear destruction (and even we reactor people are only slightly less beset with such guilt than are our weaponeering colleagues)."[21]

Our instinct of self-preservation, one should have thought, would make us immune to the blandishments of guilt-ridden

"Even an economist might well ask": In this remarkable sentence, two of Schumacher's grand themes—disdain for economists and their worship of economic growth, and reverence for life and nature—joined in protest against nuclear radiation and its proliferation via nuclear power.

—CHARLES KOMANOFF

As Amory Lovins and others (myself included) have calculated, of all the possible means of reducing greenhouse gas emissions, nuclear reactors are the most costly and inefficient. Society will be far better served by putting reactor dollars into energy efficiency measures and conservation programs.

—CHARLES KOMANOFF

scientific optimism or the unproved promises of pecuniary advantages. "It is not too late at this point for us to reconsider old decisions and make new ones," says a recent American commentator. "For the moment at least, the choice is available."[22] Once many more centres of radioactivity have been created, there will be no more choice, whether we can cope with the hazards or not.

It is clear that certain scientific and technological advances of the last thirty years have produced, and are continuing to produce, hazards of an altogether intolerable kind. At the Fourth National Cancer Conference in America in September 1960, Lester Breslow of the California State Department of Public Health reported that tens of thousands of trout in western hatcheries suddenly acquired liver cancers, and continued thus:

> Technological changes affecting man's environment are being introduced at such a rapid rate and with so little control that it is a wonder man has thus far escaped the type of cancer epidemic occurring this year among the trout.[23]

To mention these things, no doubt, means laying oneself open to the charge of being against science, technology, and progress. Let me therefore, in conclusion, add a few words about future scientific research. Man cannot live without science and technology any more than he can live against nature. What needs the most careful consideration, however, is the *direction* of scientific research. We cannot leave this to the scientists alone. As Einstein himself said,[24] "almost all scientists are economically completely dependent," and "the number of scientists who possess a sense of social responsibility is so small" that they cannot determine the direction of research. The latter dictum applies, no doubt, to all specialists, and the task therefore falls to the intelligent layman, to people like those who form the National Society for Clean Air and other, similar societies concerned with *conservation*. They must work on public opinion, so that the politicians, depending on public opinion, will free themselves from the thraldom of economism and attend to the things that really matter. What matters, as I said, is the *direction* of research, that the direction should be towards non-violence rather than violence; towards an harmonious cooperation with nature rather than a warfare against nature; towards the noiseless, low-energy, elegant, and economical solutions normally applied in nature rather than the noisy, high-energy, brutal, wasteful, and clumsy solutions of our present-day sciences.

The continuation of scientific advance in the direction of ever-increasing violence, culminating in nuclear fission and moving on to nuclear fusion, is a prospect of terror threatening the abolition of man. Yet it is not written in the stars that this must be the direction. There is also a life-giving and life-enhancing possibility, the conscious exploration and cultivation of all relatively non-violent, harmonious, organic methods of cooperating with that enormous, wonderful, incomprehensible system of God-given nature, of which we are a part and which we certainly have not made ourselves.

This statement, which was part of a lecture given before the National Society for Clean Air in October 1967, was received with thoughtful applause by a highly responsible audience, but was subsequently ferociously attacked by the authorities as "the height of irresponsibility." The most priceless remark was reportedly made by Richard Marsh, then Her Majesty's Minister of Power, who felt it necessary to "rebuke" the author. The lecture, he said, *was one of the more extraordinary and least profitable contributions to the current debate on nuclear and coal cost. (Daily Telegraph, 21 October 1967.)

However, times change. A report on the Control of Pollution, presented in February 1972 to the Secretary of State for the Environment by an officially appointed Working Party, published by Her Majesty's Stationery Office and entitled Pollution: Nuisance or Nemesis?, has this to say:

The main worry is about the future, and in the international context. The economic prosperity of the world seems to be linked with nuclear energy. At the moment, nuclear energy provides only one per cent of the total electricity generated in the world. By the year 2000, if present plans go ahead, this will have increased to well over fifty per cent and the equivalent of two new 500 MWe reactors—each of the size of the one at Trawsfynydd in Snowdonia—will be opened every day.[25]

Ecological design is a comparatively new discipline involving more than using renewable resources like solar and wind energy in lieu of fossil fuels or nuclear power. It has been codified as a scientific discipline and successfully implemented in a number of fields. Predicated upon an unprecedented partnership with the natural world, ecological design has generated a science of stewardship and new and hybrid forms of technology. This technology, literally drawing on the intelligence encoded in the processes of evolution, incorporates elements from the living world in the form of thousands of selected organisms. These are inoculated into a contained ecosystem which is designed to perform a specific task.

Harnessing natural intelligence in this way is a new step in the co-evolution of human and natural systems. This partnership of human ➡

> ➡ *ingenuity and resilient biological self-organization, maintenance, and repair has the potential to replace the present industrial systems and technological infrastructure with sustainable living technologies—the potential foundation for an economics of permanence.*
>
> —NANCY JACK TODD

On radioactive wastes of nuclear reactors:

> The biggest cause of worry for the future is the storage of the long-lived radioactive wastes.... Unlike other pollutants, there is no way of destroying radioactivity.... So there is no alternative to permanent storage....
>
> In the United Kingdom, strontium-90 is at the present time stored as a liquid in huge stainless steel tanks at Windscale in Cumberland. They have to be continually cooled with water, since the heat given off by the radiation would otherwise raise the temperature to above boiling point. We shall have to go on cooling these tanks for many years, even if we build no more nuclear reactors. But with the vast increase of strontium-90 expected in the future, the problem may prove far more difficult. Moreover, the expected switch to fast breeder reactors will aggravate the situation even further, for they produce large quantities of radioactive substances with very long half-lives.
>
> In effect, we are consciously and deliberately accumulating a toxic substance on the off-chance that it may be possible to get rid of it at a later date. We are committing future generations to tackle a problem which we do not know how to handle.

Finally, the report issues a very clear warning:

> The evident danger is that man may have put all his eggs in the nuclear basket before he discovers that a solution cannot be found. There would then be powerful political pressures to ignore the radiation hazards and continue using the reactors which had been built. It would be only prudent to slow down the nuclear power programme until we have solved the waste disposal problem.... Many responsible people would go further. They feel that no more nuclear reactors should be built until we know how to control their wastes.

And how is the ever-increasing demand for energy to be satisfied?

Since planned demand for electricity cannot be satisfied without nuclear power, they consider mankind must develop societies which are less extravagant in their use of electricity and other forms of energy. Moreover, they see the need for this change of direction as immediate and urgent.

No degree of prosperity could justify the accumulation of large amounts of highly toxic substances which nobody knows how to make "safe" and which remain an incalculable danger to the whole of creation for historical or even geological ages. To do such a thing is a transgression against life itself, a transgression infinitely more serious than any crime ever perpetrated by man. The idea that a civilisation could sustain itself on the basis of such a transgression is an ethical, spiritual, and metaphysical monstrosity. It means conducting the economic affairs of man as if people really did not matter at all.

CHAPTER 10

TECHNOLOGY WITH
A HUMAN FACE

THE MODERN WORLD has been shaped by its metaphysics, which has shaped its education, which in turn has brought forth its science and technology. So, without going back to metaphysics and education, we can say that the modern world has been shaped by technology. It tumbles from crisis to crisis; on all sides there are prophecies of disaster and, indeed, visible signs of breakdown.

If that which has been shaped by technology, and continues to be so shaped, looks sick, it might be wise to have a look at technology itself. If technology is felt to be becoming more and more inhuman, we might do well to consider whether it is possible to have something better—a technology with a human face.

Strange to say, technology, although of course the product of man, tends to develop by its own laws and principles, and these are very different from those of human nature or of living nature in general. Nature always, so to speak, knows where and when to stop. Greater even than the mystery of natural growth is the mystery of the natural cessation of growth. There is measure in all natural things—in their size, speed, or violence. As a result, the system of nature, of which man is a part, tends to be self-balancing, self-adjusting, self-cleansing. Not so with technology, or perhaps I should say: not so with man dominated by technology and specialisation. Technology recognises no self-limiting principle—in terms, for instance, of size, speed, or violence. It therefore does not possess the virtues of being self-balancing, self-adjusting, and self-cleansing. In the subtle system of nature, technology, and in particular the super-technology of the modern world, acts like a foreign body, and there are now numerous signs of rejection.

Suddenly, if not altogether surprisingly, the modern world, shaped by modern technology, finds itself involved in three crises simultaneously. First, human nature revolts against inhuman technological, organisational, and political patterns, which it experiences as suffocating and debilitating; second, the living environment which supports human life aches and groans and gives signs of partial breakdown; and, third, it is clear to anyone fully knowledgeable in the subject matter that the inroads being made into the world's non-renewable resources, particularly those of fossil fuels, are such that serious bottlenecks and virtual exhaustion loom ahead in the quite foreseeable future.

Any one of these three crises or illnesses can turn out to be deadly. I do not know which of the three is the most likely to be the direct cause of collapse. What is quite clear is that a way of life that bases itself on materialism, i.e. on permanent, limitless expansionism in a finite environment, cannot last long, and that its life expectation is the shorter the more successfully it pursues its expansionist objectives.

If we ask where the tempestuous developments of world industry during the last quarter-century have taken us, the answer is somewhat discouraging. Everywhere the problems seem to be growing faster than the solutions. This seems to apply to the rich countries just as much as to the poor. There is nothing in the experience of the last twenty-five years to suggest that modern technology, as we know it, can really help us to alleviate world poverty, not to mention the problem of unemployment which already reaches levels like thirty per cent in many so-called developing countries, and now threatens to become endemic also in many of the rich countries. In any case, the apparent yet illusory successes of the last twenty-five years cannot be repeated: the threefold crisis of which I have spoken will see to that. So we had better face the question of technology—what does it do and what should it do? Can we develop a technology which really helps us to solve our problems—a technology with a human face?

The primary task of technology, it would seem, is to lighten the

Schumacher would certainly have supported the Gaia hypothesis, the view that planet earth is a self-regulating system. But there is nothing self-regulating about technology, which is still driven by notions of limitless growth, labor-saving, and perpetual expansion of consumption.
—GEORGE McROBIE

We are creating so many
unnecessary technologies for
the home environment that
we have made housing unaf-
fordable for most people.
When we go to the roots of
technologies in housing, we
recognize that what we
had before was adequate—
people were sheltered
sufficiently from the
elements. In our drive to
create technologies that
protect us and save our time
and energy, we are losing
energy by producing gadgets
that are not necessary to
begin with.
—AVI FRIEDMAN

burden of work man has to carry in order to stay alive and develop his potential. It is easy enough to see that technology fulfills this purpose when we watch any particular piece of machinery at work—a computer, for instance, can do in seconds what it would take clerks or even mathematicians a very long time, if they can do it at all. It is more difficult to convince oneself of the truth of this simple proposition when one looks at whole societies. When I first began to travel the world, visiting rich and poor countries alike, I was tempted to formulate the first law of economics as follows: "The amount of real leisure a society enjoys tends to be in inverse proportion to the amount of labour-saving machinery it employs." It might be a good idea for the professors of economics to put this proposition into their examination papers and ask their pupils to discuss it. However that may be, the evidence is very strong indeed. If you go from easy-going England to, say, Germany or the United States, you find that people there live under much more strain than here. And if you move to a country like Burma, which is very near to the bottom of the league table of industrial progress, you find that people have an enormous amount of leisure really to enjoy themselves. Of course, as there is so much less labour-saving machinery to help them, they "accomplish" much less than we do; but that is a different point. The fact remains that the burden of living rests much more lightly on their shoulders than on ours.

The question of what technology actually does for us is therefore worthy of investigation. It obviously greatly reduces some kinds of work while it increases other kinds. The type of work which modern technology is most successful in reducing or even eliminating is skillful, productive work of human hands, in touch with real materials of one kind or another. In an advanced industrial society, such work has become exceedingly rare, and to make a decent living by doing such work has become virtually impossible. A great part of the modern neurosis may be due to this very fact; for the human being, defined by Thomas Aquinas as a being with brains and hands, enjoys nothing more than to be creatively, usefully, productively engaged with both his hands and his brains. Today, a person has to be wealthy to be able to enjoy this simple thing, this very great luxury: he has to be able to afford space and good tools; he has to be lucky enough to find a good teacher and plenty of free time to learn and practise. He really has to be rich enough not to need a job; for the number of jobs that would be satisfactory in these respects is very small indeed.

The extent to which modern technology has taken over the work of human hands may be illustrated as follows. We may ask how much of "total social time"—that is to say, the time all of us have together, twenty-four hours a day each—is actually engaged in real production. Rather less than one-half of the total population of this country is, as they say, gainfully occupied, and about one-third of these are actual producers in agriculture, mining, construction, and industry. I do mean *actual producers,* not people who tell other people what to do, or account for the past, or plan for the future, or distribute what other people have produced. In other words, rather less than one-sixth of the total population is engaged in actual production; on average, each of them supports five others beside himself, of which two are gainfully employed on things other than real production and three are not gainfully employed. Now, a fully employed person, allowing for holidays, sickness, and other absence, spends about one-fifth of his total time on his job. It follows that the proportion of "total social time" spent on actual production—in the narrow sense in which I am using the term—is, roughly, one-fifth of one-third of one-half, i.e. $3^1/2$ per cent. The other $96^1/2$ per cent of "total social time" is spent in other ways, including sleeping, eating, watching television, doing jobs that are not *directly* productive, or just killing time more or less humanely.

Although this bit of figuring work need not be taken too literally, it quite adequately serves to show what technology has enabled us to do: namely, to reduce the elementary sense to such a tiny percentage of total social time that it pales into insignificance, that it carries no real weight, let alone prestige. When you look at industrial society in this way, you cannot be surprised to find what prestige is carried by those who help fill the other $96^1/2$ percent of total social time, primarily the entertainers but also the executors of Parkinson's Law. In fact, one might put the following proposition to students of sociology: "The prestige carried by people in modern industrial society varies in inverse proportion to their closeness to actual production."

There is a further reason for this. The process of confining

Schumacher believed that making things with your hands and physical labor not only provides employment and houses, food, clothes, shoes, and furniture; it also heals your psyche by using the imagination and creativity. Work fulfills many functions—spiritual, creative, economic, and social. Many benefits of economic activity are lost when we only work on a computer and consume mass-produced goods.
—SATISH KUMAR

productive time to $3^1/_2$ per cent of total social time has had the inevitable effect of taking all normal human pleasure and satisfaction out of the time spent on this work. Virtually all real production has been turned into an inhuman chore which does not enrich a man but empties him. "From the factory," it has been said, "dead matter goes out improved, whereas men there are corrupted and degraded."

We may say, therefore, that modern technology has deprived man of the kind of work that he enjoys most, creative, useful work with hands and brains, and given him plenty of work of a fragmented kind, most of which he does not enjoy at all. It has multiplied the number of people who are exceedingly busy doing kinds of work which, if it is productive at all, is so only in an indirect or "roundabout" way, and much of which would not be necessary at all if technology were rather less modern. Karl Marx appears to have foreseen much of this when he wrote: "They want production to be limited to useful things, but they forget that the production of too many useful things results in too many useless people," to which we might add: particularly when the processes of production are joyless and boring. All this confirms our suspicion that modern technology, the way it has developed, is developing, and promises further to develop, is showing an increasingly inhuman face, and that we might do well to take stock and reconsider our goals.

Taking stock, we can say that we possess a vast accumulation of new knowledge, splendid scientific techniques to increase it further, and immense experience in its application. All this is truth of a kind. This truthful knowledge, as such, does *not* commit us to a technology of giantism, supersonic speed, violence, and the destruction of human work-enjoyment. The use we have made of our knowledge is only one of its possible uses and, as is now becoming even more apparent, often an unwise and destructive use.

As I have shown, directly productive time in our society has already been reduced to about $3^1/_2$ per cent of total social time, and the whole drift of modern technological development is to reduce it further, asymptotically* to zero. Imagine we set ourselves a goal in the opposite direction—to increase it sixfold, to about twenty per cent, so that twenty per cent of total social time would be used for

---

*Asymptote: A mathematical line continually approaching some curve but never meeting it within a finite distance.

actually producing things, employing hands and brains and, naturally, excellent tools. An incredible thought! Even children would be allowed to make themselves useful, even old people. At one-sixth of present-day productivity, we should be producing as much as at present. There would be six times as much time for any piece of work we chose to undertake—enough to make a really good job of it, to enjoy oneself, to produce real quality, even to make things beautiful. Think of the therapeutic value of real work; think of its educational value. No one would then want to raise the school-leaving age or to lower the retirement age, so as to keep people off the labour market. Everybody would be welcome to lend a hand. Everybody would be admitted to what is now the rarest privilege, the opportunity of working usefully, creatively, with his own hands and brains, in his own time, at his own pace—and with excellent tools. Would this mean an enormous extension of working hours? No, people who work in this way do not know the difference between work and leisure. Unless they sleep or eat or occasionally choose to do nothing at all, they are always agreeably, productively engaged. Many of the "on-cost jobs" would simply disappear; I leave it to the reader's imagination to identify them. There would be little need for mindless entertainment or other drugs, and unquestionably much less illness.

Now, it might be said that this is a romantic, a utopian, vision. True enough. What we have today, in modern industrial society, is not romantic and certainly not utopian, as we have it right here. But it is in very deep trouble and holds no promise of survival. We jolly well have to have the courage to dream if we want to survive and give our children a chance of survival. The threefold crisis of which I have spoken will not go away if we simply carry on as before. It will become worse and end in disaster, until or unless we develop a new life-style which is compatible with the real needs of human nature, with the health of living nature around us, and with the resource endowment of the world.

Now, this is indeed a tall order, not because a new life-style to meet these critical requirements and facts is impossible to conceive, but because the present consumer society is like a drug addict who, no matter how miserable he may feel, finds it extremely

It has been said that modern technology is like a steamroller—you are either part of the steamroller or you are part of the road! But the last time I checked, a steamroller did not have much room for human beings. And if you are lucky enough to be on board, there is always somebody trying to push or pull you off to take your place. It's dog-eat-dog out there. You can take nothing for granted, no matter what your job.
—ROBERT BATEMAN

The "developing" world was developed in very damaging ways on the 1980s' borrowed money. Billions were spent on mega-projects, very few of which did any good for the vast majority of the people, and in most cases, harmed them. The World Bank loans for dams, for example, displaced 10 million people from their homes, farms, and villages. A few people got very rich and much of the money disappeared into the pockets of the leaders and their cronies. Borrowing for military build-up in the Third World is, if anything, even more wasteful and certainly destructive. The tragedy is that the ordinary people of these nations must now suffer under austerity programs and struggle with inflation and debt to repay international bankers.

—ROBERT BATEMAN

difficult to get off the hook. The problem children of the world—from this point of view and in spite of many other considerations that could be adduced—are the rich societies and not the poor.

It is almost like a providential blessing that we, the rich countries, have found it in our heart at least to consider the Third World and to try to mitigate its poverty. In spite of the mixture of motives and the persistence of exploitative practices, I think that this fairly recent development in the outlook of the rich is an honourable one. And it could save us; for the poverty of the poor makes it in any case impossible for them successfully to adopt our technology. Of course, they often try to do so, and then have to bear the more dire consequences in terms of mass unemployment, mass migration into cities, rural decay, and intolerable social tensions. They need, in fact, the very thing I am talking about, which we also need: a *different* kind of technology, a technology with a human face, which, instead of making human hands and brains redundant, helps them to become far more productive than they have ever been before.

As Gandhi said, the poor of the world cannot be helped by mass production, only by production by the masses. The system of *mass production,* based on sophisticated, highly capital-intensive, high energy-input dependent, and human labour-saving technology, presupposes that you are already rich, for a great deal of capital investment is needed to establish one single workplace. The system of *production by the masses* mobilises the priceless resources which are possessed by all human beings, their clever brains and skillful hands, *and supports them with first-class tools.* The technology of *mass production* is inherently violent, ecologically damaging, self-defeating in terms of non-renewable resources, and stultifying for the human person. The technology of *production by the masses,* making use of the best of modern knowledge and experience, is conducive to decentralisation, compatible with the laws of ecology, gentle in its use of scarce resources, and designed to serve the human person instead of making him the servant of machines. I have named it *intermediate technology* to signify that it is vastly superior to the primitive technology of bygone ages but at the same time much simpler, cheaper, and freer than the super-technology of the rich. One can also call it self-help technology, or democratic or people's technology—a technology to which everybody can gain admittance and which is not reserved to those already rich and powerful. It will be more fully discussed in later chapters.

Although we are in possession of all requisite knowledge, it still requires a systematic, creative effort to bring this technology into active existence and make it generally visible and available. It is my experience that it is rather more difficult to recapture directness and simplicity than to advance in the direction of ever more sophistication and complexity. Any third-rate engineer or researcher can increase complexity; but it takes a certain flair of real insight to make things simple again. And this insight does not come easily to people who have allowed themselves to become alienated from real, productive work and from the self-balancing system of nature, which never fails to recognise measure and limitation. Any activity which fails to recognise a self-limiting principle is of the devil. In our work with the developing countries we are at least forced to recognise the limitations of poverty, and this work can therefore be a wholesome school for all of us in which, while genuinely trying to help others, we may also gain knowledge and experience of how to help ourselves.

I think we can already see the conflict of attitudes which will decide our future. On the one side, I see the people who think they can cope with our threefold crisis by the methods current, only more so; I call them the people of the forward stampede. On the other side, there are people in search of a new life-style, who seek to return to certain basic truths about man and his world; I call them homecomers. Let us admit that the people of the forward stampede, like the devil, have all the best tunes or at least the most popular and familiar tunes. You cannot stand still, they say; standing still means going down; you must go forward; there is nothing wrong with modern technology except that it is as yet incomplete; let us complete it. Dr. Sicco Mansholt, one of the most prominent chiefs of the European Economic Community, may be quoted as a typical representative of this group. "More, further, quicker, richer," he says, "are the watchwords of present-day society." And he thinks we must help people to adapt "for there is no alternative." This is the authentic voice of the forward stampede, which talks in much the

In the past few decades we have created a culture of overconsumption. We consume far more than we need and can afford. By doing so, we work extremely hard to justify or get the means to buy gadgets that we don't need. This overconsumption is related to the housing market, which perpetuates the notion that the only house to buy or start life with must be huge and lavish. And people accept this norm without seeing that it is unnecessary.

We have developed the Grow Home in Montreal, Canada. When we introduced these homes, which measure only 1000 square feet, the demand was enormous. People told us, "This is what we need. We don't want to spend money on a huge place." In addition, we have encouraged people to participate in their own housing, which Schumacher advocated. The Grow Home is a strategy that enables people to complete their ➡

➡ *homes by themselves. We leave some open unfinished space in the basement or second floor to be finished as needed. A survey of Grow Home purchasers indicated that 92 percent did complete their homes by themselves. When you challenge people to work for cost reduction and simplicity, they embrace it.*

—AVI FRIEDMAN

same tone as Dostoyevsky's Grand Inquisitor: "Why have you come to hinder us?" They point to the population explosion and to the possibilities of world hunger. Surely, we must take our flight forward and not be fainthearted. If people start protesting and revolting, we shall have to have more police and have them better equipped. If there is trouble with the environment, we shall need more stringent laws against pollution, and faster economic growth to pay for anti-pollution measures. If there are problems about natural resources, we shall turn to synthetics; if there are problems about fossil fuels, we shall move from slow reactors to fast breeders and from fission to fusion. There *are* no insoluble problems. The slogans of the people of the forward stampede burst into the newspaper headlines every day with the message, "a breakthrough a day keeps the crisis at bay."

And what about the other side? This is made up of people who are deeply convinced that technological development has taken a wrong turn and needs to be redirected. The term "home-comer" has, of course, a religious connotation. For it takes a good deal of courage to say "no" to the fashions and fascinations of the age and to question the presuppositions of a civilisation which appears destined to conquer the whole world; the requisite strength can be derived only from deep convictions. If it were derived from nothing more than fear of the future, it would be likely to disappear at the decisive moment. The genuine "home-comer" does not have the best tunes, but he has the most exalted text, nothing less than the Gospels. For him, there could not be a more concise statement of his situation, of *our* situation, than the parable of the prodigal son. Strange to say, the Sermon on the Mount gives pretty precise instructions on how to construct an outlook that could lead to an Economics of Survival.

> —How blessed are those who know that they are poor:
>   the Kingdom of Heaven is theirs.
> —How blessed are the sorrowful;
>   they shall find consolation.
> —How blessed are those of a gentle spirit;
>   they shall have the earth for their possession.

—How blessed are those who hunger and thirst to see right
  prevail; they shall be satisfied.
—How blessed are the peacemakers;
  God shall call them his sons.

It may seem daring to connect these beatitudes with matters of
technology and economics. But may it not be that we are in trouble
precisely because we have failed for so long to make this connection? It is not difficult to discern what these beatitudes may mean
for us today:

*The struggle for environ-
mental preservation is
intimately linked with our
struggle for cultural survival
and self-determination. The
land is our life. That is our
fundamental challenge
to power.*
  —WINONA LADUKE

—We are poor, not demigods.
—We have plenty to be sorrowful about, and are not emerging into a golden age.
—We need a gentle approach, a non-violent spirit, and
  small is beautiful.
—We must concern ourselves with justice and see right
  prevail.
—And all this, only this, can enable us to become peacemakers.

The home-comers base themselves upon a different picture of
man from that which motivates the people of the forward stampede. It would be very superficial to say that the latter believe in
"growth" while the former do not. In a sense, everybody believes in
growth, and rightly so, because growth is an essential feature of life.
The whole point, however, is to give to the idea of growth a qualitative determination; for there are always many things that ought to
be growing and many things that ought to be diminishing.

Equally, it would be very superficial to say that the home-comers
do not believe in progress, which also can be said to be an essential
feature of all life. The whole point is to determine what constitutes
progress. And the home-comers believe that the direction which
modern technology has taken and is continuing to pursue—towards ever-greater size, ever-higher speeds, and ever-increased violence, in defiance of all laws of natural harmony—is the opposite of
progress. Hence the call for taking stock and finding a new orienta-

The good news is that there is a growing number of home-comers who believe that technological development must be redirected towards sustainable lifestyles. We must ask of technology that not only does it make money for its owners, but also, is it good for people, the environment, and the resource base. In modern industrial societies, home-comers are mostly organized in voluntary, nongovernmental organizations. Two in which Schumacher played a leading part are the Intermediate Technology Development Group and the Soil Association. Both address the need to create technologies that directly benefit people and are nonviolent towards the environment.

—GEORGE M^CROBIE

tion. The stocktaking indicates that we are destroying our very basis of existence, and the reorientation is based on remembering what human life is really about.

In one way or another everybody will have to take sides in this great conflict. To "leave it to the experts" means to side with the people of the forward stampede. It is widely accepted that politics is too important a matter to be left to experts. Today, the main content of politics is economics, and the main content of economics is technology. If politics cannot be left to the experts, neither can economics and technology.

The case for hope rests on the fact that ordinary people are often able to take a wider view, and a more "humanistic" view, than is normally being taken by experts. The power of ordinary people, who today tend to feel utterly powerless, does not lie in starting new lines of action, but in placing their sympathy and support with minority groups which have already started. I shall give two examples, relevant to the subject here under discussion. One relates to agriculture, still the greatest single activity of man on earth, and the other relates to industrial technology.

Modern agriculture relies on applying to soil, plants, and animals ever-increasing quantities of chemical products, the long-term effect of which on soil fertility and health is subject to very grave doubts. People who raise such doubts are generally confronted with the assertion that the choice lies between "poison or hunger." There are highly successful farmers in many countries who obtain excellent yields without resort to such chemicals and without raising any doubts about long-term soil fertility and health. For the last twenty-five years, a private, voluntary organisation, the Soil Association, has been engaged in exploring the vital relationships between soil, plant, animal, and man; has undertaken and assisted relevant research; and has attempted to keep the public informed about developments in these fields. Neither the successful farmers nor the Soil Association have been able to attract official support or recognition. They have generally been dismissed as "the muck and mystery people," because they are obviously outside the mainstream of modern technological progress. Their methods bear the mark of non-violence and humility towards the infinitely subtle system of natural harmony, and this stands in opposition to the life-style of the modern world. But if we now realise that the modern life-style is putting us into mortal danger, we may find it in our hearts to support and even join these pioneers rather than to ignore or ridicule them.

On the industrial side, there is the Intermediate Technology Development Group. It is engaged in the systematic study of how to help people to help themselves. While its work is primarily concerned with giving technical assistance to the Third World, the results of its research are attracting increasing attention also from those who are concerned about the future of the rich societies. For they show that an intermediate technology, a technology with a human face, is in fact possible; that it is viable; and that it re-integrates the human being, with his skillful hands and creative brain, into the productive process. It serves *production by the masses* instead of *mass production*. Like the Soil Association, it is a private, voluntary organisation depending on public support.

I have no doubt that it is possible to give a new direction to technological development, a direction that shall lead it back to the real needs of man, and that also means: *to the actual size of man*. Man is small, and, therefore, small is beautiful. To go for giantism is to go for self-destruction. And what is the cost of a reorientation? We might remind ourselves that to calculate the cost of survival is perverse. No doubt, a price has to be paid for anything worth while: to redirect technology so that it serves man instead of destroying him requires primarily an effort of the imagination and an abandonment of fear.

Technology without wisdom is a recipe for disaster. Hammers to make homes or holes in a head. Glues for arrows to bring home food or scalps. Matches to light the hearth fire or cannons. The real question is how to find and implement wisdom about anything.

—PETER WARSHALL

PART III

THE THIRD WORLD

CHAPTER II

DEVELOPMENT

A BRITISH GOVERNMENT WHITE PAPER on Overseas Development some years ago stated the aims of foreign aid as follows:

> To do what lies within our power to help the developing countries to provide their people with the material opportunities for using their talents, of living a full and happy life and steadily improving their lot.

It may be doubtful whether equally optimistic language would be used today, but the basic philosophy remains the same. There is, perhaps, some disillusionment: the task turns out to be much harder than may have been thought—and the newly independent countries are finding the same. Two phenomena, in particular, are giving rise to world-wide concern—mass unemployment and mass migration into cities. For two-thirds of mankind, the aim of a "full and happy life" with steady improvements of their lot, if not actually receding, seems to be as far away as ever. So we had better have a new look at the whole problem.

Many people are having a new look and some say the trouble is that there is too little aid. They admit that there are many unhealthy and disrupting tendencies but suggest that with more massive aid one ought to be able to over-compensate them. If the available aid cannot be massive enough for everybody, they suggest that it should be concentrated on the countries where the promise of success seems most credible. Not surprisingly, this proposal has failed to win general acceptance.

Conventional development thinking implicitly defines equity as a problem of the poor. Facing the gap separating the rich from the poor, developmentalists perceive this gap as a deficit of the powerless and not as a fault of the powerful. They launch themselves into raising the living standards of the poor toward the level of the rich. They work for lifting the bottom rather than lowering the top. However, with the emergence of biophysical limits to growth, the classical notions of justice, which were devised in a perspective of finitude and not in a perspective of infinity, acquire new relevance: justice is about changing the rich and not about changing the poor.

As our research has shown, if industrialized countries aspire to become good global neighbors, they will have to reduce their resource consumption by a factor of 10 within the next 50 years. ➥

One of the unhealthy and disruptive tendencies in virtually all the developing countries is the emergence, in an ever more accentuated form, of the "dual economy," in which there are two different patterns of living as widely separated from each other as two different worlds. It is not a matter of some people being rich and others being poor, both being united by a common way of life: it is a matter of two ways of life existing side by side in such a manner that even the humblest member of the one disposes of a daily income which is a high multiple of the income accruing to even the hardest working member of the other. The social and political tensions arising from the dual economy are too obvious to require description.

In the dual economy of a typical developing country, we may find fifteen per cent of the population in the modern sector, mainly confined to one or two big cities. The other eighty-five per cent exist in the rural areas and small towns. For reasons which will be discussed, most of the development effort goes into the big cities, which means that eighty-five per cent of the population are largely by-passed. What is to become of them? Simply to assume that the modern sector in the big cities will grow until it has absorbed almost the entire population—which is, of course, what has happened in many of the highly developed countries—is utterly unrealistic. Even the richest countries are groaning under the burden which such a maldistribution of population inevitably imposes.

In every branch of modern thought, the concept of "evolution" plays a central role. Not so in development economics, although the words "development" and "evolution" would seem to be virtually synonymous. Whatever may be the merit of the theory of evolution in specific cases, it certainly reflects our experience of economic and technical development. Let us imagine a visit to a modern industrial establishment, say, a great refinery. As we walk around in its vastness, through all its fantastic complexity, we might well wonder how it was possible for the human mind to conceive such a thing. What an immensity of knowledge, ingenuity, and experience is here incarnated in equipment! How is it possible? The answer is that it did not spring ready-made out of any person's mind—it came by a process of evolution. It started quite simply, then this was added and that was modified, and so the whole thing became more and more complex. But even what we actually see in this refinery is only, as we might say, the tip of an iceberg.

What we cannot see on our visit is far greater than what we can see: the immensity and complexity of the arrangements that allow crude oil to flow into the refinery and ensure that a multitude of consignments of refined products, properly prepared, packed and labelled, reaches innumerable consumers through a most elaborate distribution system. All this we cannot see. Nor can we see the intellectual achievements behind the planning, the organising, the financing and marketing. Least of all can we see the great educational background which is the precondition of all, extending from primary schools to universities and specialised research establishments, and without which nothing of what we actually see would be there. As I said, the visitor sees only the tip of the iceberg: there is ten times as much somewhere else, which he cannot see, and without the "ten," the "one" is worthless. And if the "ten" is not supplied by the country or society in which the refinery has been erected, either the refinery simply does not work or it is, in fact, a foreign body depending for most of its life on some other society. Now, all this is easily forgotten, because the modern tendency is to see and become conscious of only the visible and to forget the invisible things that are making the visible possible and keep it going.

Could it be that the relative failure of aid, or at least our disappointment with the effectiveness of aid, has something to do with our materialist philosophy which makes us liable to overlook the most important preconditions of success, which are generally invisible? Or if we do not entirely overlook them, we tend to treat them just as we treat material things—things that can be planned and scheduled and purchased with money according to some all-comprehensive development plan. In other words, we tend to think of development, not in terms of evolution, but in terms of creation.

Our scientists incessantly tell us with the utmost assurance that everything around us has evolved by small mutations sieved out through natural selection. Even the Almighty is not credited with having been able to create anything complex. Every complexity, we are told, is the result of evolution. Yet our development planners

➡ *No doubt, this enormous challenge would amount to a civilization transition of sorts, bringing both technological talents and new public virtues to bear. But sufficiency has been the hallmark of justice before the dreams of infinity took over; it is bound to become the axis around which any post-developmental notion of justice will revolve. From now on, justice is about taking less rather than giving more.*

—WOLFGANG SACHS

Employment prospects are no better today. In Opening the Marketplace to Small Enterprises *(1991), de Wilde et al. report that over the next 10 years, 1.2 billion will come of age to work, but only a quarter of them will be able to find it. That leaves 900 million without a regular income. The International Fund for Agricultural Development says that more than one billion people in developing countries already live below the poverty line (based on internationally accepted measures), likely increasing to 1.3 billion within a few years. This is human misery on an unprecedented scale.*
—GEORGE McROBIE

seem to think that they can do better than the Almighty, that they can create the most complex things at one throw by a process called planning, letting Athene spring, not out of the head of Zeus, but out of nothingness, fully armed, resplendent, and viable.

Now, of course, extraordinary and unfitting things can occasionally be done. One can successfully carry out a project here or there. It is always possible to create small ultra-modern islands in a pre-industrial society. But such islands will then have to be defended, like fortresses, and provisioned, as it were, by helicopter from far away, or they will be flooded by the surrounding sea. Whatever happens, whether they do well or badly, they produce the "dual economy" of which I have spoken. They cannot be integrated into the surrounding society, and tend to destroy its cohesion.

We may observe in passing that similar tendencies are at work even in some of the richest countries, where they manifest as a trend towards excessive urbanisation, towards "megalopolis," and leave, in the midst of affluence, large pockets of poverty-stricken people, "drop-outs," unemployed, and unemployables.

Until recently, the development experts rarely referred to the dual economy and its twin evils of mass unemployment and mass migration into cities. When they did so, they merely deplored them and treated them as transitional. Meanwhile, it has become widely recognised that time alone will not be the healer. On the contrary, the dual economy, unless consciously counteracted, produces what I have called a "process of mutual poisoning," whereby successful industrial development in the cities destroys the economic structure of the hinterland, and the hinterland takes its revenge by mass migration into the cities, poisoning them and making them utterly unmanageable. Forward estimates made by the World Health Organisation and by experts like Kingsley Davies predict cities of twenty, forty, and even sixty million inhabitants, a prospect of "immiseration" for multitudes of people that beggars the imagination.

Is there an alternative? That the developing countries cannot do without a modern sector, particularly where they are in direct contact with the rich countries, is hardly open to doubt. What needs to be questioned is the implicit assumption that the modern sector can be expanded to absorb virtually the entire population and that this can be done fairly quickly. The ruling philosophy of development over the last twenty years has been: "What is best for the rich must be best for the poor." This belief has been carried to truly astonishing lengths, as can be seen by inspecting the list of developing countries in which the Americans and their allies and in some cases also the Russians have found it necessary and wise to establish "peaceful" nuclear reactors—Taiwan, South Korea, Philippines, Vietnam, Thailand, Indonesia, Iran, Turkey, Portugal, Venezuela—all of them countries whose overwhelming problems are agriculture and the rejuvenation of rural life, since the great majority of their poverty-stricken peoples live in rural areas.

The starting point of all our considerations is poverty, or rather, a degree of poverty which means misery, and degrades and stultifies the human person; and our first task is to recognise and understand the boundaries and limitations which this degree of poverty imposes. Again, our crudely materialistic philosophy makes us liable to see only "the material opportunities" (to use the words of the White Paper which I have already quoted) and to overlook the immaterial factors. Among the causes of poverty, I am sure, the material factors are entirely secondary—such things as a lack of natural wealth, or a lack of capital, or an insufficiency of infrastructure. The primary causes of extreme poverty are immaterial; they lie in certain deficiencies in education, organisation, and discipline.

Development does not start with goods; it starts with people and their education, organisation, and discipline. Without these three, all resources remain latent, untapped, potential. There are prosperous societies with but the scantiest basis of natural wealth, and we have had plenty of opportunity to observe the primacy of the invisible factors after the war. Every country, no matter how devastated, which had a high level of education, organisation, and discipline, produced an "economic miracle." In fact, these were miracles only for people whose attention is focused on the tip of the iceberg. The tip had been smashed to pieces, but the base, which is education, organisation, and discipline, was still there.

Here, then, lies the central problem of development. If the primary causes of poverty are deficiencies in these three respects, then

Moving toward the local may seem impractical or utopian. One reason is the belief that an emphasis on the local economy means total self-reliance on a village level, without any trade at all. The most urgent issue today, however, isn't whether people have oranges in cold climates, but whether their wheat, eggs, or milk should travel thousands of miles when they could all be produced within a 50-mile radius. Individuals are becoming dependent for their everyday needs on products that have been transported thousands of miles, often unnecessarily. The goal of localization would not be to eliminate all trade but to reduce unnecessary transport while encouraging changes that would strengthen and diversify economies at both the community and national levels. The degree of diversification, the goods produced, and the amount of trade would naturally vary from region to region. ➡

➡ *Another stumbling block is the belief that a greater degree of self-reliance in the North would undermine the economies of the "Third World," where people supposedly need northern markets to lift themselves out of poverty. The truth of the matter is that a shift toward smaller scale and more localized production would benefit both North and South, and allow for more meaningful work and fuller employment all around. Today, a large proportion of the South's natural resources is delivered to the North, on increasingly unfavorable terms, in the form of raw materials. The South's best agricultural land is devoted to growing food, fibers, even flowers for the North, and a good deal of the South's labor is used to manufacture goods for northern markets. Rather than further impoverishing the South, producing more ourselves would allow the South to keep more of its resources and labor for itself.*

—HELENA
NORBERG-HODGE

the alleviation of poverty depends primarily on the removal of these deficiencies. Here lies the reason why development cannot be an act of creation, why it cannot be ordered, bought, comprehensively planned: why it requires a process of evolution. Education does not "jump"; it is a gradual process of great subtlety. Organisation does not "jump"; it must gradually evolve to fit changing circumstances. And much the same goes for discipline. All three must evolve step by step, and the foremost task of development policy must be to speed this evolution. All three must become the property not merely of a tiny minority, but of the whole society.

If aid is given to introduce certain new economic activities, these will be beneficial and viable only if they can be sustained by the already existing educational level of fairly broad groups of people, and they will be truly valuable only if they promote and spread advances in education, organisation, and discipline. There can be a process of stretching—never a process of jumping. If new economic activities are introduced which depend on *special* education, *special* organisation, and *special* discipline, such as are in no way inherent in the recipient society, the activity will not promote healthy development but will be more likely to hinder it. It will remain a foreign body that cannot be integrated and will further exacerbate the problems of the dual economy.

It follows from this that development is not primarily a problem for economists, least of all for economists whose expertise is founded on a crudely materialistic philosophy. No doubt, economists of whatever philosophical persuasion have their usefulness at certain stages of development and for strictly circumscribed technical jobs, but only if the general guidelines of a development policy *to involve the entire population* are already firmly established.

The new thinking that is required for aid and development will be different from the old because it will take poverty seriously. It will not go on mechanically, saying: "What is good for the rich must also be good for the poor." It will care for people—from a severely practical point of view. Why care for people? Because people are the primary and ultimate source of any wealth whatsoever. If they are left out, if they are pushed around by self-styled experts and high-handed planners, then nothing can ever yield real fruit.

The following chapter is a slightly shortened version of a paper prepared in 1965 for a Conference on the Application of Science and Technology to the Development of Latin America, organised by UNESCO in Santiago, Chile. At that time, discussions on economic development almost invariably tended to take technology simply as "given"; the question was how to transfer the given technology to those not yet in possession of it. The latest was obviously the best, and the idea that it might not serve the urgent needs of developing countries because it failed to fit into the actual conditions and limitations of poverty, was treated with ridicule. However, the paper became the basis on which the Intermediate Technology Development Group was set up in London.

It isn't the human-scale hardware flowing out of intermediate and appropriate technology centers around the world that has had the most profound impact on society. As Schumacher well recognized, it is the software of the industrial nations that needs to change if the world is to provide a just and equitable life for all. It is that "search for a new lifestyle" and "return to certain basic truths about man and his world" that is now on the verge of promising a bright new future for all of humanity.
—BILL ELLIS

SOCIAL AND ECONOMIC PROBLEMS CALLING FOR THE DEVELOPMENT OF INTERMEDIATE TECHNOLOGY

INTRODUCTION

IN MANY PLACES in the world today the poor are getting poorer while the rich are getting richer, and the established processes of foreign aid and development planning appear to be unable to overcome this tendency. In fact, they often seem to promote it, for it is always easier to help those who can help themselves than to help the helpless. Nearly all the so-called developing countries have a modern sector where the patterns of living and working are similar to those of the developed countries, but they also have a non-modern sector, accounting for the vast majority of the total population, where the patterns of living and working are not only profoundly unsatisfactory but also in a process of accelerating decay.

I am concerned here exclusively with the problem of helping the people in the non-modern sector. This does not imply the suggestion that constructive work in the modern sector should be discontinued, and there can be no doubt that it will continue in any case. But it does imply the conviction that all successes in the modern sector are likely to be illusory unless there is also a healthy growth—or at least a healthy condition of stability—among the very great numbers of people today whose life is characterised not only by dire poverty but also by hopelessness.

THE NEED FOR INTERMEDIATE TECHNOLOGY

The Condition of the Poor

What is the typical condition of the poor in most of the so-called developing countries? Their work opportunities are so restricted that they cannot work their way out of misery. They are underemployed or totally unemployed, and when they do find occasional work their productivity is exceedingly low. Some of them have land, but often too little. Many have no land and no prospect of ever getting any. There is no hope for them in the rural areas and hence they drift into the big cities. But there is no work for them in the big cities either and, of course, no housing. All the same, they flock into the cities because the chances of finding some work appear to be greater there than in the villages, where they are nil.

The open and disguised unemployment in the rural areas is often thought to be due entirely to population growth, and no doubt this is an important contributory factor. But those who hold this view still have to explain why additional people cannot do additional work. It is said that they cannot work because they lack "capital." But what is "capital"? It is the product of human work. The lack of capital can explain a low level of productivity, but it cannot explain a lack of work opportunities.

The fact remains, however, that great numbers of people do not work or work only intermittently, and that they are therefore poor and helpless and often desperate enough to leave the village to search for some kind of existence in the big city. Rural unemployment produces mass migration into cities, leading to a rate of urban growth which would tax the resources of even the richest societies. Rural unemployment becomes urban unemployment.

Help to Those who Need it Most

The problem may therefore be stated quite simply thus: What can be done to bring health to economic life outside the big cities, in the

I first met Fritz Schumacher in 1968 while working in the Science Policy Division of UNESCO. His concept of intermediate technology had become the driving force behind a shift in technological aid to the Third World. In the following decade, intermediate technology centers had sprung up all over the world. Papua New Guinea, Nepal, Ghana, Colombia, and India were only a few of the nations of the Third World developing small-scale, low-cost technologies. Water wheels, composting privies, solar pumps, bicycle-driven threshers, and other intermediate hardware filled the gap between the primitive hand tools used by most of the people of the world and the hi-tech, high-cost, complex hardware and infrastructure being foisted on these countries by the "development experts." The industrial countries too caught Fritz's small-is-beautiful bug.
—BILL ELLIS

small towns and villages which still contain—in most cases—eighty to ninety per cent of the total population? As long as the development effort is concentrated mainly on the big cities, where it is easiest to establish new industries, to staff them with managers and men, and to find finance and markets to keep them going, the competition from these industries will further disrupt and destroy non-agricultural production in the rest of the country, will cause additional unemployment outside, and will further accelerate the migration of destitute people into towns that cannot absorb them. The "process of mutual poisoning" will not be halted.

It is necessary, therefore, that at least an important part of the development effort should by-pass the big cities and be directly concerned with the creation of an "agro-industrial structure" in the rural and small-town areas. In this connection it is necessary to emphasise that the primary need is workplaces, literally millions of workplaces. No one, of course, would suggest that output-per-man is unimportant; but the primary consideration cannot be to maximise output per man; it must be to maximise work opportunities for the unemployed and the underemployed. For a poor man the chance to work is the greatest of all needs, and even poorly paid and relatively unproductive work is better than idleness. "Coverage must come before perfection," to use the words of Mr. Gabriel Ardant.[1]

> It is important that there should be enough work for all because that is the only way to eliminate anti-productive reflexes and create a new state of mind—that of a country where labour has become precious and must be put to the best possible use.

In other words, the economic calculus which measures success in terms of output or income, without consideration of the number of jobs, is quite inappropriate in the conditions here under consideration, for it implies a static approach to the problem of development. The dynamic approach pays heed to the needs and reactions of people: their first need is to start work of some kind that brings some reward, however small; it is only when they experience that their time and labour is of value that they can become interested in making it more valuable. It is therefore more important that everybody should produce something than that a few people should each produce a great deal, and this remains true even if in some exceptional cases the total output under the former arrangement should be smaller than it would be under the latter arrangement. It will not remain smaller, because this is a dynamic situation capable of generating growth.

An unemployed man is a desperate man and he is practically forced into migration. This is another justification for the assertion that the provision of work opportunities is the primary need and should be the primary objective of economic planning. Without it, the drift of people into the large cities cannot be mitigated, let alone halted.

The Nature of the Task
The task, then, is to bring into existence millions of new workplaces in the rural areas and small towns. That modern industry, as it has arisen in the developed countries, cannot possibly fulfill this task should be perfectly obvious. It has arisen in societies which are rich in capital and short of labour and therefore cannot possibly be appropriate for societies short of capital and rich in labour. Puerto Rico furnishes a good illustration of the point. To quote from a recent study:

> Development of modern factory-style manufacturing makes only a limited contribution to employment. The Puerto Rican development programme has been unusually vigorous and successful; but from 1952–62 the average increase of employment in E.D.A.-sponsored plants was about 5,000 a year. With present labour force participation rates, and in the absence of net emigration to the mainland, annual additions to the Puerto Rican labour force would be of the order of 40,000....
>
> Within manufacturing, there should be imaginative exploration of small-scale, more decentralised, more labour-using forms of organisation such as have persisted in the

In the experience of the Intermediate Technology Development Group, a number of developing countries have adopted policies that promote the introduction of appropriate—small-scale and relatively labor intensive—technologies. These include Costa Rica, Eritrea, Ghana, India, Uganda, and Peru. Several other countries have encouraged the Group to set up local Intermediate Technology centers in their territories.

—GEORGE MᶜROBIE

The central tenet of appropriate technology (AT) is that
a technology should be
designed to fit into and be
compatible with its local
setting. Examples of current
projects generally classified as
AT include: passive solar
design; active solar collectors
for heating and cooling;
small windmills to provide
electricity; roof-top gardens
and hydroponic greenhouses;
permaculture; and worker-
managed craft industries.
There is general agreement,
however, that the main goal
of the AT movement is to
enhance the self-reliance of
people on a local level. Characteristics of self-reliant
communities that AT can
help facilitate include: low
resource usage coupled with
extensive recycling; preference for renewable over
nonrenewable resources;
emphasis on environmental
harmony; emphasis on
small-scale industries; and a
high degree of social cohesion
and sense of community.

—MARK ROSELAND

Japanese economy to the present day and have contributed materially to its vigorous growth.[2]

Equally powerful illustrations could be drawn from many other countries, notably India and Turkey, where highly ambitious five-year plans regularly show a greater volume of unemployment at the end of the five-year period than at the beginning, even assuming that the plan is fully implemented.

The real task may be formulated in four propositions:

First, that workplaces have to be created in the areas where the people are living now, and not primarily in metropolitan areas into which they tend to migrate.

Second, that these workplaces must be, on average, cheap enough so that they can be created in large numbers without this calling for an unattainable level of capital formation and imports.

Third, that the production methods employed must be relatively simple, so that the demands for high skills are minimised, not only in the production process itself but also in matters of organisation, raw material supply, financing, marketing, and so forth.

Fourth, that production should be mainly from local materials and mainly for local use.

These four requirements can be met only if there is a "regional" approach to development and, second, if there is a conscious effort to develop and apply what might be called an "intermediate technology." These two conditions will now be considered in turn.

The Regional or District Approach

A given political unit is not necessarily of the right size for economic development to benefit those whose need is the greatest. In some cases it may be too small, but in the generality of cases today it is too large. Take, for example, the case of India. It is a very large political unit, and it is no doubt desirable from many points of view that this unity should be maintained. But if development policy is

concerned merely—or primarily—with "India-as-a-whole," the natural drift of things will concentrate development mainly in a few
metropolitan areas, in the modern sector. Vast areas within the
country, containing eighty per cent of the population or more, will
benefit little and may indeed suffer. Hence the twin evils of mass
unemployment and mass migration into the metropolitan areas.
The result of "development" is that a fortunate minority have their
fortunes greatly increased, while those who really need help are left
more helpless than ever before. If the purpose of development is to
bring help to those who need it most, each "region" or "district"
within the country needs its own development. This is what is
meant by a "regional" approach.

A further illustration may be drawn from Italy, a relatively
wealthy country. Southern Italy and Sicily do not develop merely as
a result of successful economic growth in "Italy-as-a-whole." Italian
industry is concentrated mainly in the north of the country, and its
rapid growth does not diminish, but on the contrary tends to inten-
sify, the problem of the south. Nothing succeeds like success and,
equally, nothing fails like failure. Competition from the north destroys production in the south and drains all talented and enterprising men out of it. Conscious efforts have to be made to counteract
these tendencies, for if the population of any region within a country is by-passed by development it becomes actually worse off than
before, is thrown into mass unemployment, and forced into mass
migration. The evidence of this truth can be found all over the
world, even in the most highly developed countries.

In this matter it is not possible to give hard and fast definitions.
Much depends on geography and local circumstances. A few thousand people, no doubt, would be too few to constitute a "district" for
economic development; but a few hundred thousand people, even
if fairly widely scattered, may well deserve to be treated as such. The
whole of Switzerland has less than six million inhabitants; yet it is
divided into more than twenty "cantons," each of which is a kind of
development district, with the result that there is a fairly even
spread of population and of industry and no tendency towards the
formation of excessive concentrations.

Each "district," ideally speaking, would have some sort of inner

cohesion and identity and possess at least one town to serve as a district centre. There is need for a "cultural structure" just as there is
need for an "economic structure"; thus, while every village would
have a primary school, there would be a few small market towns
with secondary schools, and the district centre would be big enough
to carry an institution of higher learning. The bigger the country,
the greater is the need for internal "structure" and for a decen-
tralised approach to development. If this need is neglected, there is
no hope for the poor.

The Need for an Appropriate Technology
It is obvious that this "regional" or "district" approach has no
chance of success unless it is based on the employment of a suitable
technology. The establishment of each workplace in modern industry costs a great deal of capital—something of the order of, say,
£2,000 on average. A poor country, naturally, can never afford to
establish more than a very limited number of such workplaces
within any given period of time. A "modern" workplace, moreover,
can be really productive only within a modern environment, and for
this reason alone is unlikely to fit into a "district" consisting of rural
areas and a few small towns. In every "developing country" one can
find industrial estates set up in rural areas, where high-grade modern equipment is standing idle most of the time because of a lack of
organisation, finance, raw material supplies, transport, marketing
facilities, and the like. There are then complaints and recrim-
inations; but they do not alter the fact that a lot of scarce capital
resources—normally imports paid from scarce foreign exchange—
are virtually wasted.

The distinction between "capital-intensive" and "labour-intensive" industries is, of course, a familiar one in development theory.
Although it has an undoubted validity, it does not really make contact with the essence of the problem; for it normally induces people
to accept the technology of any given line of production as given
and unalterable. If it is then argued that developing countries
should give preference to "labour-intensive" rather than "capital-intensive" industries, no intelligent action can follow, because the
choice of industry, in practice, will be determined by quite other,

much more powerful criteria, such as raw material base, markets, entrepreneurial interest, etc. The choice of industry is one thing; but the choice of technology to be employed *after* the choice of industry has been made, is quite another. It is therefore better to speak directly of technology, and not cloud the discussion by choosing terms like "capital intensity" or "labour intensity" as one's point of departure. Much the same applies to another distinction frequently made in these discussions, that between "large-scale" and "small-scale" industry. It is true that modern industry is often organised in very large units, but "large-scale" is by no means one of its essential and universal features. Whether a given industrial activity is appropriate to the conditions of a developing district does not directly depend on "scale," but on the technology employed. A small-scale enterprise with an average cost per workplace of £2,000 is just as inappropriate as a large-scale enterprise with equally costly workplaces.

I believe, therefore, that the best way to make contact with the essential problem is by speaking of technology: economic development in poverty-stricken areas can be fruitful only on the basis of what I have called "intermediate technology." In the end, intermediate technology will be "labour-intensive" and will lend itself to use in small-scale establishments. But neither "labour-intensive" nor "small-scale" implies "intermediate technology."

Definition of Intermediate Technology
If we define the level of technology in terms of "equipment cost per workplace," we can call the indigenous technology of a typical developing country—symbolically speaking—a £1-technology, while that of the developed countries could be called a £1,000-technology. The gap between these two technologies is so enormous that a transition from the one to the other is simply impossible. In fact, the current attempt of the developing countries to infiltrate the £1,000-technology into their economies inevitably kills off the £1-technology at an alarming rate, destroying traditional workplaces much faster than modern workplaces can be created, and thus leaves the poor in a more desperate and helpless position than ever before. If effective help is to be brought to those who need it most, a

In 1965, a group of us helped Schumacher start the Intermediate Technology Development Group in London. Our starting point was that mass unemployment and rural misery could be overcome only by creating new workplaces in the rural areas—low-cost workplaces that could be created in large numbers, where production methods and associated services were relatively simple, and used local materials for local use.

We used the term "intermediate" to indicate that, in terms of cost per workplace, the technology appropriate to a poor country would be somewhere between the almost nil cost of a primitive hand tool, and the £40,000-cost of a combine harvester. Thus if a developing country insisted on technologies that needed £40,000 for each new workplace, obviously, being short of capital, relatively few jobs could be created. But with a technology that cost £500, the country could create ➡

technology is required which would range in some intermediate position between the £1-technology and the £1,000-technology. Let us call it—again symbolically speaking—a £100-technology.

Such an intermediate technology would be immensely more productive than the indigenous technology (which is often in a condition of decay), but it would also be immensely cheaper than the sophisticated, highly capital-intensive technology of modern industry. At such a level of capitalisation, very large numbers of workplaces could be created within a fairly short time; and the creation of such workplaces would be "within reach" for the more enterprising minority within the district, not only in financial terms but also in terms of their education, aptitude, organising skill, and so forth.

This last point may perhaps be elucidated as follows:

The average annual income per worker and the average capital per workplace in the developed countries appear at present to stand in a relationship of roughly 1 : 1. This implies, in general terms, that it takes one man-year to create one workplace, or that a man would have to save one month's earnings a year for twelve years to be able to own a workplace. If the relationship were 1 : 10, it would require ten man-years to create one workplace, and a man would have to save a month's earnings a year for 120 years before he could make himself owner of a workplace. This, of course, is an impossibility, and it follows that the £1,000-technology transplanted into a district which is stuck on the level of a £1-technology simply cannot spread by any process of normal growth. It cannot have a positive "demonstration effect"; on the contrary, as can be observed all over the world, its "demonstration effect" is wholly negative. The people, to whom the £1,000-technology is inaccessible, simply "give up" and often cease doing even those things which they had done previously.

The intermediate technology would also fit much more smoothly into the relatively unsophisticated environment in which it is to be utilised. The equipment would be fairly simple and therefore understandable, suitable for maintenance and repair on the spot. Simple equipment is normally far less dependent on raw materials of great purity or exact specifications and much more adaptable to market fluctuations than highly sophisticated equipment.

Men are more easily trained; supervision, control, and organisation are simpler; and there is far less vulnerability to unforeseen difficulties.

Objections Raised and Discussed

Since the idea of intermediate technology was first put forward, a number of objections have been raised. The most immediate objections are psychological: "You are trying to withhold the best and make us put up with something inferior and outdated." This is the voice of those who are not in need, who can help themselves and want to be assisted in reaching a higher standard of living at once. It is not the voice of those with whom we are here concerned, the poverty-stricken multitudes who lack any real basis of existence, whether in rural or in urban areas, who have neither "the best" nor "the second best" but go short of even the most essential means of subsistence. One sometimes wonders how many "development economists" have any real comprehension of the condition of the poor.

There are economists and econometricians who believe that development policy can be derived from certain allegedly fixed ratios, such as the capital/output ratio. Their argument runs as follows: The amount of available capital is given. Now, you may concentrate it on a small number of highly capitalised workplaces, or you may spread it thinly over a large number of cheap workplaces. If you do the latter, you obtain less total output than if you do the former; you therefore fail to achieve the quickest possible rate of economic growth. Dr. Kaldor, for instance, claims that "research has shown that the most modern machinery produces much more output per unit of capital invested than less sophisticated machinery which employs more people." Not only "capital" but also "wages goods" are held to be a given quantity, and this quantity determines "the limits on wages employment in any country at any given time."

If we can employ only a limited number of people in wage labour, then let us employ them in the most productive way, so that they make the biggest possible contribution to the national output, because that will also give the quickest rate of

➡ *80 times as many jobs. The best engineering talent available, we argued, should be engaged in the task of creating low-cost technologies: tools and equipment that could be owned and controlled by the rural and urban poor with which they could work themselves out of poverty.*

—GEORGE McROBIE

economic growth. You should not go deliberately out of your way to reduce productivity in order to reduce the amount of capital per worker. This seems to me nonsense because you may find that by increasing capital per worker tenfold you increase the output per worker twentyfold. There is no question from every point of view of the superiority of the latest and more capitalistic technologies.[4]

The first thing that might be said about these arguments is that they are evidently static in character and fail to take account of the dynamics of development. To do justice to the real situation it is necessary to consider the reactions and capabilities of people, and not confine oneself to machinery or abstract concepts. As we have seen before, it is wrong to assume that the most sophisticated equipment, transplanted into an unsophisticated environment, will be regularly worked at full capacity, and if capacity utilisation is low, then the capital/output ratio is also low. It is therefore fallacious to treat capital/output ratios as technological facts, when they are so largely dependent on quite other factors.

The question must be asked, moreover, whether there is such a law, as Dr. Kaldor asserts, that the capital/output ratio grows if capital is concentrated on fewer workplaces. No one with the slightest industrial experience would ever claim to have noticed the existence of such a "law," nor is there any foundation for it in any science. Mechanisation and automation are introduced to increase the productivity of labour, i.e. the worker/output ratio, and their effect on the capital/output ratio may just as well be negative as it may be positive. Countless examples can be quoted where advances in technology eliminate workplaces at the cost of an additional input of capital without affecting the volume of output. It is therefore quite untrue to assert that a given amount of capital invariably and necessarily produces the biggest total output when it is concentrated on the smallest number of workplaces.

The greatest weakness of the argument, however, lies in taking "capital"—and even "wages goods"—as "given quantities" in an underemployed economy. Here again, the static outlook inevitably leads to erroneous conclusions. The central concern of development policy, as I have argued already, must be the creation of work opportunities for those who, being unemployed, are consumers—on however miserable a level—without contributing anything to the fund of either "wages goods" or "capital." Employment is the very precondition of everything else. The output of an idle man is nil, whereas the output of even a poorly equipped man can be a positive contribution, and this contribution can be to "capital" as well as to "wages goods." The distinction between those two is by no means as definite as the econometricians are inclined to think, because the definition of "capital" itself depends decisively on the level of technology employed.

Let us consider a very simple example. Some earth-moving job has to be done in an area of high unemployment. There is a wide choice of technologies, ranging from the most modern earth-moving equipment to purely manual work without tools of any kind. The "output" is fixed by the nature of the job, and it is quite clear that the capital/output ratio will be highest if the input of "capital" is kept lowest. If the job were done without any tools, the capital/output ratio would be infinitely large, but the productivity per man would be exceedingly low. If the job were done at the highest level of modern technology, the capital/output ratio would be low and the productivity per man very high. Neither of these extremes is desirable, and a middle way has to be found. Assume some of the unemployed men were first set to work to make a variety of tools, including wheelbarrows and the like, while others were made to produce various "wages goods." Each of these lines of production in turn could be based on a wide range of different technologies, from the simplest to the most sophisticated. The task in every case would be to find an intermediate technology which obtains a fair level of productivity without having to resort to the purchase of expensive and sophisticated equipment. The outcome of the whole venture would be an economic development going far beyond the completion of the initial earth-moving project. With a total input of "capital" from outside which might be much smaller than would have been involved in the acquisition of the most modern earth-moving equipment, and an input of (previously unemployed) labour much greater than the "modern" method would have demanded, not only

Sustainable community economic development provides a means of integrating sustainable development and Buddhist economics at the community level. Community economic development can be characterized as a process by which communities can initiate and generate their own solutions to their common economic problems and thereby build long-term community capacity and foster the integration of economic, social, and environmental objectives.
—MARK ROSELAND

a given project would have been completed, but a whole community would have been set on the path of development.

I say, therefore, that the dynamic approach to development, which treats the choice of appropriate, intermediate technologies as the central issue, opens up avenues of constructive action, which the static, econometric approach totally fails to recognise.

This leads to the next objection which has been raised against the idea of intermediate technology. It is argued that all this might be quite promising if it were not for a notorious shortage of entrepreneurial ability in the underdeveloped countries. This scarce resource should therefore be utilised in the most concentrated way, in places where it has the best chances of success, and should be endowed with the finest capital equipment the world can offer. Industry, it is thus argued, should be established in or near the big cities, in large integrated units, and on the highest possible level of capitalisation per workplace.

The argument hinges on the assumption that "entrepreneurial ability" is a fixed and given quantity, and thus again betrays a purely static point of view. It is, of course, neither fixed nor given, being largely a function of the technology to be employed. Men quite incapable of acting as entrepreneurs on the level of modern technology may nonetheless be fully capable of making a success of a small-scale enterprise set up on the basis of intermediate technology—for reasons already explained above. In fact, it seems to me that the apparent shortage of entrepreneurs in many developing countries today is precisely the result of the "negative demonstration effect" of a sophisticated technology infiltrated into an unsophisticated environment. The introduction of an appropriate, intermediate technology would not be likely to founder on any shortage of entrepreneurial ability. Nor would it diminish the supply of entrepreneurs for enterprises in the modern sector; on the contrary, by spreading familiarity with systematic, technical modes of production over the entire population, it would undoubtedly help to increase the supply of the required talent.

Two further arguments have been advanced against the idea of intermediate technology—that its products would require protection within the country and would be unsuitable for export. Both arguments are based on mere surmise. In fact a considerable number of design studies and costings, made for specific products in specific districts, have universally demonstrated that the products of an intelligently chosen intermediate technology could actually be cheaper than those of modern factories in the nearest big city. Whether or not such products could be exported is an open question; the unemployed are not contributing to exports now, and the primary task is to put them to work so that they will produce useful goods from local materials for local use.

Applicability of Intermediate Technology
The applicability of intermediate technology is, of course, not universal. There are products which are themselves the typical outcome of highly sophisticated modern industry and cannot be produced except by such an industry. These products, at the same time, are not normally an urgent need of the poor. What the poor need most of all is simple things—building materials, clothing, household goods, agricultural implements—and a better return for their agricultural products. They also most urgently need in many places: trees, water, and crop storage facilities. Most agricultural populations would be helped immensely if they could themselves do the first stages of processing their products. All these are ideal fields for intermediate technology.

There are, however, also numerous applications of a more ambitious kind. I quote two examples from a recent report:

The first relates to the recent tendency [fostered by the policy of most African, Asian and Latin American governments of having oil refineries in their own territories, however small their markets] for international firms to design small petroleum refineries with low capital investment per unit of output and a low total capacity, say from 5,000 to 30,000 barrels daily. These units are as efficient and low-cost as the much bigger and more capital-intensive refineries corresponding to conventional design. The second example relates to "package plants" for ammonia production, also recently designed for small markets. According to some provisional data, the investment cost per ton in a "package plant" with a sixty-tons-a-day capacity may be about 30,000 dollars, whereas a conventionally designed unit, with a daily capacity of 100 tons [which is, for a conventional plant, very small] would require an investment of approximately 50,000 dollars per ton.[5]

The idea of intermediate technology does not imply simply a "going back" in history to methods now outdated, although a systematic study of methods employed in the developed countries, say, a hundred years ago could indeed yield highly suggestive results. It is too often assumed that the achievement of Western science, pure and applied, lies mainly in the apparatus and machinery that have been developed from it, and that a rejection of the apparatus and machinery would be tantamount to a rejection of science. This is an excessively superficial view. The real achievement lies in the accumulation of precise knowledge, and this knowledge can be applied in a great variety of ways, of which the current application in modern industry is only one. The development of an intermediate technology, therefore, means a genuine forward movement into new territory, where the enormous cost and complication of production methods for the sake of labour saving and job elimination is avoided and technology is made appropriate for labour-surplus societies.

That the applicability of intermediate technology is extremely wide, even if not universal, will be obvious to anyone who takes the trouble to look for its actual applications today. Examples can be found in every developing country and, indeed, in the advanced countries as well. What, then, is missing? It is simply that the brave and able practitioners of intermediate technology do not know of one another, do not support one another, and cannot be of assistance to those who want to follow a similar road but do not know how to get started. They exist, as it were, outside the mainstream of official and popular interest. "The catalogue issued by the European or United States exporter of machinery is still the prime source of technical assistance"[6] and the institutional arrangements for dispensing aid are generally such that there is an unsurmountable bias in favour of large-scale projects on the level of the most modern technology.

If we could turn official and popular interest away from the grandiose projects and to the real needs of the poor, the battle could be won. A study of intermediate technologies as they exist today already would disclose that there is enough knowledge and experience to set everybody to work, and where there are gaps, new design studies could be made very quickly. Professor Gadgil, director of the Gokhale Institute of Politics and Economics at Poona, has outlined three possible approaches to the development of intermediate technology, as follows:

One approach may be to start with existing techniques in traditional industry and to utilise knowledge of advanced techniques to transform them suitably. Transformation implies retaining some elements in existing equipment, skills and procedures.... This process of improvement of traditional technology is extremely important, particularly for that part of the transition in which a holding operation for preventing added technological unemployment appears necessary....

Another approach would be to start from the end of the most advanced technology and to adapt and adjust so as to meet the requirements of the intermediate.... In some cases, the process would also involve adjustment to special local circumstances such as type of fuel or power available.

A third approach may be to conduct experimentation and research in a direct effort to establish intermediate technology. However, for this to be fruitfully undertaken it would be necessary to define, for the scientist and the technician, the limiting economic circumstances. These are chiefly the scale of operations aimed at and the relative costs of capital and labour and the scale of their inputs—possible or desirable. Such direct effort at establishing intermediate technology would undoubtedly be conducted against the background of knowledge of advanced technology in the field. However, it could cover a much wider range of possibilities than the effort through the adjustment and adaptation approach.

In today's terminology, appropriate technologies (AT) are those products and processes that promote sustainable livelihoods and reorient development strategies toward increased employment, enhanced income and gender equity, the protection and rehabilitation of the biophysical environment, and the provision of basic needs. Many AT practitioners today describe what they do as community economic development.

—MARK ROSELAND

Professor Gadgil goes on to plead that:

> The main attention of the personnel on the applied side of National Laboratories, technical institutes and the large university departments must be concentrated on this work. The advancement of advanced technology in every field is being adequately pursued in the developed countries; the special adaptations and adjustments required in India are not and are not likely to be given attention in any other country. They must, therefore, obtain the highest priority in our plans. Intermediate technology should become a national concern and not, as at present, a neglected field assigned to a small number of specialists, set apart.[7]

A similar plea might be made to supranational agencies which would be well-placed to collect, systematise, and develop the scattered knowledge and experience already existing in this vitally important field.

In summary we can conclude:

1. The "dual economy" in the developing countries will remain for the foreseeable future. The modern sector will not be able to absorb the whole.
2. If the non-modern sector is not made the object of special development efforts, it will continue to disintegrate; this disintegration will continue to manifest itself in mass unemployment and mass migration into metropolitan areas; and this will poison economic life in the modern sector as well.
3. The poor can be helped to help themselves, but only by making available to them a technology that recognises the economic boundaries and limitations of poverty—an intermediate technology.
4. Action programmes on a national and supranational basis are needed to develop intermediate technologies suitable for the promotion of full employment in developing countries.

CHAPTER 13

TWO MILLION VILLAGES

THE RESULTS of the second development decade will be no better than those of the first unless there is a conscious and determined shift of emphasis from goods to people. Indeed, without such a shift the results of aid will become increasingly destructive.

If we talk of promoting development, what have we in mind—goods or people? If it is people—which particular people? Who are they? Where are they? Why do they need help? If they cannot get on without help, what, precisely, is the help they need? How do we communicate with them? Concern with people raises countless questions like these. Goods, on the other hand, do not raise so many questions. Particularly when econometricians and statisticians deal with them, goods even cease to be anything identifiable, and become GNP, imports, exports, savings, investment, infrastructure, or what not. Impressive models can be built out of these abstractions, and it is a rarity for them to leave any room for actual people. Of course, "populations" may figure in them, but as nothing more than a mere quantity to be used as a divisor after the dividend, i.e. the quantity of available goods, has been determined. The model then shows that "development," that is, the growth of the dividend, is held back and frustrated if the divisor grows as well.

It is much easier to deal with goods than with people—if only because goods have no minds of their own and raise no problems of communication. When the emphasis is on people, communications problems become paramount. Who are the helpers and who are those to be helped? The helpers, by and large, are rich, educated (in a somewhat specialised sense), and town-based. Those who

Schumacher's favorite economic system was the Gandhian decentralized model. In India today, the rural village economy is still very strong, especially in agriculture and crafts, despite Bombay, Calcutta, and New Delhi, where citizens prefer the globalized, international economy. Sixty to 70 percent of Indian villagers are practicing their crafts and small-scale agriculture without chemicals, fertilizers, and genetically modified and engineered patent seeds, and so on.

—SATISH KUMAR

most need help are poor, uneducated, and rurally based. This means that three tremendous gulfs separate the former from the latter: the gulf between rich and poor; the gulf between educated and uneducated; and the gulf between city-men and country-folk, which includes that between industry and agriculture. The first problem of development aid is how to bridge these three gulfs. A great effort of imagination, study, and compassion is needed to do so. The methods of production, the patterns of consumption, the systems of ideas and of values that suit relatively affluent and educated city people are unlikely to suit poor, semi-illiterate peasants. Poor peasants cannot suddenly acquire the outlook and habits of sophisticated city people. If the people cannot adapt themselves to the methods, then the methods must be adapted to the people. This is the whole crux of the matter.

There are, moreover, many features of the rich man's economy which are so questionable in themselves and, in any case, so inappropriate for poor communities that successful adaptation of the people to these features would spell ruin. If the nature of change is such that nothing is left for the fathers to teach their sons, or for the sons to accept from their fathers, family life collapses. The life, work, and happiness of all societies depend on certain "psychological structures" which are infinitely precious and highly vulnerable. Social cohesion, cooperation, mutual respect, and above all, self-respect, courage in the face of adversity, and the ability to bear hardship—all this and much else disintegrates and disappears when these "psychological structures" are gravely damaged. A man is destroyed by the inner conviction of uselessness. No amount of economic growth can compensate for such losses—though this may be an idle reflection, since economic growth is normally inhibited by them.

None of these awesome problems figures noticeably in the cosy theories of most of our development economists. The failure of the first development decade is attributed simply to an insufficiency of aid appropriations or, worse still, to certain alleged defects inherent in the societies and populations of the developing countries. A study of the current literature could lead one to suppose that the decisive question was whether aid was dispensed multilaterally or bilaterally, or that an improvement in the terms of trade for primary commodities, a removal of trade barriers, guarantees for private investors, or the effective introduction of birth control, were the only things that really mattered.

Now, I am far from suggesting that any of these items are irrelevant, but they do not seem to go to the heart of the matter, and there is in any case precious little constructive action flowing from the innumerable discussions which concentrate on them. The heart of the matter, as I see it, is the stark fact that world poverty is primarily a problem of two million villages, and thus a problem of two thousand million villagers. The solution cannot be found in the cities of the poor countries. Unless life in the hinterland can be made tolerable, the problem of world poverty is insoluble and will inevitably get worse.

All important insights are missed if we continue to think of development mainly in quantitative terms and in those vast abstractions—like GNP, investment, savings, etc.—which have their usefulness in the study of developed countries but have virtually no relevance to development problems as such. (Nor did they play the slightest part in the actual development of the rich countries!) Aid can be considered successful only if it helps to mobilise the labour-power of the masses in the receiving country and raises productivity without "saving" labour. The common criterion of success, namely the growth of GNP, is utterly misleading and, in fact, must of necessity lead to phenomena which can only be described as neo-colonialism.

I hesitate to use this term because it has a nasty sound and appears to imply a deliberate intention on the part of the aid-givers. Is there such an intention? On the whole, I think, there is not. But this makes the problem greater instead of smaller. Unintentional neo-colonialism is far more insidious and infinitely more difficult to combat than neocolonialism intentionally pursued. It results from the mere drift of things, supported by the best intentions. Methods of production, standards of consumption, criteria of success or failure, systems of values, and behaviour patterns establish themselves in poor countries which, being (doubtfully) appropriate only to conditions of affluence already achieved, fix the poor countries ever

Our growth economy is based on greed and envy stimulated by aggressive advertising to levels beyond that provided by original sin. Our modern alchemists, the economists, promise to transmute the sinful dross of private greed into the virtuous gold of public riches by the catalyst of the market, guided by their invisible hand. But even when the invisible hand produces wealth, private greed ultimately finds a way to defeat it, by concentrating increasing riches in visible but fewer hands. To meet the still unmet needs of the poor we are urged to give still freer rein to greed by allowing the consumption of natural and social capital and falsely counting it as income. Greed thus takes from the future as well as the present.
—HERMAN DALY

more inescapably in a condition of utter dependence on the rich. The most obvious example and symptom is increasing indebtedness. This is widely recognised, and well-meaning people draw the simple conclusion that grants are better than loans, and cheap loans better than dear ones. True enough. But increasing indebtedness is not the most serious matter. After all, if a debtor cannot pay he ceases to pay—a risk the creditor must always have had in mind.

Far more serious is the dependence created when a poor country falls for the production and consumption patterns of the rich. A textile mill I recently visited in Africa provides a telling example. The manager showed me with considerable pride that his factory was at the highest technological level to be found anywhere in the world. Why was it so highly automated? "Because," he said, "African labour, unused to industrial work, would make mistakes, whereas automated machinery does not make mistakes. The quality standards demanded today," he explained, "are such that my product must be perfect to be able to find a market." He summed up his policy by saying: "Surely, my task is to eliminate the human factor." Nor is this all. Because of inappropriate quality standards, all his equipment had to be imported from the most advanced countries; the sophisticated equipment demanded that all higher management and maintenance personnel had to be imported. Even the raw materials had to be imported because the locally grown cotton was too short for top-quality yarn and the postulated standards demanded the use of a high percentage of man-made fibres. This is not an untypical case. Anyone who has taken the trouble to look systematically at actual "development" projects—instead of merely studying development plans and econometric models—knows of countless such cases: soap factories producing luxury soap by such sensitive processes that only highly refined materials can be used, which must be imported at high prices while the local raw materials are exported at low prices; food-processing plants; packing stations; motorisation, and so on—all on the rich man's pattern. In many cases, local fruit goes to waste because the consumer allegedly demands quality standards which relate solely to eye-appeal and can be met only by fruit imported from Australia or California, where the application of an immense science and a fantastic technology ensures that every apple is of the same size and without the slightest visible blemish. The examples could be multiplied without end. Poor countries slip—and are pushed—into the adoption of production methods and consumption standards which destroy the possibilities of self-reliance and self-help. The results are unintentional neocolonialism and hopelessness for the poor.

How, then, is it possible to help these two million villages? First, the quantitative aspect. If we take the total of Western aid, after eliminating certain items which have nothing to do with development, and divide it by the number of people living in the developing countries, we arrive at a per-head figure of rather less than £2 a year. Considered as an income supplement, this is, of course, negligible and derisory. Many people therefore plead that the rich countries ought to make a much bigger financial effort—and it would be perverse to refuse to support this plea. But what is it that one could reasonably expect to achieve? A per-head figure of £3 a year, or £4 a year? As a subsidy, a sort of "public assistance" payment, even £4 a year is hardly less derisory than the present figure.

To illustrate the problem further, we may consider the case of a small group of developing countries which receive supplementary income on a truly magnificent scale—the oil producing countries of the Middle East, Libya, and Venezuela. Their tax and royalty income from the oil companies in 1968 reached £2,349 million, or roughly £50 per head of their populations. Is this input of funds producing healthy and stable societies, contented populations, the progressive elimination of rural poverty, a flourishing agriculture, and widespread industrialisation? In spite of some very limited successes, the answer is certainly no. Money alone does not do the trick. The quantitative aspect is quite secondary to the qualitative aspect. If the policy is wrong, money will not make it right; and if the policy is right, money may not, in fact, present an unduly difficult problem.

Let us turn then to the qualitative aspect. If we have learnt anything from the last ten or twenty years of development effort, it is that the problem presents an enormous *intellectual* challenge. The aid-givers—rich, educated, town-based—know how to do things in

Schumacher hoped for pluralistic economic systems rather than a global monoculture, which is the hallmark of industrial society. Today wherever you go, you find the same market economy—the same kind of food, clothes, and buildings, such as Coca-Cola and McDonald's. Schumacher did not want any one economic model. He liked to see cultural and economic diversity worldwide.

—SATISH KUMAR

their own way; but do they know how to assist self-help among two million villages, among two thousand million villagers—poor, uneducated, country-based? They know how to do a few big things in big towns; but do they know how to do thousands of small things in rural areas? They know how to do things with lots of capital; but do they know how to do them with lots of labour—initially untrained labour at that?

On the whole, they do not know; but there are many experienced people who do know, each of them in their own limited field of experience. In other words, the necessary knowledge, by and large, exists; but it does not exist in an organised, readily accessible form. It is scattered, unsystematic, unorganised, and no doubt also incomplete.

The best aid to give is intellectual aid, a gift of useful knowledge. A gift of knowledge is infinitely preferable to a gift of material things. There are many reasons for this. Nothing becomes truly "one's own" except on the basis of some genuine effort or sacrifice. A gift of material goods can be appropriated by the recipient without effort or sacrifice; it therefore rarely becomes "his own" and is all too frequently and easily treated as a mere windfall. A gift of intellectual goods, a gift of knowledge, is a very different matter. Without a genuine effort of appropriation on the part of the recipient there is no gift. To appropriate the gift and to make it one's own is the same thing, and "neither moth nor rust doth corrupt." The gift of material goods makes people dependent, but the gift of knowledge makes them free—provided it is the right kind of knowledge, of course. The gift of knowledge also has far more lasting effects and is far more closely relevant to the concept of "development." Give a man a fish, as the saying goes, and you are helping him a little bit for a very short while; teach him the art of fishing, and he can help himself all his life. On a higher level: supply him with fishing tackle; this will cost you a good deal of money, and the result remains doubtful; but even if fruitful, the man's continuing livelihood will still be dependent upon you for replacements. But teach him to make his own fishing tackle and you have helped him to become not only self-supporting, but also self-reliant and independent.

This, then, should become the ever-increasing preoccupation of aid programmes—to make men self-reliant and independent by the generous supply of the appropriate intellectual gifts, gifts of relevant knowledge on the methods of self-help. This approach, incidentally, also has the advantage of being relatively cheap, that is to say, of making money go a very long way. For £100 you may be able to equip one man with certain means of production; but for the same money you may well be able to teach a hundred men to equip themselves. Perhaps a little "pump-priming" by way of material goods will in some cases be helpful to speed the process; but this would be purely incidental and secondary, and if the goods are rightly chosen, those who need them can probably pay for them.

A fundamental reorientation of aid in the direction I advocate would require only a marginal reallocation of funds. If Britain is currently giving aid to the tune of about £250 million a year, the diversion of merely one per cent of this sum to the organisation and mobilisation of "gifts of knowledge" would, I am certain, change all prospects and open a new and much more hopeful era in the history of "development." One per cent, after all, is about £2¹/₂ million—a sum of money which would go a very, very long way for this purpose if intelligently employed. And it might make the other ninety-nine per cent immensely more fruitful.

Once we see the task of aid as primarily one of supplying relevant knowledge, experience, know-how, etc.—that is to say, intellectual rather than material goods—it is clear that the present organisation of the overseas development effort is far from adequate. This is natural as long as the main task is seen as one of making *funds* available for a variety of needs and projects proposed by the recipient country, the availability of the knowledge factor being more or less taken for granted. What I am saying is simply that this availability cannot be taken for granted, that it is precisely this knowledge factor which is conspicuously lacking, that this is the gap, the "missing link," in the whole enterprise. I am not saying that no knowledge is currently being supplied: this would be ridiculous. No, there is a plentiful flow of know-how, but it is based on the implicit assumption that what is good for the rich must obviously be good for the poor. As I have argued above, this assumption is wrong, or at least, only very partially right and preponderantly wrong.

So we get back to our two million villages and have to see how we can make relevant knowledge available to *them*. To do so, we must first possess this knowledge ourselves. Before we can talk about giving aid, we must have something to give. We do not have thousands of poverty-stricken villages in our country; so what do *we* know about effective methods of self-help in such circumstances? The beginning of wisdom is the admission of one's own lack of knowledge. As long as we think we know, when in fact we do not, we shall continue to go to the poor and demonstrate to them all the marvellous things they could do if they were already rich. This has been the main failure of aid to date.

But we do know something about the organisation and systematisation of knowledge and experience; we do have facilities to do almost any job, provided only that we clearly understand what it is. If the job is, for instance, to assemble an effective guide to methods and materials for low-cost building in tropical countries, and, with the aid of such a guide, to train local builders in developing countries in the appropriate technologies and methodologies, there is no doubt we can do this, or—to say the least—that we can immediately take the steps which will enable us to do this in two or three years' time. Similarly, if we clearly understand that one of the basic needs in many developing countries is water, and that millions of villagers would benefit enormously from the availability of systematic knowledge on low-cost, self-help methods of water storage, protection, transport, and so on—if this is clearly understood and brought into focus, there is no doubt that we have the ability and resources to assemble, organise, and communicate the required information.

As I have said already, poor people have relatively simple needs, and it is primarily with regard to their basic requirements and activities that they want assistance. If they were not capable of self-help and self-reliance, they would not survive today. But their own methods are all too frequently too primitive, too inefficient, and ineffective; these methods require upgrading by the input of new knowledge, new to them, but not altogether new to everybody. It is quite wrong to assume that poor people are generally unwilling to change; but the proposed change must stand in some organic relationship to what they are doing already, and they are rightly suspicious of, and resistant to, radical changes proposed by town-based and office-bound innovators who approach them in the spirit of: "You just get out of my way and I shall show you how useless you are and how splendidly the job can be done with a lot of foreign money and outlandish equipment."

Because the needs of poor people are relatively simple, the range of studies to be undertaken is fairly limited. It is a perfectly manageable task to tackle systematically, but it requires a different organisational set-up from what we have at present (a set-up primarily geared to the disbursement of *funds*). At present, the development effort is mainly carried on by government officials, both in the donor and in the recipient country; in other words, by administrators. They are not, by training and experience, either entrepreneurs or innovators, nor do they possess specific technical knowledge of productive processes, commercial requirements, or communication problems. Assuredly, they have an essential role to play, and one could not—and would not—attempt to proceed without them. But they can do nothing by themselves alone. They must be closely associated with other social groups, with people in industry and commerce, who are trained in the "discipline of viability"—if they cannot pay their wages on Fridays, they are out!—and with professional people, academics, research workers, journalists, educators, and so on, who have time, facilities, ability, and inclination to think, write, and communicate. Development work is far too difficult to be done successfully by any one of these three groups working in isolation. Both in the donor countries and in the recipient countries it is necessary to achieve what I call the A-B-C combination, where A stands for administrators; B stands for businessmen; and C stands for communicators—that is intellectual workers, professionals of various descriptions. It is only when the A-B-C combination is effectively achieved that a real impact on the appallingly difficult problems of development can be made.

In the rich countries, there are thousands of able people in all these walks of life who would like to be involved and make a contribution to the fight against world poverty, a contribution that goes

It is a mistake for Western societies to give complicated technologies to developing countries to "ameliorate" their living conditions. If you have complicated machinery, you have to get parts, and parts cannot be made affordably in countries that cannot produce the machinery themselves. So by giving them our technology, we cripple them because they need wealth to support it.
—AVI FRIEDMAN

beyond forking out a bit of money; but there are not many outlets for them. And in the poor countries, the educated people, a highly privileged minority, all too often follow the fashions set by the rich societies—another aspect of unintentional neocolonialism—and attend to any problem except those directly concerned with the poverty of their fellow-countrymen. They need to be given strong guidance and inspiration to deal with the urgent problems of their own societies.

The mobilisation of relevant knowledge to help the poor to help themselves, through the mobilisation of the willing helpers who exist everywhere, both here and overseas, and the tying together of these helpers in "A-B-C-Groups," is a task that requires some money, but not very much. As I said, a mere one per cent of the British aid programme would be enough—more than enough—to give such an approach all the financial strength it could possibly require for quite a long time to come. There is therefore no question of turning the aid programmes upside down or inside out. It is the thinking that has to be changed and also the method of operating. It is not enough merely to have a new policy: new methods of organisation are required, because *the policy is in the implementation*.

To implement the approach here advocated, action groups need to be formed not only in the donor countries but also, and this is most important, in the developing countries themselves. These action groups, on the A-B-C pattern, should ideally be outside the government machine, in other words, they should be non-governmental voluntary agencies. They may well be set up by voluntary agencies already in development work.

There are many such agencies, both religious and secular, with large numbers of workers at the "grass roots level," and they have not been slow in recognising that "intermediate technology" is precisely what they have been trying to practise in numerous instances, but that they are lacking any organised technical backing to this end. Conferences have been held in many countries to discuss their common problems, and it has become ever more apparent that even the most self-sacrificing efforts of the voluntary workers cannot bear proper fruit unless there is a systematic organisation of knowledge and an equally systematic organisation of communication—in other words, unless there is something that might be called an "intellectual infrastructure."

Attempts are being made to create such an infrastructure, and they should receive the fullest support from governments and from the voluntary fund-raising organisations. At least four main functions have to be fulfilled:

The function of communications—to enable each field worker or group of field workers to know what other work is going on in the geographical or "functional" territory in which they are engaged, so as to facilitate the direct exchange of information.

The function of information brokerage—to assemble on a systematic basis and to disseminate relevant information on appropriate technologies for developing countries, particularly on low-cost methods relating to building, water, and power, crop storage and processing, small-scale manufacturing, health services, transportation, and so forth. Here the essence of the matter is not to hold all the information in one centre but to hold "information on information" or "know-how on know-how."

The function of "feed-back," that is to say, the transmission of technical problems from the field workers in developing countries to those places in the advanced countries where suitable facilities for their solution exist.

The function of creating and coordinating "substructures," that is to say, action groups and verification centres in the developing countries themselves.

People all over the world are taking their own progress into their own hands. In the Third World and industrial countries, citizens have moved beyond waiting for the government or the market to solve their local problems. Local exchange and trading systems, community supported agriculture, community land trusts, food co-ops, cohousing, homesteading, homeschooling, ecovillages, and other soft appropriate technologies have proliferated in the last two decades. The voice of the people, with some help from the Internet, is now being heard.
—BILL ELLIS

These are matters which can be fully clarified only by trial and error. In all this one does not have to begin from scratch—a great deal exists already, but it now wants to be pulled together and systematically developed. The future success of development aid will depend on the organisation and communication of the right kind of knowledge—a task that is manageable, definite, and wholly within the available resources.

Why is it so difficult for the rich to help the poor? The all-per-

The combination of software transitions are the roots of an emerging civil world governance. In the sphere of government, Civil Society is now recognized as the third leg of governance. And it is Civil Society that government and corporations are meant to serve.

—BILL ELLIS

vading disease of the modern world is the total imbalance between city and countryside, an imbalance in terms of wealth, power, culture, attraction, and hope. The former has become overextended and the latter has atrophied. The city has become the universal magnet, while rural life has lost its savour. Yet it remains an unalterable truth that, just as a sound mind depends on a sound body, so the health of the cities depends on the health of the rural areas. The cities, with all their wealth, are merely secondary producers, while primary production, the precondition of all economic life, takes place in the countryside. The prevailing lack of balance, based on the age-old exploitation of countryman and raw material producer, today threatens all countries throughout the world, the rich even more than the poor. To restore a proper balance between city and rural life is perhaps the greatest task in front of modern man. It is not simply a matter of raising agricultural yields so as to avoid world hunger. There is no answer to the evils of mass unemployment and mass migration into cities, unless the whole level of rural life can be raised, and this requires the development of an agro-industrial culture, so that each district, each community, can offer a colourful variety of occupations to its members.

The crucial task of this decade, therefore, is to make the development effort appropriate and thereby more effective, so that it will reach down to the heartland of world poverty, to two million villages. If the disintegration of rural life continues, there is no way out—no matter how much money is being spent. But if the rural people of the developing countries are helped to help themselves, I have no doubt that a genuine development will ensue, without vast shanty towns and misery belts around every big city and without the cruel frustrations of bloody revolution. The task is formidable indeed, but the resources that are waiting to be mobilised are also formidable.

Economic development is something much wider and deeper than economics, let alone econometrics. Its roots lie outside the economic sphere, in education, organisation, discipline and, beyond that, in political independence and a national consciousness of self-reliance. It cannot be "produced" by skillful grafting operations carried out by foreign technicians or an indigenous élite that has lost contact with the ordinary people. It can succeed only if it is carried forward as a broad, popular "movement of reconstruction" with primary emphasis on the full utilisation of the drive, enthusiasm, intelligence, and labour power of everyone. Success cannot be obtained by some form of magic produced by scientists, technicians, or economic planners. It can come only through a process of growth involving the education, organisation, and discipline of the whole population. Anything less than this must end in failure.

CHAPTER 14

THE PROBLEM OF UNEMPLOYMENT IN INDIA

A Talk to the India Development Group in London

WHEN SPEAKING of unemployment I mean the non-utilisation or gross under-utilisation of available labour. We may think of a productivity scale that extends from zero, i.e. the productivity of a totally unemployed person, to 100 per cent, i.e. the productivity of a fully and most effectively occupied person. The crucial question for any poor society is how to move up on this scale. When considering productivity in any society it is not sufficient to take account only of those who are employed or self-employed and to leave out of the reckoning all those who are unemployed and whose productivity therefore is zero.

Economic development is primarily a question of getting more work done. For this, there are four essential conditions. First, there must be motivation; second, there must be some know-how; third, there must be some capital; and fourth, there must be an outlet: additional output requires additional markets.

As far as the motivation is concerned, there is little to be said *from the outside*. If people do not want to better themselves, they are best left alone—this should be the first principle of aid. Insiders may take a different view, and they also carry different responsibilities. For the aid-giver, there are always enough people who *do* wish to better themselves, but they do not know how to do it. So we come to the question of know-how. If there are millions of people who want to better themselves but do not know how to do it, who is going to show them? Consider the size of the problem in India. We are not talking about a few thousands or a few millions, but rather about a few hundred millions of people. The size of the problem puts it beyond any kind of little amelioration, any little reform, improvement, or inducement, and makes it a matter of basic political philosophy. The whole matter can be summed in the question: what is education for? I think it was the Chinese, before World War II, who calculated that it took the work of thirty peasants to keep one man or woman at a university. If that person at the university took a five-year course, by the time he had finished he would have consumed 150 peasant-work-years. How can this be justified? Who has the right to appropriate 150 years of peasant work to keep one person at university for five years, and what do the peasants get back for it? These questions lead us to the parting of the ways: is education to be a "passport to privilege" or is it something which people take upon themselves almost like a monastic vow, a sacred obligation to serve the people? The first road takes the educated young person into a fashionable district of Bombay, where a lot of other highly educated people have already gone and where he can join a mutual admiration society, a "trade union of the privileged," to see to it that his privileges are not eroded by the great masses of his contemporaries who have not been educated. This is one way. The other way would be embarked upon in a different spirit and would lead to a different destination. It would take him back to the people who, after all, directly or indirectly, had paid for his education by 150 peasant-work-years; having consumed the fruits of their work, he would feel in honour bound to return something to them.

The problem is not new. Leo Tolstoy referred to it when he wrote: "I sit on a man's back, choking him, and making him carry me, and yet assure myself and others that I am very sorry for him and wish to ease his lot by any means possible, except getting off his back." So this is the first question I suggest we have to face. Can we establish an ideology, or whatever you like to call it, which insists that the educated have taken upon themselves an obligation and have not simply acquired a "passport to privilege"? This ideology is of course well supported by all the higher teachings of mankind. As a Christian, I may be permitted to quote from St. Luke: "Much will be expected of the man to whom much has been given. More will be asked of him because he was entrusted with more." It is, you might well say, an elementary matter of justice.

Schumacher's opportunity to address this task came in 1962 when India's then prime minister Nehru, having read "Buddhist Economics," asked him to advise on rural development in his country. It was then that Fritz came up with his concept of an intermediate technology. Conventional Western technology, he argued, was very large-scale and expensive, capital- and energy-intensive, and environmentally damaging. There was no way it could provide the millions of new workplaces desperately needed in India and other developing countries. That need could be met only by technologies specially designed to fit small rural economies. The technologies would be relatively small, simple, and capital-saving instead of labor-saving, and environmentally benign—tools and equipment that could be owned and operated by poor people. The technologies would be "intermediate" between, say, the sickle ➡

If this ideology does not prevail, if it is taken for granted that education is a passport to privilege, then the content of education will not primarily be something to serve the people, but something to serve ourselves, the educated. The privileged minority will wish to be educated in a manner that sets them apart and will inevitably learn and teach the wrong things, that is to say, things that do set them apart, with a contempt for manual labour, a contempt for primary production, a contempt for rural life, etc., etc. Unless virtually all educated people see themselves as servants of their country—and that means after all as servants of the common people—there cannot possibly be enough leadership and enough communication of know-how to solve this problem of unemployment or unproductive employment in the half million villages of India. It is a matter of 500 million people. For helping people to help themselves you need at least two persons to look after 100 and that means an obligation to raise ten million helpers, that is, the whole educated population of India. Now you may say this is impossible, but if it is, it is not so because of any laws of the universe, but because of a certain inbred, ingrained selfishness on the part of the people who are quite prepared to receive and not prepared to give. As a matter of fact, there is evidence that the problem is not insoluble; but it can be solved only at the political level.

Now let me turn to the third factor, after motivation and after know-how, the factor I have called capital, which is of course closely related to the matter of know-how. According to my estimates there is in India an immediate need for something like fifty million new jobs. If we agree that people cannot do productive work unless they have some capital—in the form of equipment and also of working capital—the question arises: How much capital can you afford to establish one new job? If it costs £10 to establish a job you need £500 million for fifty million jobs. If it costs £100 to establish a job you need £5,000 million, and if it cost £5,000 per job, which is what it might cost in Britain and the U.S.A., to set up fifty million jobs you require £250,000 million.

The national income of the country we are talking about, of India, is about £15,000 million a year. So the first question is how much can we offer for each job, and the second question, how much time have we to do it in? Let us say we want fifty million jobs in ten years. What proportion of national income (which I identify as about £15,000 million) can one reasonably expect to be available for the establishment of this capital fund for job creation? I would say, without going into any details, you are lucky if you can make it five per cent. Therefore, if you have five per cent of £15,000 million for ten years you have a total of £7,500 million for the establishment of jobs. If you want fifty million jobs in those ten years, you can afford to spend an average of £150 per workplace. At that level of capital investment per workplace, in other words, you could afford to set up five million workplaces a year. Let us assume, however, that you say: "No, £150 is too mean; it will not buy more than a set of tools; we want £1,500 per workplace," then you cannot have five million new jobs a year but only half a million. And if you say: "Only the best is good enough; we want all to be little Americans right away, and that means £5,000 per workplace," then you cannot have half a million new jobs a year, let alone five million, but only about 170,000. Now, you have no doubt noticed already that I have simplified this matter very much because, in the ten years with investment in jobs, you would have an increase in the national income; but I have also left out the increase in the population, and I would suggest that these two factors cancel one another in their effect on my calculation.

It follows, I suggest, that the biggest single collective decision that any country in the position of India has to take is the choice of technology. I am not laying down the law of what ought to be. I am simply saying that these are the hard facts of life. A lot of things you can argue against, but you cannot argue against arithmetic. So you can have a few jobs at a high level of capitalisation or you can have many jobs at a relatively low level of capitalisation.

Now, all this of course links up with the other factors I have mentioned, with education, motivation, and know-how. In India there are about fifty million pupils in primary schools; almost fifteen million in secondary schools; and roughly one and a half million in institutions of higher learning. To maintain an educational machine on this kind of scale would of course be pointless unless at the end of the pipeline there was something for them to do, with a

➥ *and the combine harvester, or the hoe and the tractor. They would be appropriate to the needs and resources of the poor.*
—GEORGE McROBIE

chance to apply their knowledge. If there is not, the whole thing is nothing but a ghastly burden. This rough picture of the educational effort suffices to show that one really does have to think in terms of five million new jobs a year and not in terms of a few hundred thousand jobs.

Now, until quite recently, that is to say, some fifty to seventy years ago, the way we did things was, by present standards, quite primitive. In this connection, I should like to refer to chapter II of John Kenneth Galbraith's *The New Industrial Estate.*[1] It contains a fascinating report on the Ford Motor Company. The Ford Motor Company was set up on 16 June 1903, with an authorised capital of $150,000, of which $100,000 was issued but only $28,500 was paid for in cash. So the total cash which went into this enterprise was of the order of $30,000. They set up in June 1903 and the first car to reach the market appeared in October 1903, that is to say, after four months. The employment in 1903, of course, was small— 125 people, and the capital investment per workplace was somewhat below £100. That was in 1903. If we now move sixty years forward, to 1963, we find that the Ford Motor Company decided to produce a new model, the Mustang. The preparation required three and a half years. Engineering and styling costs were $9 million; the costs of tooling up for this new model were $50 million. Meanwhile the assets employed by the company were $6,000 million, which works out at almost £10,000 per person employed, about a hundred times as much as sixty years earlier.

Galbraith draws certain conclusions from all this which are worth studying. They describe what happened over these sixty years. The first is that a vast increased span of time now separates the beginning of an enterprise from the completion of the job. The first Ford car, from the beginning of the work to its appearance on the market, took four months, while a mere change of model now takes four years. Second, a vast increase in capital committed to production. Investment per unit of output in the original Ford factory was infinitesimal; material and parts were there only briefly; no expensive specialists gave them attention; only elementary machines were used to assemble them into a car; it helped that the frame of the car could be lifted by only two men. Third, in those sixty years, a vast increase of inflexibility. Galbraith comments: "Had Ford and his associates [in 1903] decided at any point to shift from gasoline to steam power, the machine shop could have accommodated itself to the change in a few hours." If they now try to change even one screw, it takes that many months. Fourth, increasingly specialised manpower, not only on the machinery, but also on the planning, the foreseeing of the future in the uttermost detail. Fifth, a vastly different type of organisation to integrate all these numerous specialists, none of whom can do anything more than just one small task inside the complicated whole. "So complex, indeed, will be the job for organising specialists that there will be specialists of organisation. More even than machinery, massive and complex business organisations are being tangible manifestations of advanced technology." Finally, the necessity for long-range planning, which, I can assure you, is a highly sophisticated job, and also highly frustrating. Galbraith comments: "In the early days of Ford, the future was very near at hand. Only days elapsed between the commitment of machinery and materials to production and their appearance as a car. If the future is near at hand, it can be assumed to be very much like the present," and the planning and forecasting is not very difficult.

Now what is the upshot of all this? The upshot is that the more sophisticated the technology, the greater in general will be the foregoing requirements. When the simple things of life, which is all I am concerned with, are produced by ever more sophisticated processes, then the need to meet these six requirements moves ever more beyond the capacity of any poor society. As far as simple products are concerned—food, clothing, shelter, and culture—the greatest danger is that people should automatically assume that only the 1963 model is relevant and not the 1903 model; because the 1963 way of doing things is inaccessible to the poor, as it presupposes great wealth. Now, without wishing to be rude to my academic friends, I should say that this point is almost universally overlooked by them. The question of how much you can afford for each workplace when you need millions of them is hardly ever raised. To fulfill the requirements that have arisen over the last fifty or sixty years in fact involves a quantum jump. Everything was

In designing sustainable communities, we made a community effort to think small. We found that to use land efficiently to build small homes, we didn't have to consume great tracts of land. We didn't have to build complicated infrastructures that consume a lot of energy, require many roads, and need many trees. And yet in most of our developments, there was enough space available for people to grow their own food.
—AVI FRIEDMAN

quite continuous in human history till about the beginning of this century; but in the last half-century there has been a quantum jump, the sort of jump as with the capitalisation of Ford, from $30,000 to $6,000 million.

In a developing country it is difficult enough to get Henry Fords, at the 1903 level. To get Henry super-Fords, to move from practically nowhere on to the 1963 level, is virtually impossible. No one can start at this level. This means that no one can do anything at this level unless he is already established, is already operating at that level. This is absolutely crucial for our understanding of the modern world. At this level no *creations* are possible, only extensions, and this means that the poor are more dependent on the rich than ever before in human history, *if* they are wedded to that level. They can only be gap-fillers for the rich, for instance, where low wages enable them to produce cheaply this and that trifle. People ferret around and say: "Here, in this or that poor country, wages are so low that we can get some part of a watch, or of a carburettor, produced more cheaply than in Britain. So let it be produced in Hong Kong or in Taiwan or wherever it might be." The role of the poor is to be gap-fillers in the requirements of the rich. It follows that at this level of technology it is impossible to attain either full employment or independence. The choice of technology is the most important of all choices.

It is a strange fact that some people say that there are no technological choices. I read an article by a well-known economist from the U.S.A. who asserts that there is only one way of producing any particular commodity: the way of 1971. Had these commodities never been produced before? The basic things of life have been needed and produced since Adam left Paradise. He says that the only machinery that can be procured is the very latest. Now that is a different point and it may well be that the only machinery that can be procured *easily* is the latest. It is true that at any one time there is only one kind of machinery that tends to dominate the market and this creates the impression as if we had no choice and as if the amount of capital in a society determined the amount of employment it could have. Of course this is absurd. The author whom I am quoting also knows that it is absurd, and he then corrects himself and points to examples of Japan, Korea, Taiwan, etc., where people achieve a high level of employment and production with very modest capital equipment.

The importance of technological choice is gradually entering the consciousness of economists and development planners. There are four stages. The first stage has been laughter and scornful rejection of anyone who talked about this. The second stage has now been reached and people give lip service to it, but no action follows and the drift continues. The third stage would be active work in the mobilisation of the knowledge of this technological choice; and the fourth stage will then be the practical application. It is a long road, but I do not wish to hide the fact that there are political possibilities of going straight to the fourth stage. If there is a political ideology that sees development as being about people, then one can immediately employ the ingenuity of hundreds of millions of people and go straight to the fourth stage. There are indeed some countries which are going straight to the fourth stage.

However, it is not for me to talk politics. If it is now being increasingly understood that this technological choice is of absolutely pivotal importance, how can we get from stage two to stage three, namely from just giving lip service to actually doing work? To my knowledge this work is being done systematically only by one organisation, the Intermediate Technology Development Group (ITDG). I do not deny that some work is also being done on a commercial basis, but not systematically. ITDG set itself the task to find out what are the technological choices. I will only give one example out of the many activities of this purely private group. Take foundry work and woodworking, metal and wood being the two basic raw materials of industry. Now, what are the alternative technologies that can be employed, arranged in the order of capital intensity from the most primitive, when people work with the simplest tools, to the most complicated? This is shown in what we call an industrial profile, and these industrial profiles are supported by instruction manuals at each level of technology and by a directory of equipment with addresses where it can be obtained.

The only criticism that can be levelled against this activity is that it is too little and too late. It is not good enough that in this crucial matter one should be satisfied with one little group of private enthusiasts doing this work. There ought to be dozens of solid, well-endowed organisations in the world doing it. The task is so great that even some overlapping would not matter. In any case, I should hope that this work will be taken up on a really substantial scale in India, and I am delighted to see that already some beginnings have been made.

I shall now turn to the fourth factor, namely markets. There is, of course, a very real problem here, because poverty means that markets are small and there is very little free purchasing power. All the purchasing power that exists already, is, as it were, bespoken, and if I start a new production of, say, sandals or shoes in a poor area, my fellow-sufferers in the area will not have any money to buy the shoes when I have made them. Production is sometimes easier to start than it is to find markets, and then, of course, we get very quickly the advice to produce for export, because exports are mainly for the rich countries and their purchasing power is plentiful. But if I start from nothing in a rural area, how could I hope to be competitive in the world market?

There are two reasons for this extraordinary preoccupation with exports, as far as I can see. One is real; the other not so good. I shall first talk about the second one. It is really a hangover of the economic thinking of the days of colonialism. Of course, the metropolitan power moved into a territory not because it was particularly interested in the local population, but in order to open up resources needed for its own industry. One moved into Tanzania for sisal, into Zambia for copper, etc., and into some other place for trade. The whole thinking was shaped by these interests.

"Development" meant the development of raw material or food supplies or of trading profits. The colonial power was primarily interested in supplies and profits, not in the development of the natives, and this meant it was primarily interested in the colony's exports and not in its internal market. This outlook has stuck to such an extent that even the Pearson Report considers the expansion of exports the main criterion of success for developing countries. But, of course, people do not live by exporting, and what they produce for themselves and for each other is of infinitely greater importance to them than what they produce for foreigners.

The other point, however, is a more real one. If I produce for export into a rich country, I can take the availability of purchasing power for granted, because my own little production is as nothing compared with what exists already. But if I start new production in a poor country there can be no local market for my products unless I divert the flow of purchasing power from some other product to mine. A dozen different productions should all be started together: then for every one of the twelve producers the other eleven would be his market. There would be additional purchasing power to absorb the additional output. But it is extremely difficult to start many different activities at once. So the conventional advice is: "Only production for export is proper development." Such production is not only highly limited in scope, its employment effect is also extremely limited. To compete in world markets, it is normally necessary to employ the highly capital-intensive and labour-saving technology of the rich countries. In any case, there is no multiplier effect: my goods are sold for foreign exchange, and the foreign exchange is spent on imports (or the repayment of debt), and that is the end of it.

The need to start many complementary productive activities simultaneously presents a very severe difficulty for development, but the difficulty can be mitigated by "pump-priming" through public works. The virtues of a massive public works programme for job creation have often been extolled. The only point I should like to make in this context is the following: if you can get new purchasing power into a rural community by way of a public works programme financed from outside, see to it that the fullest possible use is made of the "multiplier effect." The people employed on the public works want to spend their wages on "wages goods," that is to say, consumers' goods of all kinds. If these wages goods can be locally produced, the new purchasing power made available through the public works programme does not seep away but goes on circulating in the local market, and the total employment effect could be prodigious. Public works are very desirable and can do a great deal of good; but if they are not backed up by the indigenous production of additional wages goods, the additional purchasing power will flow into imports and the country may experience serious foreign exchange difficulties. Even so, it is misleading to deduce from this truism that exports are specially important for development. After

Colonialism, development, and now "free trade" and globalization have meant that the best land in the South is used to grow crops for northern markets. Shifting the emphasis to diversified production for local consumption would not only improve the economies of rural communities, but also lessen the gap between rich and poor while eliminating much of the hunger that is now so endemic in the so-called "developing" parts of the world.
—HELENA
NORBERG-HODGE

all, for mankind as a whole there are no exports. We did not start development by obtaining foreign exchange from Mars or from the moon. Mankind is a closed society. India is quite big enough to be a relatively closed society in that sense—a society in which the able-bodied people work and produce what they need.

Everything sounds very difficult and in a sense it is very difficult if it is done *for* the people, instead of *by* the people. But let us not think that development or employment is anything but the most natural thing in the world. It occurs in every healthy person's life. There comes a point when he simply sets to work. In a sense this is much easier to do now than it has ever been in human history. Why? Because there is so much more knowledge. There are so much better communications. You can tap all this knowledge (this is what the Indian Development Group is there for). So let's not mesmerise ourselves by the difficulties, but recover the common-sense view that to work is the most natural thing in the world. Only one must not be blocked by being too damn clever about it. We are always having all sorts of clever ideas about optimising something before it even exists. I think the stupid man who says "something is better than nothing" is much more intelligent than the clever chap who will not touch anything unless it is optimal. What is stopping us? Theories, planning. I have come across planners at the Planning Commission who have convinced themselves that even within fifteen years it is not possible to put the willing labour power of India to work. If they say it is not possible in fifteen months, I accept that, because it takes time to get around. But to throw up the sponge and say it is not possible to do the most elementary thing within fifteen years, this is just a sort of degeneracy of the intellect. What is the argument behind it? Oh! The argument is very clever, a splendid piece of model building. They have ascertained that in order to put a man to work you need on average so much electricity, so much cement, and so much steel. This is absurd. I should like to remind you that a hundred years ago electricity, cement, and steel did not even exist in any significant quantity at all. (I should like to remind you that the Taj Mahal was built without electricity, cement, and steel and that all the cathedrals of Europe were built without them. It is a fixation in the mind, that unless you can have the latest you can't do anything at all, and this is the thing that has to be over-come.) You may say, again, this is not an economic problem, but basically a political problem. It is basically a problem of compassion with the ordinary people of the world. It is basically a problem, not of conscripting the ordinary people, but of getting a kind of voluntary conscription of the educated.

Another example: we are told by theorists and planners that the number of people you can put to work depends upon the amount of capital you have, as if you could not put people to work to produce capital goods. We are told there is no choice of technology, as if production had started in the year 1971. We are told that it cannot be economic to use anything but the latest methods, as if anything could be more uneconomic than having people doing absolutely nothing. We are told that it is necessary to "eliminate the human factor."

The greatest deprivation anyone can suffer is to have no chance of looking after himself and making a livelihood. There is no conflict between growth and employment. Not even a conflict as between the present and the future. You will have to construct a very absurd example to demonstrate that by letting people work you create a conflict between the present and the future. No country that has developed has been able to develop without letting the people work. On the one hand, it is quite true to say that these things are difficult; on the other hand, let us never lose sight of the fact that we are talking about man's most elementary needs and that we must not be prevented by all these high-faluting and very difficult considerations from doing the most elementary and direct things.

Now, at the risk of being misunderstood, I will give you the simplest of all possible examples of self-help. The Good Lord has not disinherited any of his children and as far as India is concerned he has given her a variety of trees unsurpassed anywhere in the world. There are trees for almost all human needs. One of the greatest teachers of India was the Buddha, who included in his teaching the obligation of every good Buddhist that he should plant and see to the establishment of one tree at least every five years. As long as this was observed, the whole large area of India was covered with trees, free of dust, with plenty of water, plenty of shade, plenty of food and

When we look at a tree, we can see two aspects. One is utilitarian—that the tree will make firewood, furniture, and houses. We need the wood for human benefit, therefore we must plant the trees. This is an anthropocentric view. The Schumacherian reverential ecology view is that the tree has intrinsic value—it is beautiful and good in itself as it is. It is good not because it is beneficial to humans, but because it is a living tree, a tree of life.

—SATISH KUMAR

materials. Just imagine you could establish an ideology which would make it obligatory for every able-bodied person in India, man, woman, and child, to do that little thing—to plant and see to the establishment of one tree a year, five years running. This, in a five-year period, would give you 2,000 million established trees. Anyone can work it out on the back of an envelope that the economic value of such an enterprise, intelligently conducted, would be greater than anything that has ever been promised by any of India's five-year plans. It could be done without a penny of foreign aid; there is no problem of savings and investment. It would produce foodstuffs, fibres, building material, shade, water, almost anything that man really needs.

I just leave this as a thought, not as the final answer to India's enormous problems. But I ask: What sort of an education is this if it prevents us from thinking of things ready to be done immediately? What makes us think we need electricity, cement, and steel before we can do anything at all? The really helpful things will not be done from the centre; they cannot be done by big organisations; but they can be done by the people themselves. If we can recover the sense that it is the most natural thing for every person born into this world to use his hands in a productive way and that it is not beyond the wit of man to make this possible, then I think the problem of unemployment will disappear and we shall soon be asking ourselves how we can get all the work done that needs to be done.

PART IV

ORGANISATION AND OWNERSHIP

CHAPTER 15

A MACHINE TO FORETELL THE FUTURE?

T HE REASON FOR INCLUDING a discussion on predictability in this volume is that it represents one of the most important metaphysical—and therefore practical—problems with which we are faced. There have never been so many futurologists, planners, forecasters, and model-builders as there are today, and the most intriguing product of technological progress, the computer, seems to offer untold new possibilities. People talk freely about "machines to foretell the future." Are not such machines just what we have been waiting for? All men at all times have been wanting to know the future.

The ancient Chinese used to consult the *I Ching,* also called *The Book of Changes* and reputed to be the oldest book of mankind. Some of our contemporaries do so even today. The *I Ching* is based on the conviction that, while everything changes all the time, change itself is unchanging and conforms to certain ascertainable metaphysical laws. "To everything there is a season," said Ecclesiastes, "and a time to every purpose under heaven...a time to break down and a time to build up...a time to cast away stones and a time to gather stones together," or, as we might say, a time for expansion and a time for consolidation. And the task of the wise man is to understand the great rhythms of the Universe and to gear in with them. While the Greeks—and I suppose most other nations—went to living oracles, to their Pythias, Cassandras, prophets, and seers, the Chinese, remarkably, went to a book setting out the universal and necessary pattern of changes, the very Laws of Heaven to which all nature conforms inevitably and to which man will conform

Our mainstream culture encourages a linear view of progress, one in which the goal is to free ourselves from our past and from the laws of nature. The modern-day mantra, "we cannot go back, we cannot go back," is deeply ingrained in our thinking. Of course we could not go back, even if we wanted to, but our search for a future that works is inevitably bringing us back to certain fundamental patterns that are in greater harmony with nature—including human nature.
—HELENA
NORBERG-HODGE

freely as a result of insight gained either from wisdom or from suffering. Modern man goes to the computer.

Tempting as it may be to compare the ancient oracles and the modern computer, only a comparison by contrast is possible. The former deal exclusively with qualities; the latter, with quantities. The inscription over the Delphic temple was "Know Thyself," while the inscription on an electronic computer is more likely to be: "Know Me," that is, "Study the Operating Instructions before Plugging In." It might be thought that the *I Ching* and the oracles are metaphysical while the computer model is "real"; but the fact remains that a machine to foretell the future is based on metaphysical assumptions of a very definite kind. It is based on the implicit assumption that "the future is already here," that it exists already in a determinate form, so that it requires merely good instruments and good techniques to get it into focus and make it visible. The reader will agree that this is a very far-reaching metaphysical assumption, in fact, a most extraordinary assumption which seems to go against all direct personal experience. It implies that human freedom does not exist or, in any case, that it cannot alter the predetermined course of events. We cannot shut our eyes to the fact, on which I have been insisting throughout this book, that such an assumption, like all metaphysical theses, whether explicit or implicit, has decisive practical consequences. The question is simply: Is it true or is it untrue?

When the Lord created the world and people to live in it—an enterprise which, according to modern science, took a very long time—I could well imagine that he reasoned with himself as follows: "If I make everything predictable, these human beings, whom I have endowed with pretty good brains, will undoubtedly learn to predict everything, and they will thereupon have no motive do anything at all, because they will recognise that the future is totally determined and cannot be influenced by any human action. On the other hand, if I make everything unpredictable, they will gradually discover that there is no rational basis for any decision whatsoever and, as in the first case, they will thereupon have no motive to do anything at all. Neither scheme would make sense. I must therefore create a mixture of the two. Let some things be predictable and let others be unpredictable. They will then, amongst many other things, have the very important task of finding out which is which."

And this, indeed, is a very important task, particularly today, when people try to devise machines to foretell the future. Before anyone makes a prediction, he should be able to give a convincing reason why the factor to which his prediction refers is inherently predictable.

Planners, of course, proceed on the assumption that the future is not "already here," that they are not dealing with a predetermined—and therefore predictable—system, that they can determine things by their own free will, and that their plans will make the future different from what it would have been had there been no plan. And yet it is the planners, more than perhaps anyone else, who would like nothing better than to have a machine to foretell the future. Do they ever wonder whether the machine might incidentally also foretell their own plans before they have been conceived?

NEED FOR SEMANTICS

However this may be, it is clear that the question of predictability is not only important but also somewhat involved. We talk happily about estimating, planning, forecasting, budgeting, about surveys, programmes, targets, and so forth, and we tend to use these terms as if they were freely interchangeable and as if everybody would automatically know what was meant. The result is a great deal of confusion, because it is in fact necessary to make a number of fundamental distinctions. The terms we use may refer to the past or to the future; they may refer to acts or to events; and they may signify certainty or uncertainty. The number of combinations possible where there are three pairs of this kind is 2^3, or 8, and we really ought to have eight different terms to be quite certain of what we are talking about. Our language, however, is not as perfect as that. The most important distinction is generally that between acts and events. The eight possible cases may therefore be ordered as follows:

As this century draws to a close, we are living in a time when technology dominates our relationship with the domestic environment, work environment, and even nature. It has a powerful influence in most of our decision-making. So we need to question whether we are using technology just for the sake of using it.
—AVI FRIEDMAN

1. Act
   Past
   Certain

2. Act
   Future
   Certain

3. Act
   Past
   Uncertain

4. Act
   Future
   Uncertain

5. Event
   Past
   Certain

6. Event
   Future
   Certain

7. Event
   Past
   Uncertain

8. Event
   Future
   Uncertain

The distinction between acts and events is as basic as that between active and passive or between "within my control" or "outside my control." To apply the word "planning" to matters outside the planner's control is absurd. Events, as far as the planner is concerned, simply happen. He may be able to forecast them and this may well influence his plan; but they cannot possibly be part of the plan.

The distinction between the past and the future proved to be necessary for our purpose, because, in fact, words like "plan" or "estimate" are being used to refer to either. If I say: "I shall not visit Paris without a plan," this can mean: "I shall arm myself with a street plan for orientation" and would therefore refer to case 5. Or it can mean: "I shall arm myself with a plan which outlines in advance where I am going to go and how I am going to spend my time and money"—case 2 or 4. If someone claims that "to have a plan is indispensable," it is not without interest to find out whether he means the former or the latter. The two are *essentially* different.

Similarly, the word "estimate," which denotes uncertainty, may apply to the past or to the future. In an ideal world, it would not be necessary to make estimates about things that had already happened. But in the actual world, there is much uncertainty even about matters which, in principle, could be fully ascertained. Cases 3, 4, 7, and 8 represent four different types of estimates. Case 3 relates to something I have done in the past; case 7, to something that has happened in the past. Case 4 relates to something I plan to do in the future, while case 8 relates to something I expect to happen in the future. Case 8, in fact, is a forecast in the proper sense of the term and has nothing whatever to do with "planning." How often, however, are forecasts presented as if they were plans—and vice versa! The British "National Plan" of 1965 provides an outstanding example and, not surprisingly, came to nothing.

Can we ever speak of future acts or events as certain (cases 2 and 6)? If I have made a plan with full knowledge of all the relevant facts, being inflexibly resolved to carry it through—case 2—I may, in this respect, consider my future actions as certain. Similarly, in laboratory science, dealing with carefully isolated deterministic systems, future events may be described as certain. The real world, however, is not a deterministic system; we may be able to talk with certainty about acts or events of the past—cases 1 or 5—but we can do so *about future events only on the basis of assumptions.* In other words, we can formulate conditional statements about the future, such as: "*If* such and such a trend of events continued for another x years, this is where it would take us." This is not a forecast or prediction, which must always be uncertain in the real world, but an exploratory calculation, which, being conditional, has the virtue of mathematical certainty.

Endless confusion results from the semantic muddle in which we find ourselves today. As mentioned before, "plans" are put forward which upon inspection turn out to relate to events totally outside the control of the planner. "Forecasts" are offered which upon inspection turn out to be conditional sentences, in other words, exploratory calculations. The latter are misinterpreted as if they were forecasts or predictions. "Estimates" are put forward which upon inspection turn out to be plans. And so on and so forth. Our academic teachers would perform a most necessary and really helpful task if they taught their students to make the distinctions discussed above and developed a terminology which fixed them in words.

PREDICTABILITY

Let us now return to our main subject—predictability. Is prediction or forecasting—the two terms would seem to be interchangeable—

The 1980s saw the culmination of the bigger-is-better, growth- and greed-philosophy. Based on the assumption that accelerating growth is desirable or even possible, large-scale borrowing became the watchword. Happy bankers with their eyes closed to reality doled out billions in loans, which now are impossible to repay and will remain as debts into future generations. It was really fun to borrow from our grandchildren during the 1980s.

—ROBERT BATEMAN

possible at all? The future does not exist; how could there be knowledge about something non-existent? This question is only too well justified. In the strict sense of the word, knowledge can only be about the past. The future is always in the making, but it is being made *largely* out of existing material, about which a great deal can be known. The future, there, is *largely* predictable, if we have solid and extensive knowledge of the past. *Largely,* but by no means wholly; for into the making of the future there enters that mysterious and irrepressible factor called human freedom. It is the freedom of a being of which it has been said that it was made in the image of God the Creator: the freedom of creativity.

Strange to say, under the influence of laboratory science many people today seem to use their freedom only for the purpose of denying its existence. Men and women of great gifts find their purest delight in magnifying every "mechanism," every "inevitability," everything where human freedom does not enter or does not appear to enter. A great shout of triumph goes up whenever anybody has found some further evidence—in physiology or psychology or sociology or economics or politics—of unfreedom, some further indication that people cannot help being what they are and doing what they are doing, no matter how inhuman their actions might be. The denial of freedom, of course, is a denial of responsibility: there are no acts, but only events; everything simply happens; no one is responsible. And this is no doubt the main cause of the semantic confusion to which I have referred above. It is also the cause for the belief that we shall soon have a machine to foretell the future.

To be sure, if everything simply happened, if there were no element of freedom, choice, human creativity, and responsibility, everything would be perfectly predictable, subject only to accidental and temporary limitations of knowledge. The absence of freedom would make human affairs suitable for study by the natural sciences or at least by their methods, and reliable results would no doubt quickly follow the systematic observation of facts. Professor Phelps Brown, in his presidential address to the Royal Economic Society, appears to adopt precisely this point of view when talking about "The Underdevelopment of Economics." "Our own science," he says, "has hardly yet reached its seventeenth century." Believing

that economics is *metaphysically* the same as physics, he quotes another economist, Professor Morgenstern, approvingly, as follows:

> The decisive break which came in physics in the seventeenth
> century, specifically in the field of mechanics, was possible
> only because of previous developments in astronomy. It was
> backed by several millennia of systematic, scientific, astro-
> nomical observation.... Nothing of this sort has occurred in
> economic science. It would have been absurd in physics to
> have expected Kepler and Newton without Tycho—and
> there is no reason to hope for an easier development in eco-
> nomics.

Professor Phelps Brown concludes therefore that we need many,
many more years of observations of behaviour. *"Until then, our
mathematisation is premature."*

It is the intrusion of human freedom and responsibility that
makes economics metaphysically different from physics and
makes human affairs largely unpredictable. We obtain predictability, of course, when we or others are acting according to a plan. But
this is so precisely because a plan is the result of an exercise in the
freedom of choice: the choice has been made; all alternatives have
been eliminated. If people stick to their plan, their behaviour is predictable simply because they have chosen to surrender their freedom to act otherwise than prescribed in the plan.

In principle, everything which is immune to the intrusion of
human freedom, like the movements of the stars, is predictable,
and everything subject to this intrusion is unpredictable. Does that
mean that all human actions are unpredictable? No, because most
people, most of the time, make no use of their freedom and act
purely mechanically. Experience shows that when we are dealing
with large numbers of people many aspects of their behaviour are
indeed predictable; for out of a large number, at any one time, only
a tiny minority are using their power of freedom, and they often do
not significantly affect the total outcome. Yet all really important in-
novations and changes normally start from tiny minorities of people who *do* use their creative freedom.

It is true that social phenomena acquire a certain steadiness and predictability from the non-use of freedom, which means that the great majority of people respond to a given situation in a way that does not alter greatly in time, unless there are really overpowering new causes.

We can therefore distinguish as follows:

1. Full predictability (in principle) exists only in the absence of human freedom, i.e. in "sub-human" nature. The limitations of predictability are purely limitations of knowledge and technique.
2. Relative predictability exists with regard to the behaviour pattern of very large numbers of people doing "normal" things (routine).
3. Relatively full predictability exists with regard to human actions controlled by a plan which eliminates freedom, e.g. railway timetable.
4. Individual decisions by individuals are in principle unpredictable.

SHORT-TERM FORECASTS

In practice all prediction is simply extrapolation, modified by known "plans." But how do you extrapolate? How many years do you go back? Assuming there is a record of growth, what precisely do you extrapolate—the average rate of growth, or the increase in the rate of growth, or the annual increment in absolute terms? As a matter of fact, there are no rules:* it is just a matter of "feel" or judgement.

It is good to know of all the different possibilities of using the same time series for extrapolations with very different results. Such knowledge will prevent us from putting undue faith in any extrapolation. At the same time, and by the same token, the development of (what purport to be) better forecasting techniques can become a vice. In short-term forecasting, say, for next year, a refined technique rarely produces significantly different results from those of a crude technique. After a year of growth—what can you predict?

---

*When there are seasonal or cyclical patterns, it is, of course, necessary to go back by at least a year or a cycle; but it is a matter of judgement to decide how many years or cycles.

1. that we have reached a (temporary) ceiling;
2. that growth will continue at the same, or a slower, or a faster rate;
3. that there will be a decline.

Now, it seems clear that the choice between these three basic alternative predictions cannot be made by "forecasting technique" but only by informed judgement. It depends, of course, on what you are dealing with. When you have something that is normally growing very fast, like the consumption of electricity, your threefold choice is between the same rate of growth, a faster rate, or a slower rate.

It is not so much forecasting technique, as a full understanding of the current situation that can help in the formation of a sound judgement for the future. If the present level of performance (or rate of growth) is known to be influenced by quite abnormal factors which are unlikely to apply in the coming year, it is, of course, necessary to take these into account. The forecast, "same as last year," may imply a "real" growth or a "real" decline on account of exceptional factors being present this year, and this, of course, must be made explicit by the forecaster.

I believe, therefore, that all effort needs to be put into understanding the current situation, to identify and, if need be, eliminate "abnormal" and non-recurrent factors from the current picture. This having been done, the method of forecasting can hardly be crude enough. No amount of refinement will help one come to the fundamental judgement—is next year going to be the same as last year, or better, or worse?

At this point, it may be objected that there ought to be great possibilities of short-term forecasting with the help of electronic computers, because they can very easily and quickly handle a great mass of data and fit to them some kind of mathematical expression. By means of "feedback" the mathematical expression can be kept up to date almost instantaneously, and once you have a really good mathematical fit, the machine can predict the future.

Once again, we need to have a look at the metaphysical basis of such claims. What is the meaning of a "good mathematical fit"? Simply that a sequence of quantitative changes in the past has been

In the 1970s, when new power plants were big enough to serve the average needs of nearly a million households or a hundred thousand commercial customers, suggestions that it might make more sense (and money) to match the plants' size more closely to the size of their loads were ridiculed by the energy industries. But many utilities had financial near-death experiences as they defied Miss Piggy's Fourth Law, "Never try to eat more than you can lift." The giant-power-plant business soon collapsed: competitive economies simply stopped buying them because financial markets did not have a big enough appetite for risk. As smaller but better technologies emerged—combined-cycle gas plants, co- and tri-generation, renewables, and (cheapest of all) more efficient end-use—U.S. orders for all fossil-fueled steam plants fell back to Victorian levels. ➥

➡ *The U.S. generators being commissioned in the 1990s are back to the sizes that prevailed in the 1940s (megawatts to tens of megawatts), and within a few years will be at 1920s sizes (kilowatts to tens of kilowatts)—about a million-fold smaller than the 1980s behemoths, nicely matched to customers' needs, and a far better buy.*
—AMORY LOVINS

elegantly described in precise mathematical language. But the fact that I—or the machine—have been able to describe this sequence so exactly by no means establishes a presumption that the pattern will continue. It could continue only if (a) there were no human freedom and (b) there was no possibility of any change in the causes that have given rise to the observed pattern.

I should accept the claim that a very clear and very strongly established pattern (of stability, growth, or decline) can be expected to continue for a little longer, unless there is definite knowledge of the arrival of new factors likely to change it. But I suggest that for the detection of such clear, strong and persistent patterns the non-electronic human brain is normally cheaper, faster, and more reliable than its electronic rival. Or to put it the other way around: if it is really necessary to apply such highly refined methods of mathematical analysis for the detection of a pattern that one needs an electronic computer, the pattern is too weak and too obscure to be a suitable basis for extrapolation in real life.

Crude methods of forecasting—after the current picture has been corrected for abnormalities—are not likely to lead into the errors of spurious verisimilitude and spurious detailing—the two greatest vices of the statistician. Once you have a formula and an electronic computer, there is an awful temptation to squeeze the lemon until it is dry and to present a picture of the future which through its very precision and verisimilitude carries conviction. Yet a man who uses an imaginary map, thinking it a true one, is likely to be worse off than someone with no map at all; for he will fail to inquire wherever he can, to observe every detail on his way, and to search continuously with all his senses and all his intelligence for indications of where he should go.

The person who makes the forecasts may still have a precise appreciation of the assumptions on which they are based. But the person who uses the forecasts may have no idea at all that the whole edifice, as is often the case, stands and falls with one single, unverifiable assumption. He is impressed by the thoroughness of the job done, by the fact that everything seems to "add up," and so forth. If the forecasts were presented quite artlessly, as it were, on the back

of an envelope, he would have a much better chance of appreciating
their tenuous character and the fact that, forecasts or no forecasts,
someone has to take an entrepreneurial decision about the unknown future.

PLANNING

I have already insisted that a plan is something essentially different
from a forecast. It is a statement of intention, of what the planners—or their masters—intend to do. Planning (as I suggest the
term should be used) is inseparable from power. It is natural and
indeed desirable that everybody wielding any kind of power should
have some sort of a plan, that is to say, that he should use power deliberately and consciously, looking some distance ahead in time. In
doing so he must consider what other people are likely to do; in
other words, he cannot plan sensibly without doing a certain
amount of forecasting. This is quite straightforward as long as that
which has to be forecast is, in fact, "forecastable," if it relates either
to matters into which human freedom does not enter, or to the routine actions of a very large number of individuals, or to the established plans of other people wielding power. Unfortunately, the
matters to be forecast very often belong to none of these categories
but are dependent on the individual decisions of single persons or
small groups of persons. In such cases forecasts are little more than
"inspired guesses," and no degree of improvement in forecasting
technique can help. Of course, some people may turn out to make
better guesses than others, but this will not be due to their possess-
ing a better forecasting technique or better mechanical equipment
to help them in their computations.

What, then, could be the meaning of a "national plan" in a free
society? It cannot mean the concentration of all power at one point,
because that would imply the end of freedom: genuine planning is
coextensive with power. It seems to me that the only intelligible
meaning of the words "a national plan" in a free society would be
the fullest possible statement of intentions by all people wielding

substantial economic power, such statements being collected and collated by some central agency. The very inconsistencies of such a composite "plan" might give valuable pointers.

LONG-TERM FORECASTS AND FEASIBILITY STUDIES

The fabric of industrial society is to a great extent determined by the interaction of science, technology, and a narrow economic paradigm—an interaction that is leading to ever-greater centralization and specialization. Since the Industrial Revolution, the perspective of the individual has become more limited while political and economic units have grown larger. I have become convinced that we need to decentralize our political and economic structures and broaden our approach to knowledge if we are to find our way to a more balanced and sane society. In Ladakh, I have seen how human-scale structures nurture intimate bonds with the earth and an active and participatory democracy, while supporting strong and vital communities, healthy families, and a greater balance between male and female. These structures in turn provide the security needed for ➡

Let us now turn to long-term forecasting, by which I mean producing estimates five or more years ahead. It must be clear that, change being a function of time, the longer-term future is even less predictable than the short-term. In fact, all long-term forecasting is somewhat presumptuous and absurd, unless it is of so general a kind that it merely states the obvious. All the same, there is often a practical necessity for "taking a view" on the future, as decisions have to be taken and long-term commitments entered. Is there nothing that could help?

Here I should like to emphasise again the distinction between forecasts on the one hand and "exploratory calculations" or "feasibility studies" on the other. In the one case I assert that this or that will be the position in, say, twenty years' time. In the other case I merely explore the long-term effect of certain assumed tendencies. It is unfortunately true that in macro-economics feasibility studies are very rarely carried beyond the most rudimentary beginnings. People are content to rely on general forecasts which are rarely worth the paper they are written on.

It may be helpful if I give a few examples. It is very topical these days to talk about the development of underdeveloped countries and countless "plans" (so-called) are being produced to this end. If we go by the expectations that are being aroused all over the world, it appears to be assumed that within a few decades most people the world over are going to be able to live more or less as the Western Europeans are living today. Now, it seems to me, it would be very instructive if someone undertook to make a proper, detailed feasibility study of this project. He might choose the year 2000 as the terminal date and work backwards from there. What would be the required output of foodstuffs, fuels, metals, textile fibres, and so forth? What would be the stock of industrial capital? Naturally, he would have to introduce many new assumptions as he went along. Each assumption could then become the object of a further feasibility study. He might then find that he could not solve his equations unless he introduced assumptions which transcended all bounds of reasonable probability. This might prove highly instructive. It might conceivably lead to the conclusion that, while most certainly there ought to be substantial economic development throughout the countries where great masses of people live in abject misery, there are certain choices between alternative *patterns* of development that could be made, and that some types of development would appear more feasible than others.

Long-term thinking, supported by conscientious feasibility studies, would seem to be particularly desirable with regard to all non-renewable raw materials of limited availability, that is to say, mainly fossil fuels and metals. At present, for instance, there is a replacement of coal by oil. Some people seem to assume that coal is on the way out. A careful feasibility study, making use of all available evidence of coal, oil, and natural gas reserves, proved as well as merely assumed to exist, would be exceedingly instructive.

On the subject of population increase and food supplies, we have had the nearest thing to feasibility studies so far, coming mainly from United Nations organisations. They might be carried much further, giving not only the totals of food production to be attained by 1980 or 2000, but also showing in much greater detail than has so far been done the timetable of specific steps that would have to be taken in the near future if these totals are to be attained.

In all this, the most essential need is a purely intellectual one: a clear appreciation of the difference between a forecast and a feasibility study. It is surely a sign of statistical illiteracy to confuse the two. A long-term forecast, as I said, is presumptuous; but a long-term feasibility study is a piece of humble and unpretentious work which we shall neglect at our peril.

Again the question arises whether this work could be facilitated by more mechanical aids such as electronic computers. Personally, I am inclined to doubt it. It seems to me that the endless multiplication of mechanical aids in fields which require judgement more than anything else is one of the chief dynamic forces behind

➡ *individual well-being and, paradoxically, for a sense of freedom.*

The emerging global economy and the growing domination of science and technology are not only severing our connection to nature and to one another but also breaking down natural and cultural diversity. In so doing, we are threatening our very existence.

It is in robust, local-scale economies that we find genuinely "free" markets; free of corporate manipulation, hidden subsidies, waste, and immense promotional costs that characterize today's global market.

Decentralization is a prerequisite for the rekindling of community in Western society. Mobility erodes community, but as we put down roots and feel attachment to a place, our human relationships deepen, become more secure, and as they continue over time, more reliable.

—HELENA
NORBERG-HODGE

Parkinson's Law. Of course, an electronic computer can work out a vast number of permutations, employing varying assumptions, within a few seconds or minutes, while it might take the non-electronic brain as many months to do the same job. But the point is that the non-electronic brain need never attempt to do that job. By the power of judgement it can concentrate on a few decisive parameters which are quite sufficient to outline the ranges of reasonable probability. Some people imagine that it would be possible and helpful to set up a machine for long-range forecasting into which current "news" could be fed continuously and which, in response, would produce continual revisions of some long-term forecasts. No doubt, this would be possible; but would it be helpful? Each item of "news" has to be judged for its long-term relevance, and a sound judgement is generally not possible immediately. Nor can I see any value in the continual revision of long-term forecasts, as a matter of mechanical routine. A forecast is required only when a long-term decision has to be taken or reviewed, which is a comparatively rare event even in the largest of businesses, and then it is worth while deliberately and conscientiously to assemble the best evidence, to judge each item in the light of accumulated experience, and finally to come to a view which appears reasonable to the best brains available. It is a matter of self-deception that this laborious and uncertain process could be short-circuited by a piece of mechanical apparatus.

When it comes to feasibility studies, as distinct from forecasts, it may occasionally seem useful to have apparatus which can quickly test the effect of variations in one's assumptions. But I have yet to be convinced that a slide rule and a set of compound interest tables are not quite sufficient for the purpose.

UNPREDICTABILITY AND FREEDOM

If I hold a rather negative opinion about the usefulness of "automation" in matters of economic forecasting and the like, I do not underestimate the value of electronic computers and similar apparatus for other tasks, like solving mathematical problems or programming production runs. These latter tasks belong to the exact sciences or their applications. Their subject matter is non-human, or perhaps I should say, sub-human. Their very exactitude is a sign of the absence of human freedom, the absence of choice, responsibility, and dignity. As soon as human freedom enters, we are in an entirely different world where there is great danger in any proliferation of mechanical devices. The tendencies which attempt to obliterate the distinction should be resisted with the utmost determination. Great damage to human dignity has resulted from the misguided attempt of the social sciences to adopt and imitate the methods of the natural sciences. Economics, and even more so applied economics, is not an exact science; it is in fact, or ought to be, something much greater: a branch of wisdom. Mr. Colin Clark once claimed "that long-period world economic equilibria develop themselves in their own peculiar manner, entirely independently of political and social changes." On the strength of this metaphysical heresy he wrote a book, in 1941, entitled *The Economics of 1960.*[1] It would be unjust to say that the picture he drew bears no resemblance to what actually came to pass; there is, indeed, the kind of resemblance which simply stems from the fact that man uses his freedom within an unchanged setting of physical laws of nature. But the lesson from Mr. Clark's book is that his metaphysical assumption is untrue; that, in fact, world economic equilibria, even in the longer run, are highly dependent on political and social changes; and that the sophisticated and ingenious methods of forecasting employed by Mr. Clark merely served to produce a work of spurious verisimilitude.

CONCLUSION

I thus come to the cheerful conclusion that life, including economic life, is still worth living because it is sufficiently unpredictable to be interesting. Neither the economist nor the statistician will get it "taped." Within the limits of the physical laws of nature, we are still masters of our individual and collective destiny, for good or ill.

Like great social thinkers that came before him—Buber, Gandhi, Kropotkin, Tagore, Tolstoy—Schumacher understood that economic renewal is tied inextricably to cultural, social, and ecological renewal. His library, housed at the E.F. Schumacher Society in Great Barrington, Massachusetts, reflects this understanding. The economics books are far outnumbered by books on philosophy, religious thinking of all traditions, psychology, social history, art, gardening, technology, and the environment. This integration of concerns most closely mirrors the human experience of community, and yields in Schumacher's work an economic theory profoundly moral in nature.
—SUSAN WITT

Schumacher's feasibility studies have become the "scenario" industry, oddly championed by Shell Oil at the same time as his book appeared. The World Business Council for Sustainable Development now has sustainability scenarios. Forecasting is improved in weather and gene-based diseases. But, as Schumacher says, it's worse in everything else.

—PETER WARSHALL

But the know-how of the economist, the statistician, the natural scientist, and engineer, and even of the genuine philosopher can help to clarify the limits within which our destiny is confined. The future cannot be forecast, but it can be explored. Feasibility studies can show us where we appear to be going, and this is more important today than ever before, since "growth" has become a keynote of economics all over the world.

In his urgent attempt to obtain reliable knowledge about his essentially indeterminate future, the modern man of action may surround himself by ever-growing armies of forecasters, by ever-growing mountains of factual data to be digested by ever more wonderful mechanical contrivances: I fear that the result is little more than a huge game of make-believe and an ever more marvellous vindication of Parkinson's Law. The best decisions will still be based on the judgements of mature non-electronic brains possessed by men who have looked steadily and calmly at the situation and seen it whole. "Stop, look, and listen" is a better motto than "Look it up in the forecasts."

CHAPTER 16

TOWARDS A THEORY OF LARGE-SCALE ORGANISATION

ALMOST EVERY DAY we hear of mergers and takeovers; Britain enters the European Economic Community to open up larger markets to be served by even larger organisations. In the socialist countries, nationalisation has produced vast combines to rival or surpass anything that has emerged in the capitalist countries. The great majority of economists and business efficiency experts supports this trend towards vastness.

In contrast, most of the sociologists and psychologists insistently warn us of its inherent dangers—dangers to the integrity of the individual when he feels as nothing more than a small cog in a vast machine and when the human relationships of his daily working life become increasingly dehumanised; dangers also to efficiency and productivity, stemming from ever-growing Parkinsonian bureaucracies.

Modern literature, at the same time, paints frightening pictures of a brave new world sharply divided between *us* and *them,* torn by mutual suspicion, with a hatred of authority from below and a contempt of people from above. The masses react to their rulers in a spirit of sullen irresponsibility, while the rulers vainly try to keep things moving by precise organisation and coordination, fiscal inducements, incentives, endless exhortations, and threats.

Undoubtedly this is all a problem of communications. But the only really effective communication is from man to man, face to face. Franz Kafka's nightmarish novel, *The Castle,* depicts the devastating effects of remote control. Mr. K., the land surveyor, has been hired by the authorities, but nobody quite knows how and

Schumacher emphasized the importance of the small in the era of gigantism. This encouraged denial of what was going on: globalization, global loss of species and cultures, and global climate change. In an age that over-emphasizes gigantism, he could have said: "Confront it boldly!" Then maybe activists would have had a jump start on processes they oppose today. So the red flags of globalization were waved, and we tried for communes, dropping out, self-sufficiency, and other forms of isola-tionism. It took almost 20 years to catch on that it's necessary to both think and act locally and globally.

—PETER WARSHALL

why. He tries to get his position clarified, because the people he meets all tell him: "Unfortunately we have no need of a land sur-veyor. There would not be the least use for one here."

So, making every effort to meet authority face to face, Mr. K. ap-proaches various people who evidently carry some weight; but oth-ers tell him: "You haven't once up till now come into real contact with our authorities. All these contacts are merely illusory, but ow-ing to your ignorance... you take them to be real."

He fails utterly to do any real work and then receives a letter from The Castle: "The surveying work which you have carried out thus far has my recognition.... Do not slacken your efforts! Bring your work to a successful conclusion. Any interruption would dis-please me.... I shall not forget you."

Nobody really likes large-scale organisation; nobody likes to take orders from a superior who takes orders from a superior who takes orders.... Even if the rules devised by bureaucracy are out-standingly humane, nobody likes to be ruled by rules, that is to say, by people whose answer to every complaint is: "I did not make the rules: I am merely applying them."

Yet, it seems, large-scale organisation is here to stay. Therefore it is all the more necessary to think about it and to theorise about it. The stronger the current, the greater the need for skillful naviga-tion.

The fundamental task is to achieve smallness *within* large or-ganisation.

Once a large organisation has come into being, it normally goes through alternating phases of *centralising* and *decentralising*, like swings of a pendulum. Whenever one encounters such *opposites*, each of them with persuasive arguments in its favour, it is worth looking into the depth of the problem for something more than compromise, more than a half-and-half solution. Maybe what we really need is not *either-or* but *the-one-and-the-other-at-the-same-time*.

This very familiar problem pervades the whole of real life, al-though it is highly unpopular with people who spend most of their time on laboratory problems from which all extraneous factors have been carefully eliminated. For whatever we do in real life, we must try to do justice to a situation which includes all so-called extraneous factors. And we always have to face the simultaneous requirement for order and freedom.

In any organisation, large or small, there must be a certain clarity and orderliness; if things fall into disorder, nothing can be accomplished. Yet, orderliness, as such, is static and lifeless; so there must also be plenty of elbow-room and scope for breaking through the established order, to do the thing never done before, never anticipated by the guardians of orderliness, the new, unpredicted, and unpredictable outcome of a man's creative idea.

Therefore any organisation has to strive continuously for the orderliness of *order* and the disorderliness of creative *freedom*. And the specific danger inherent in large-scale organisation is that its natural bias and tendency favour order, at the expense of creative freedom.

We can associate many further pairs of opposites with this basic pair of order and freedom. Centralisation is mainly an idea of order; decentralisation, one of freedom. The man of order is typically the accountant and, generally, the administrator; while the man of creative freedom is the *entrepreneur*. Order requires intelligence and is conducive to efficiency; while freedom calls for, and opens the door to, intuition and leads to innovation.

The larger an organisation, the more obvious and inescapable is the need for order. But if this need is looked after with such efficiency and perfection that no scope remains for man to exercise his creative intuition, for *entrepreneurial* disorder, the organisation becomes moribund and a desert of frustration.

These considerations form the background to an attempt towards a theory of large-scale organisation which I shall now develop in the form of five principles.

The first principle is called *The Principle of Subsidiarity* or *The Principle of Subsidiary Function*. A famous formulation of this principle reads as follows: "It is an injustice and at the same time a grave evil and disturbance of right order to assign to a greater and higher association what lesser and subordinate organisations can do. For every social activity ought of its very nature to furnish help to the members of the body social and never destroy and absorb them." These sentences were meant for society as a whole, but they apply

We all recognize, I think, that these are times of rapid change when we need to welcome innovative, better ways of doing things. Many traditionally monopolistic public services need to be opened up to entrepreneurs and others with good ideas— also with good jobs if their initiatives pan out. Great ranges of activities, from transportation and sewage treatment to recycling services, products and technology, invite innovative development. But governments can and too often do discourage experimenting, and prevent or delay privately undertaken initiatives that trespass into their traditional preserves. All central planning is at odds with multiple and diverse experimenting. To be sure, small bureaucracies can be as brain-dead as big ones, but at least if they are multiple, when one says no or just doesn't get it, the old saying applies; not all the eggs are in that basket.

—JANE JACOBS

equally to the different levels within a large organisation. The higher level must not absorb the functions of the lower one, on the assumption that, being higher, it will automatically be wiser and fulfill them more efficiently. Loyalty can grow only from the smaller units to the larger (and higher) ones, not the other way round—and loyalty is an essential element in the health of any organisation.

The Principle of Subsidiary Function implies that the burden of proof lies always on those who want to deprive a lower level of its function, and thereby of its freedom and responsibility in that respect; *they* have to prove that the lower level is incapable of fulfilling this function satisfactorily and that the higher level can actually do much better. "Those in command [to continue the quotation] should be sure that the more perfectly a graduated order is preserved among the various associations, in observing the principle of subsidiary function, the stronger will be the social authority and effectiveness and the happier and more prosperous the condition of the State."[1]

The opposites of centralising and decentralising are now far behind us: the Principle of Subsidiary Function teaches us that the centre will gain in authority and effectiveness if the freedom and responsibility of the lower formations are carefully preserved, with the result that the organisation as a whole will be "happier and more prosperous."

How can such a structure be achieved? From the administrator's point of view, i.e. from the point of view of orderliness, it will look untidy, comparing most unfavourably with the clear-cut logic of a monolith. The large organisation will consist of many semi-autonomous units, which we may call *quasi-firms*. Each of them will have a large amount of freedom, to give the greatest possible chance to creativity and *entrepreneurship*.

The structure of the organisation can then be symbolised by a man holding a large number of balloons in his hand. Each of the balloons has its own buoyancy and lift, and the man himself does not lord it over the balloons, but stands beneath them, yet holding all the strings firmly in his hand. Every balloon is not only an administrative but also an *entrepreneurial* unit. The monolithic organisation, by contrast, might be symbolised by a Christmas tree, with a star at the top and a lot of nuts and other useful things underneath. Everything derives from the top and depends on it. Real freedom and *entrepreneurship* can exist only at the top.

Therefore, the task is to look at the organisation's activities one by one and set up as many quasi-firms as may seem possible and reasonable. For example, the British National Coal Board, one of the largest commercial organisations in Europe, has found it possible to set up quasi-firms under various names for its opencast mining, its brickworks, and its coal products. But the process did not end there. Special, relatively self-contained organisational forms have been evolved for its road transport activities, estates, and retail business, not to mention various enterprises falling under the heading of diversification. The board's primary activity, deep-mined coal-getting, has been organised in seventeen areas, each of them with the status of a quasi-firm. The source already quoted describes the results of such a *structurisation* as follows: "Thereby [the centre] will more freely, powerfully and effectively do all those things which belong to it alone because it alone can do them: directing, watching, urging, restraining, as occasion requires and necessity demands."

For central control to be meaningful and effective, a second principle has to be applied, which we shall call *The Principle of Vindication*. To vindicate means: to defend against reproach or accusation; to prove to be true and valid; to justify; to uphold; so this principle describes very well one of the most important duties of the central authority towards the lower formations. Good government is always government by exception. Except for exceptional cases, the subsidiary unit must be defended against reproach and upheld. This means that the exception must be sufficiently clearly defined, so that the quasi-firm is able to know without doubt whether or not it is performing satisfactorily.

Administrators taken as a pure type, namely as men of orderliness, are happy when they have everything under control. Armed with computers, they can indeed now do so and can insist on accountability with regard to an almost infinite number of items— output, productivity, many different cost items, non-operational expenditure, and so on, leading up to profit or loss. This is logical enough: but real life is bigger than logic. If a large number of criteria is laid down for accountability, every subsidiary unit can be faulted on one item or another; government by exception becomes a mockery, and no one can ever be sure how his unit stands.

In its ideal application, the Principle of Vindication would permit only one criterion for accountability in a commercial organisation, namely profitability. Of course, such a criterion would be subject to the quasi-firm's observing general rules and policies laid down by the centre. Ideals can rarely be attained in the real world, but they are none the less meaningful. They imply that any departure from the ideal has to be specially argued and justified. Unless the number of criteria for accountability is kept very small indeed, creativity and *entrepreneurship* cannot flourish in the quasi-firm.

While profitability must be the final criterion, it is not always permissible to apply it mechanically. Some subsidiary units may be exceptionally well placed, others, exceptionally badly; some may have service functions with regard to the organisation as a whole or other special obligations which have to be fulfilled without primary regard to profitability. In such cases, the measurement of profitability must be modified in advance, by what we may call *rents* and *subsidies*.

If a unit enjoys special and inescapable advantages, it must pay an appropriate *rent*, but if it has to cope with inescapable disadvantages, it must be granted a special *credit* or *subsidy*. Such a system can sufficiently equalise the profitability chances of the various units, so that profit becomes a meaningful indication of achievement. If such an equalisation is needed but not applied, the fortunate units will be featherbedded, while others may be lying on a bed of nails. This cannot be good for either morale or performance.

If, in accordance with the Principle of Vindication, an organisation adopts profitability as the primary criterion for accountability—profitability as modified, if need be, by rents and subsidies—government by exception becomes possible. The centre can then concentrate its activities on "directing, watching, urging, restraining, as occasion requires and necessity demands," which, of course, must go on all the time with regard to all its subsidiary units.

Exceptions can be defined clearly. The centre will have two opportunities for intervening exceptionally. The first occurs when the centre and the subsidiary unit cannot come to a free agreement on the rent or subsidy, as the case may be, which is to be applied. In such circumstances the centre has to undertake a full efficiency audit of the unit to obtain an objective assessment of the unit's real potential. The second opportunity arises when the unit fails to earn a profit, after allowing for rent or subsidy. The management of the unit is then in a precarious position: if the centre's efficiency audit produces highly unfavourable evidence, the management may have to be changed.

The third principle is *The Principle of Identification.* Each subsidiary unit or quasi-firm must have both a profit and loss account and a balance sheet. From the point of view of orderliness a profit and loss statement is quite sufficient, since from this one can know whether or not the unit is contributing financially to the organisation. But for the *entrepreneur,* a balance sheet is essential, even if it is used only for internal purposes. Why is it not sufficient to have but one balance sheet for the organisation as a whole?

Business operates with a certain economic substance, and this substance diminishes as a result of losses, and grows as a result of profit. What happens to the unit's profits or losses at the end of the financial year? They flow into the totality of the organisation's accounts; as far as the unit is concerned, they simply disappear. In the absence of a balance sheet, or something in the nature of a balance sheet, the unit always enters the new financial year with a nil balance. This cannot be right.

A unit's success should lead to greater freedom and financial scope for the unit, while failure—in the form of losses—should lead to restriction and disability. One wants to reinforce success and discriminate against failure. The balance sheet describes the economic substance as augmented or diminished by current results. This enables all concerned to follow the effect of operations on substance. Profits and losses are carried forward and not wiped out. Therefore, every quasi-firm should have its separate balance sheet, in which profits can appear as loans to the centre and losses as loans from the centre. This is a matter of great psychological importance.

"The real problems facing this planet are not economic or technical, they are philosophical," said Schumacher. Our high capital, low labor philosophy is pauperizing North America with downsizing and rationalizing for "efficiency." In the long run, this philosophy will be very costly and inefficient because it will destroy our consumer base, self-respect, and other delicate psychological structures of society. It is now also destroying our tax base—making governments helpless and irrelevant—just at a time when a damaged society needs more support.

—ROBERT BATEMAN

I now turn to the fourth principle, which can be called *The Principle of Motivation*. It is a trite and obvious truism that people act in accordance with their motives. All the same, for a large organisation, with its bureaucracies, its remote and impersonal controls, its many abstract rules and regulations, and above all the relative incomprehensibility that stems from its very size, motivation is the central problem. At the top, the management has no problem of motivation, but going down the scale, the problem becomes increasingly acute. This is not the place to go into the details of this vast and difficult subject.

Modern industrial society, typified by large-scale organisations, gives far too little thought to it. Managements assume that people work simply for money, for the pay-packet at the end of the week. No doubt, this is true up to a point, but when a worker, asked why he worked only four shifts last week, answers: "Because I couldn't make ends meet on three shifts' wages," everybody is stunned and feels check-mated.

Intellectual confusion exacts its price. We preach the virtues of hard work and restraint while painting utopian pictures of unlimited consumption without either work or restraint. We complain when an appeal for greater effort meets with the ungracious reply: "I couldn't care less," while promoting dreams about automation to do away with manual work, and about the computer relieving men from the burden of using their brains.

A recent Reith lecturer announced that when a minority will be "able to feed, maintain, and supply the majority, it makes no sense to keep in the production stream those who have no desire to be in it." Many have no desire to be in it, because their work does not interest them, providing them with neither challenge nor satisfaction, and has no other merit in their eyes than that it leads to a pay-packet at the end of the week. If our intellectual leaders treat work as nothing but a necessary evil soon to be abolished as far as the majority is concerned, the urge to minimise it right away is hardly a surprising reaction, and the problem of motivation becomes insoluble.

However that may be, the health of a large organisation depends to an extraordinary extent on its ability to do justice to the Principle of Motivation. Any organisational structure that is conceived without regard to this fundamental truth is unlikely to succeed.

My fifth, and last, principle is *The Principle of the Middle Axiom*. Top management in a large organisation inevitably occupies a very difficult position. It carries responsibility for everything that happens, or fails to happen, throughout the organisation, although it is far removed from the actual scene of events. It can deal with many well-established functions by means of directives, rules, and regulations. But what about new developments, new creative ideas? What about progress, the *entrepreneurial* activity *par excellence?*

We come back to our starting point: all real human problems arise from the *antinomy* of order and freedom. Antinomy means a contradiction between two laws: a conflict of authority; opposition between laws or principles that appear to be founded equally in reason.

Excellent! This is real life, full of antinomies and bigger than logic. Without order, planning, predictability, central control, accountancy, instructions to the underlings, obedience, discipline—without these, nothing fruitful can happen, because everything disintegrates. And yet—without the magnanimity of disorder, the happy abandon, the *entrepreneurship* venturing into the unknown and incalculable, without the risk and the gamble, the creative imagination rushing in where bureaucratic angels fear to tread—without this, life is a mockery and a disgrace.

The centre can easily look after order; it is not so easy to look after freedom and creativity. The centre has the power to establish order, but no amount of power evokes the creative contribution. How, then, can top management at the centre work for progress and innovation? Assuming that it knows what ought to be done: How can the management get it done throughout the organisation? This is where the Principle of the Middle Axiom comes in.

An axiom is a self-evident truth which is assented to as soon as enunciated. The centre can enunciate the truth it has discovered—that this or that is "the right thing to do." Some years ago, the most important truth to be enunciated by the National Coal Board was *concentration of output*, that is, to concentrate coal-getting on fewer coalfaces, with a higher output from each. Everybody, of course,

As the world enters its third millennium seemingly afflicted with ever-larger institutions, has the Schumacher legacy been repudiated? Not at all. True, Bigness seems to be on the march. But operating underneath galloping globalism, men and women in thousands of local communities are acting bravely in his tradition to create human scale institutions, appropriate technology, community land trusts, environmental improvement, local currencies, cooperatives, alternative health care, new energy technologies, home food production, rewarding self-employment, and entrepreneurship. The forces of the global economy, the great corporations, the international labor unions, the mega-universities, the mass media, are really powerless to stop this movement toward a new society. Indeed, the wonders of new technology have opened new possibilities for the decentralist movement. ➡

➡ *The one exception is the baneful influence of Big Government. Even as new opportunities appear for a decentralist future, Big Government constantly centralizes power over its subjects, pries into their privacy, confiscates their earnings, regulates their every activity, dictates their choices, removes what once were local civic decisions to higher and more distant bureaucracies, and all too often—alas—stifles the upwelling energies of the human spirit.*

—JOHN M^CCLAUGHRY

immediately assented to it, but, not surprisingly, very little happened.

A change of this kind requires a lot of work, a lot of new thinking and planning at every colliery, with many natural obstacles and difficulties to be overcome. How is the centre, the National Board in this case, to speed the change-over? It can, of course, preach the new doctrine. But what is the use, if everybody agrees anyhow? Preaching from the centre maintains the freedom and responsibility of the lower formations, but it incurs the valid criticism that "they only talk and do not *do* anything." Alternatively, the centre can issue instructions, but, being remote from the actual scene of operations, the central management will incur the valid criticism that "it attempts to run the industry from Headquarters," sacrificing the need for freedom to the need for order and losing the creative participation of the people at the lower formations—the very people who are most closely in touch with the actual job. Neither the soft method of government by exhortation nor the tough method of government by instruction meets the requirements of the case. What is required is something in between, a *middle axiom*, an order from above which is yet not quite an order.

When it decided to concentrate output, the National Coal Board laid down certain minimum standards for opening up new coalfaces, with the proviso that if any Area found it necessary to open a coalface that would fall short of these standards, a record of the decision should be entered into a book specially provided for the purpose, and this record should contain answers to three questions:

> Why can this particular coalface not be laid out in such a way that the required minimum size is attained?
> Why does this particular bit of coal have to be worked at all?
> What is the approximate profitability of the coalface as planned?

This was a true and effective way of applying the Principle of the Middle Axiom and it had an almost magical effect. Concentration of output really got going, with excellent results for the industry as a whole. The centre had found a way of going far beyond mere exhortation, yet without in any way diminishing the freedom and re-sponsibility of the lower formations.

Another middle axiom can be found in the device of *Impact Statistics*. Normally, statistics are collected for the benefit of the collector, who needs—or thinks he needs—certain quantitative information. Impact statistics have a different purpose, namely to make the supplier of the statistic, a responsible person at the lower formation, aware of certain facts which he might otherwise overlook. This device has been successfully used in the coal industry, particularly in the field of safety.

Discovering a middle axiom is always a considerable achievement. To preach is easy; so also is issuing instructions. But it is difficult indeed for top management to carry through its creative ideas without impairing the freedom and responsibility of the lower formations.

I have expounded five principles which I believe to be relevant to a theory of large-scale organisation, and have given a more or less intriguing name to each of them. What is the use of all this? Is it merely an intellectual game? Some readers will no doubt think so. Others—and they are the ones for whom this chapter has been written—might say: "You are putting into words what I have been trying to do for years." Excellent! Many of us have been struggling for years with the problems presented by large-scale organisation, problems which are becoming ever more acute. To struggle more successfully, we need a theory, built up from principles. But from where do the principles come? They come from observation and practical understanding.

The best formulation of the necessary interplay of theory and practice, that I know of, comes from Mao Tse-tung. Go to the practical people, he says, and learn from them: then synthesise their experience into principles and theories; and then return to the practical people and call upon them to put these principles and methods into practice so as to solve their problems and achieve freedom and happiness.[2]

CHAPTER 17

SOCIALISM

BOTH THEORETICAL considerations and practical experience have led me to the conclusion that socialism is of interest solely for its non-economic values and the possibility it creates for the overcoming of the religion of economics. A society ruled primarily by the idolatry of *enrichissez-vous,* which celebrates millionaires as its culture heroes, can gain nothing from socialisation that could not also be gained without it.

It is not surprising, therefore, that many socialists in so-called advanced societies, who are themselves—whether they know it or not—devotees of the religion of economics, are today wondering whether nationalisation is not really beside the point. It causes a lot of trouble—so why bother with it? The extinction of private ownership, by itself, does not produce magnificent results: everything worth while has still to be worked for, devotedly and patiently, and the pursuit of financial viability, *combined* with the pursuit of higher social aims, produces many dilemmas, many seeming contradictions, and imposes extra heavy burdens on management.

If the purpose of nationalisation is primarily to achieve faster economic growth, higher efficiency, better planning, and so forth, there is bound to be disappointment. The idea of conducting the entire economy on the basis of private greed, as Marx well recognised, has shown an extraordinary power to transform the world.

> The bourgeoisie, wherever it has got the upper hand, has put an end to all feudal, patriarchal, idyllic relations and has left no other nexus between man and man than naked self-interest. . . .

The bourgeoisie, by the rapid improvement of all instruments of production, by the immensely facilitated means of communication, draws all, even the most barbarian, nations into civilisation. [*Communist Manifesto*]

The strength of the idea of private enterprise lies in its terrifying simplicity. It suggests that the totality of life can be reduced to one aspect—profits. The businessman, as a private individual, may still be interested in other aspects of life—perhaps even in goodness, truth, and beauty—but *as a businessman* he concerns himself only with profits. In this respect, the idea of private enterprise fits exactly into the idea of The Market, which, in an earlier chapter, I called "the institutionalisation of individualism and non-responsibility." Equally, it fits perfectly into the modern trend towards total quantification at the expense of the appreciation of qualitative differences; for private enterprise is not concerned with what it produces but only with what it gains from production.

Everything becomes crystal clear after you have reduced reality to one—one only—of its thousand aspects. You know what to do—whatever produces profits; you know what to avoid—whatever reduces them or makes a loss. And there is at the same time a perfect measuring rod for the degree of success or failure. Let no one befog the issue by asking whether a particular action is conducive to the wealth and well-being of society, whether it leads to moral, aesthetic, or cultural enrichment. Simply find out whether it pays; simply investigate whether there is an alternative that pays better. If there is, choose the alternative.

It is no accident that successful businessmen are often astonishingly primitive; they live in a world made primitive by this process of reduction. They fit into this simplified version of the world and are satisfied with it. And when the real world occasionally makes its existence known and attempts to force upon their attention a different one of its facets, one not provided for in their philosophy, they tend to become quite helpless and confused. They feel exposed to incalculable dangers and "unsound" forces and freely predict general disaster. As a result, their judgements on actions dictated by a more comprehensive outlook on the meaning and purpose of life are generally quite worthless. It is a foregone

Too many socialists still have the same old economic ideas, just as Schumacher said. They are devotees of the classical models of efficiency, economic growth, scale, and centralization. Even though they call themselves the Third Way, the governments in Europe that are predominately socialist are still wedded to outdated models.

—HAZEL HENDERSON

Schumacher's concern about "the ruthless application of partial knowledge" is still true today. It is true not only in the economic and corporate spheres, but also in the scientific and technological. On Wall Street, for example, there is an extreme simplicity of quantification. If stocks slip in forecasted earnings by a couple of cents, they are quickly sold off. Genetically modified organisms are being created by agrobusiness in pursuit of profits and higher stock prices. Their shareholders are deeply implicated in this ecologically dangerous application of limited knowledge because Wall Street has taught a generation of shareholders that the way to provide for their children's college education and retirement is to play the stock-market.

—HAZEL HENDERSON

conclusion for them that a different scheme of things, a business, for instance, that is not based on private ownership, cannot possibly succeed. If it succeeds all the same, there must be a sinister explanation—"exploitation of the consumer," "hidden subsidies," "forced labour," "monopoly," "dumping," or some dark and dreadful accumulation of a debit account which the future will suddenly present.

But this is a digression. The point is that the real strength of the theory of private enterprise lies in this ruthless simplification, which fits so admirably also into the mental patterns created by the phenomenal successes of science. The strength of science, too, derives from a "reduction" of reality to one or the other of its many aspects, primarily the reduction of quality to quantity. But just as the powerful concentration of nineteenth-century science on the mechanical aspects of reality had to be abandoned because there was too much of reality that simply did not fit, so the powerful concentration of business life on the aspect of "profits" has had to be modified because it failed to do justice to the real needs of man. It was the historical achievement of socialists to push this development, with the result that the favourite phrase of the enlightened capitalist today is: "We are all socialists now."

That is to say, the capitalist today wishes to deny that the one final aim of all his activities is profit. He says: "Oh no, we do a lot for our employees which we do not really have to do; we try to preserve the beauty of the countryside; we engage in research that may not pay off," etc., etc. All these claims are very familiar; sometimes they are justified, sometimes not.

What concerns us here is this: private enterprise "old style," let us say, goes simply for profits; it thereby achieves a most powerful simplification of objectives and gains a perfect measuring rod of success or failure. Private enterprise "new style," on the other hand (let us assume), pursues a great variety of objectives; it tries to consider the whole fullness of life and not merely the money-making aspect; it therefore achieves no powerful simplification of objectives and possesses no reliable measuring rod of success or failure. If this is so, private enterprise "new style," as organised in large joint stock companies, differs from public enterprise only in one respect; namely that it provides an unearned income to its shareholders.

Clearly, the protagonists of capitalism cannot have it both ways. They cannot say "We are all socialists now" and maintain at the same time that socialism cannot possibly work. If they themselves pursue objectives other than that of profit-making, then they cannot very well argue that it becomes impossible to administer the nation's means of production efficiently as soon as considerations other than those of profit-making are allowed to enter. If *they* can manage without the crude yardstick of money-making, so can nationalised industry.

On the other hand, if all this is rather a sham and private enterprise works for profit and (practically) nothing else; if its pursuit of other objectives is in fact solely dependent on profit-making and constitutes merely its own choice of what to do with some of the profits, then the sooner this is made clear the better. In that case, private enterprise could still claim to possess the power of simplicity. Its case against public enterprise would be that the latter is bound to be inefficient precisely because it attempts to pursue several objectives at the same time, and the case of socialists against the former would be the traditional case, which is not primarily an economic one, namely, that it degrades life by its very simplicity, by basing all economic activity solely on the motive of private greed.

A total rejection of public ownership means a total affirmation of private ownership. This is just as great a piece of dogmatism as the opposite one of the most fanatical communist. But while all fanaticism shows intellectual weakness, a fanaticism *about the means* to be employed for reaching quite uncertain objectives is sheer feeble-mindedness.

As mentioned before, the whole crux of economic life—and indeed of life in general—is that it constantly requires the living reconciliation of opposites which, in strict logic, are irreconcilable. In macro-economics (the management of whole societies) it is necessary always to have both planning *and* freedom—not by way of a weak and lifeless compromise, but by a free recognition of the legitimacy of and need for both. Equally in micro-economics (the management of individual enterprises): on the one hand it is essential that there should be full managerial responsibility and authority; yet it is equally essential that there should be a democratic and free participation of the workers in management decisions. Again, it is

In the past decade there has been a tug of war on a global scale between public and private ownership and the role of the state and the market. The outcome has been a massive march toward privatization, a product of the Margaret Thatcher and Ronald Reagan–era policies known as the Washington consensus. We have seen the results: in countries where there is little state regulation, economic meltdowns have occurred because trying to grow economies on this gross national product–measured, Washington-consensus recipe ignores social and environmental costs. So forests are destroyed, rivers are polluted, and workers are paid slave wages. All this proves unsustainable.

The World Bank produced a draft in 1998 called "Beyond the Washington Consensus" and subtitled "Institutions Matter," which Schumacher would have ➡

➡ *loved. It admitted the importance of family, community, contracts, culture, and values—all the concerns left out of the Washington consensus. But such economic ideologies die hard.*

—HAZEL HENDERSON

not a question of mitigating the opposition of these two needs by some half-hearted compromise that satisfies neither of them, but to recognise them both. The exclusive concentration on one of the opposites—say, on planning, produces Stalinism; while the exclusive concentration on the other produces chaos. The normal answer to either is a swing of the pendulum to the other extreme. Yet the normal answer is not the only possible answer. A generous and magnanimous intellectual effort—the opposite of nagging, malevolent criticism—can enable a society, at least for a period, to find a middle way that reconciles the opposites without degrading them both.

The same applies to the choice of objectives in business life. One of the opposites—represented by private enterprise "old style"—is the need for simplicity and measurability, which is best fulfilled by a strict limitation of outlook to "profitability" and nothing else. The other opposite—represented by the original "idealistic" conception of public enterprise—is the need for a comprehensive and broad humanity in the conduct of economic affairs. The former, if exclusively adhered to, leads to the total destruction of the dignity of man; the latter, to a chaotic kind of inefficiency.

There are no "final solutions" to this kind of problem. There is only a *living* solution achieved day by day on a basis of a clear recognition *that both opposites are valid.*

Ownership, whether public or private, is merely an element of framework. It does not by itself settle the kind of objectives to be pursued within the framework. From this point of view it is correct to say that ownership is not the decisive question. But it is also necessary to recognise that private ownership of the means of production is severely limited in its freedom of choice of objectives, because it is compelled to be profit-seeking, and *tends* to take a narrow and selfish view of things. Public ownership gives *complete* freedom in the choice of objectives and can therefore be used for any purpose that may be chosen. While private ownership is an instrument that by itself largely determines the ends for which it can be employed, public ownership is an instrument the ends of which are undetermined and need to be consciously chosen.

There is therefore really no strong case for public ownership if the objectives to be pursued by nationalised industry are to be just as narrow, just as limited, as those of capitalist production: profitability and nothing else. Herein lies the real danger to nationalisation in Britain at the present time, not in any imagined inefficiency.

The campaign of the enemies of nationalisation consists of two distinctly separate moves. The first move is an attempt to convince the public at large and the people engaged in the nationalised sector that the only thing that matters in the administration of the means of production, distribution, and exchange is profitability; that any departure from this sacred standard—*and particularly a departure by nationalised industry*—imposes an intolerable burden on everyone and is directly responsible for anything that may go wrong in the economy as a whole. This campaign is remarkably successful. The second move is to suggest that since there is really nothing special at all in the behaviour of nationalised industry, and hence no promise of any progress towards a better society, any further nationalisation would be an obvious case of dogmatic inflexibility, a mere "grab" organised by frustrated politicians, untaught, unteachable, and incapable of intellectual doubt. This neat little plan has all the more chance of success if it can be supported by a governmental price policy for the products of the nationalised industries which makes it virtually impossible for them to earn a profit.

It must be admitted that this strategy, aided by a systematic smear campaign against the nationalised industries, has not been without effect on socialist thinking.

The reason is neither an error in the original socialist inspiration nor any actual failure in the conduct of the nationalised industry—accusations of that kind are quite insupportable—but a lack of vision on the part of the socialists themselves. They will not recover, and nationalisation will not fulfill its function, unless they recover their vision.

What is at stake is not economics but culture; not the standard of living but the quality of life. Economics and the standard of living can just as well be looked after by a capitalist system, moderated by a bit of planning and redistributive taxation. But culture and, generally, the quality of life, can now only be debased by such a system.

Socialists should insist on using the nationalised industries not simply to out-capitalise the capitalists—an attempt in which they

It is now abundantly demonstrated that neither the capitalist nor the state socialist economies can create viable conditions for the people of the world, nor have they been able to help developing countries to determine their own destinies. Capitalism is able to create an abundance of goods and services, but only by undermining future resources, creating increasing pollution, widening the gap between rich and poor, and unhealthily concentrating wealth and power in fewer hands. The statement "living off the future inheritance of our children" sums it up. Endeavors through regulatory forces or wider shareholding in ever-larger corporations are largely ineffective.
—GODRIC BADER

may or may not succeed—but to evolve a more democratic and dignified system of industrial administration, a more humane employment of machinery, and a more intelligent utilisation of the fruits of human ingenuity and effort. If they can do that, they have the future in their hands. If they cannot, they have nothing to offer that is worthy of the sweat of free-born men.

CHAPTER 18

OWNERSHIP

IT IS OBVIOUS, indeed, that no change of system or machinery can avert those causes of social *malaise* which consist in the egotism, greed, or quarrelsomeness of human nature. What it can do is to create an environment in which those are not the qualities which are encouraged. It cannot secure that men live up to their principles. What it can do is to establish their social order upon principles to which, if they please, they can live up and not live down. It cannot control their actions. It can offer them an end on which to fix their minds. And, as their minds are, so in the long run and with exceptions, their practical activity will be.

These words of R.H. Tawney were written many decades ago. They have lost nothing of their topicality, except that today we are concerned not only with social *malaise* but also, most urgently, with a *malaise* of the ecosystem or biosphere which threatens the very survival of the human race. Every problem touched upon in the preceding chapters leads to the question of "system or machinery," although, as I have argued all along, no system or machinery or economic doctrine or theory stands on its own feet: it is invariably built on a metaphysical foundation, that is to say, upon man's basic outlook on life, its meaning and its purpose. I have talked about the religion of economics, the idol worship of material possessions, of consumption and the so-called standard of living, and the fateful propensity that rejoices in the fact that "what were luxuries to our fathers have become necessities for us."

In March 1977, Schumacher visited The Land Institute at Salina, Kansas, a fledgling organization scarcely six months old with little to show the distinguished visitor, whose philosophy most inspired our establishment. We had arranged for this widely acclaimed author to give a public lecture in the Salina Community Theatre. To a full auditorium, he began by telling a story of a trip he had made during the 1930s with some friends, an automobile trip across America that included passage through Kansas.

They had stopped at a service station in a small Kansas town at the height of the Great Depression. Fritz engaged a local man at the station by asking, "How are things?"

"Fine," the local replied.

"What is it you do?" asked Fritz. ➡

→ *"Oh, I work on that farm
over there," he said pointing.
"I used to own that farm but
I had no money to pay the
hired hand, so I paid him in
land. Eventually he owned all
of my farm and now I work
for him."*

*"That's a very sad story,"
replied Fritz.*

*"Well, not so sad," replied
the hired hand. "He has no
money either and so he is
paying me back in land."*

—WES JACKSON

Systems are never more nor less than incarnations of man's most basic attitudes. Some incarnations, indeed, are more perfect than others. General evidence of material progress would suggest that the *modern* private enterprise system is—or has been—the most perfect instrument for the pursuit of personal enrichment. The *modern* private enterprise system ingeniously employs the human urges of greed and envy as its motive power, but manages to overcome the most blatant deficiencies of *laissez-faire* by means of Keynesian economic management, a bit of redistributive taxation, and the "countervailing power" of the trade unions.

Can such a system conceivably deal with the problems we are now having to face? The answer is self-evident: greed and envy demand continuous and limitless economic growth of a material kind, without proper regard for conservation, and this type of growth cannot possibly fit into a finite environment. We must therefore study the essential nature of the private enterprise system and the possibilities of evolving an alternative system which might fit the new situation.

The essence of private enterprise is the private ownership of the means of production, distribution, and exchange. Not surprisingly, therefore, the critics of private enterprise had advocated and in many cases successfully enforced the conversion of private ownership into so-called public or collective ownership. Let us look, first of all at the meaning of "ownership" or "property."

As regards private property, the first and most basic distinction is between (a) property that is an aid to creative work and (b) property that is an alternative to it. There is something natural and healthy about the former—the private property of the working proprietor; and there is something unnatural and unhealthy about the latter—the private property of the passive owner who lives parasitically on the work of others. This basic distinction was clearly seen by Tawney, who followed that "it is idle, therefore, to present a case for or against private property without specifying the particular forms of property to which reference is made."

For it is not private ownership, but private ownership divorced from work, which is corrupting to the principle of industry; and the idea of some socialists that private property in land or capital is necessarily mischievous is a piece of scholastic pedantry as absurd as that of those conservatives who would invest all property with some kind of mysterious sanctity.

Private enterprise carried on with property of the first category is automatically small-scale, personal, and local. It carries no wider social responsibilities. Its responsibilities to the consumer can be safeguarded by the consumer himself. Social legislation and trade union vigilance can protect the employee. No great private fortunes can be gained from small-scale enterprises, yet its social utility is enormous.

It is immediately apparent that in this matter of private owner-ship the question of scale is decisive. When we move from small-scale to medium-scale, the connection between ownership and work already becomes attenuated; private enterprise tends to be-come impersonal and also a significant social factor in the locality; it may even assume more than local significance. The very idea of *private property* becomes increasingly misleading.

1. The owner, employing salaried managers, does not need to be a proprietor to be able to do his work. His ownership, therefore, ceases to be functionally necessary. It becomes ex-ploitative if he appropriates profit in excess of a fair salary to himself and a return on his capital no higher than current rates for capital borrowed from outside sources.
2. High profits are either fortuitous or they are the achieve-ment not of the owner but of the whole organisation. It is therefore unjust and socially disruptive if they are appropri-ated by the owner alone. They should be shared with all members of the organisation. If they are "ploughed back" they should be "free capital" collectively owned, instead of accruing automatically to the wealth of the original owner.
3. Medium size, leading to impersonal relationships, poses new questions as to the exercise of control. Even autocratic control is no serious problem in small-scale enterprise which, led by a working proprietor, has almost a family char-acter. It is incompatible with human dignity and genuine

All economies are a mixture of public and private owner-ship, which is based on an underlying cultural DNA code that is the values and goals of the citizens of a society. In the United States, an example of public/private ownership is the Internet, which was funded by U.S. taxpayers and would not have happened otherwise. The Internet has become a platform in this country for private companies to tap an enormous amount of subsi-dized growth, which is still untaxed. One of the very contentious issues over the next few years will be whether to continue the subsidizing of Internet-based companies and electronic commerce to the detriment of brick and mortar, local businesses and local tax bases.

—HAZEL HENDERSON

*The issue today goes beyond
principles of ownership to
rechartering corporations.
Corporate charters were once
based on an implicit social
contract that they operate
for the public good, which
has been forgotten. We
don't have to look hard to
notice the public harm of
allowing corporations to
have all of the freedoms of
an individual without any
of the responsibilities.*
—HAZEL HENDERSON

efficiency when the enterprise exceeds a certain—very mod-est—size. There is need, then, for the conscious and systematic development of communications and consultation to allow all members of the organisation some degree of genuine participation in management.

4. The social significance and weight of the firm in its locality and its wider ramifications call for some degree of "socialisation of ownership" beyond the members of the firm itself. This "socialisation" may be effected by regularly devoting a part of the firm's profits to public or charitable purposes and bringing in trustees from outside.

There are private enterprise firms in the United Kingdom and other capitalist countries which have carried these ideas into successful practice and have thereby overcome the objectionable and socially disruptive features which are inherent in the private ownership of the means of production when extended beyond small-scale. Scott Bader & Co. Ltd., at Wollaston in Northamptonshire, is one of them. A more detailed description of their experiences and experimentation will be given in a later chapter.

When we come to large-scale enterprises, the idea of private ownership becomes an absurdity. The property is not and cannot be private in any real sense. Again, R.H. Tawney saw this with complete clarity:

> Such property may be called passive property, or property for acquisition, for exploitation, or for power, to distinguish it from the property which is actively used by its owner for the conduct of his profession or the upkeep of his household. To the lawyer the first is, of course, as fully property as the second. It is questionable, however, whether economists should call it "property" at all...since it is not identical with the rights which secure the owner the produce of his toil, but is the opposite of them.

The so-called private ownership of large-scale enterprises is in no way analogous to the simple property of the small landowner, craftsman, or entrepreneur. It is, as Tawney says, analogous to "the feudal dues which robbed the French peasant of part of his produce till the revolution abolished them."

All these rights—royalties, ground-rents, monopoly profits, surpluses of all kinds—are "property." The criticism most fatal to them...is contained in the arguments by which property is usually defended. The meaning of the institution, it is said, is to encourage industry by securing that the worker shall receive the produce of his toil. But then, precisely in proportion as it is important to preserve the property which a man has in the results of his labour, is it important to abolish that which he has in the results of the labour of someone else.

To sum up:

1. In small-scale enterprise, private ownership is natural, fruitful, and just.
2. In medium-scale enterprise, private ownership is already to a large extent functionally unnecessary. The idea of "property" becomes strained, unfruitful, and unjust. If there is only one owner or a small group of owners, there can be, and should be, a voluntary surrender of privilege to the wider group of actual workers—as in the case of Scott Bader & Co. Ltd. Such an act of generosity may be unlikely when there is a large number of anonymous shareholders, but legislation could pave the way even then.
3. In large-scale enterprise, private ownership is a fiction for the purpose of enabling functionless owners to live parasitically on the labour of others. It is not only unjust but also an irrational element which distorts all relationships within the enterprise. To quote Tawney again:

If every member of a group puts something into a common pool on condition of taking something out, they may still quarrel about the size of the shares...but, if the total is

In public talks and private discussions, Schumacher often pondered "the land question." An economic system that treats land as a commodity to be bought and sold on the market fails to foster the respect for land necessary to encourage its proper use. When an individual is allowed private ownership of a limited natural resource, that individual has an unfair economic advantage. The scarcity of arable land and a growing demand for its use result in an increase in the value of the land through no effort on the part of the landowner.

This potential for speculative gain places tremendous pressure on the landowner to maximize the dollar value of the land through excessive development and erodes the landowner's commitment to community and place. A further result of the ability to make land a commodity is that a community's capital is tied up in land. Credit for ➥

➡ *the small-business owner tightens. The region loses its diversity of enterprises, which is the basis of a more sustainable economy and a more environmentally responsible business sector.*

—ROBERT SWANN

known and the claims are admitted, that is all they can quarrel about. . . . But in industry the claims are not all admitted, for those who put nothing in demand to take something out.

There are many methods of doing away with so-called private ownership in large-scale enterprise; the most prominent one is generally referred to as "nationalisation."

But nationalisation is a word which is neither very felicitous nor free from ambiguity. Properly used it means merely ownership by a body representing . . . the general public of consumers. . . . No language possesses a vocabulary to express neatly the finer shades in the numerous possible varieties of organisation under which a public service may be carried on.

The result has been that the singularly colourless word "nationalisation" almost inevitably tends to be charged with a highly specialised and quite arbitrary body of suggestions. It has come in practice to be used as equivalent to a particular method of administration, under which officials employed by the State step into the position of the present directors of industry and exercise all the power which they exercised. So those who desire to maintain the system under which industry is carried on, not as a profession serving the public, but for the advantage of shareholders, attack nationalisation on the ground that State management is necessarily inefficient.

A number of large industries have been "nationalised" in Britain. They have demonstrated the obvious truth that the quality of an industry depends on the people who run it and not on absentee owners. Yet the nationalised industries, in spite of their great achievements, are still being pursued by the implacable hatred of certain privileged groups. The incessant propaganda against them tends to mislead even people who do not share the hatred and ought to know better. Private enterprise spokesmen never tire of asking for more "accountability" of nationalised industries. This may be thought to be somewhat ironic—since the accountability of these enterprises, which work solely in the public interest, is already very highly developed, while that of private industry, *which works avowedly for private profit,* is practically non-existent.

Ownership is not a single right, but a bundle of rights. "Nationalisation" is not a matter of simply transferring this bundle of rights from A to B, that is to say, from private persons to "the State," whatever that may mean: it is a matter of making precise choices as to where the various rights of the bundle are to be placed, all of which, before nationalisation, were deemed to belong to the so-called private owner. Tawney, therefore, says succinctly: "Nationalisation [is] a problem of Constitution-making." Once the legal device of private property has been removed, there is freedom to arrange everything anew—to amalgamate or to dissolve, to centralise or to decentralise, to concentrate power or to diffuse it, to create large units or small units, a unified system, a federal system, or no system at all. As Tawney put it:

> The objection to public ownership, in so far as it is intelligent, is in reality largely an objection to overcentralisation. But the remedy for overcentralisation is not the maintenance of functionless property in private hands, but the decentralised ownership of public property.

"Nationalisation" extinguishes private proprietary rights but does not, by itself, create any new "ownership" in the existential—as distinct from the legal—sense of the word. Nor does it, by itself, determine what is to become of the original ownership rights and who is to exercise them. It is therefore in a sense a purely negative measure which annuls previous arrangements and creates the opportunity and necessity to make new ones. These new arrangements made possible through "nationalisation," must of course fit the needs of each particular case. A number of principles may, however, be observed in all cases of nationalised enterprises providing public services.

First, it is dangerous to mix business and politics. Such a mixing normally produces inefficient business and corrupt politics.

The forces of multinational businesses are rapacious in forest destruction, decimation of fish stocks, and the earth's raw material resources. Nonetheless, if human life is to continue and become sustainable, the irreversible violation and degradation of our water, soil, flora, and fauna has to stop, and the adoption of the trusteeship principle on a local basis has to be inaugurated urgently on a global scale. Every country is now involved. I believe that trusteeship is the only viable way out of these impasses for either the developed or developing countries on any kind of sustainable basis.
—GODRIC BADER

The nationalisation act, therefore, should in every case carefully enumerate and define the rights, if any, which the political side, e.g. the minister or any other organ of government, or parliament, can exercise over the business side, that is to say, the board of management. This is of particular importance with regard to appointments.

Second, nationalised enterprises providing public services should always aim at a profit—in the sense of eating to live, not living to eat—and should build up reserves. They should never distribute profits to anyone, not even to the government. Excessive profits—and that means the building up of excessive reserves—should be avoided by reducing prices.

Third, nationalised enterprises, nonetheless, should have a statutory obligation "to serve the public interest in all respects." The interpretation of what is the "public interest" must be left to the enterprise itself, which must be structured accordingly. It is useless to pretend that the nationalised enterprise should be concerned only with profits, as if it worked for private shareholders, while the interpretation of the public interest could be left to government alone. This idea has unfortunately invaded the theory of how to run nationalised industries in Britain, so that these industries are expected to work only for profit and to deviate from this principle only if instructed by government to do so and compensated by government for doing so. This tidy division of functions may commend itself to theoreticians but has no merit in the real world, for it destroys the very ethos of management within the nationalised industries. "Serving the public interest in all respects" means nothing unless it permeates the everyday behaviour of management, and this cannot and should not be controlled, let alone financially compensated, by government. That there may be occasional conflicts between profit-seeking and serving the public interest cannot be denied. But this simply means that the task of running a nationalised industry makes higher demands than that of running private enterprise. The idea that a better society could be achieved without making higher demands is self-contradictory and chimerical.

Fourth, to enable the "public interest" to be recognised and to be safeguarded in nationalised industries, there is need for arrangements by which all legitimate interests can find expression and exercise influence, namely, those of the employees, the local community, the consumers, and also the competitors, particularly if the last-named are themselves nationalised industries. To implement this principle effectively still requires a good deal of experimentation. No perfect "models" are available anywhere. The problem is always one of safeguarding these interests without unduly impairing management's ability to manage.

Finally, the chief danger to nationalisation is the planner's addiction to overcentralisation. In general, small enterprises are to be preferred to large ones. Instead of creating a large enterprise by nationalisation—as has invariably been the practice hitherto—and then attempting to decentralise power and responsibility to smaller formations, it is normally better to create semi-autonomous small units first and then to centralise certain functions at a higher level, *if* the need for better coordination can be shown to be paramount.

No one has seen and understood these matters better than R.H. Tawney, and it is therefore fitting to close this chapter with yet another quotation from him:

> So the organisation of society on the basis of functions, instead of on that of rights, implies three things. It means, first, that proprietary rights shall be maintained when they are accompanied by the performance of service and abolished when they are not. It means, second, that the producers shall stand in a direct relation to the community for whom production is carried on, so that their responsibility to it may be obvious and unmistakable, not lost, as at present, through their immediate subordination to shareholders whose interest is not service but gain. It means, in the third place, that the obligation for the maintenance of the service shall rest upon the professional organisations of those who perform it, and that, subject to the supervision and criticism of the consumer, those organisations shall exercise so much voice in the government of industry as may be needed to secure that the obligation is discharged.

CHAPTER 19

NEW PATTERNS OF OWNERSHIP

We do not yet know what combination of social forces brought down the Berlin Wall, and the de-legitimatized communist structures in Eastern Bloc countries. Maybe similar forces will de-legitimatize the unacceptable faces of capitalism and exploitation. I would like to believe that the forces developing trusteeship principles will be paramount in transforming industrial society in the next century.

—GODRIC BADER

J.K. GALBRAITH has spoken of private affluence and public squalor. It is significant that he referred to the United States, reputedly, and in accordance with conventional measurements, the richest country in the world. How could there be public squalor in the richest country, and, in fact, much more of it than in many other countries whose Gross National Product, adjusted for size of population, is markedly smaller? If economic growth to the present American level has been unable to get rid of public squalor—or, maybe, has even been accompanied by its increase—how could one reasonably expect that further "growth" would mitigate or remove it? How is it to be explained that, by and large, the countries with the highest growth rates tend to be the most polluted and also to be afflicted by public squalor to an altogether astonishing degree? If the Gross National Product of the United Kingdom grew by, say, five per cent—or about £2,000 million a year—could we then use all or most of this money, this additional wealth, to "fulfill our nation's aspirations"?

Assuredly not; for under private ownership every bit of wealth, as it arises, is immediately and automatically *privately* appropriated. The public authorities have hardly any income of their own and are reduced to extracting from the pockets of their citizens monies which the citizens consider to be rightfully their own. Not surprisingly, this leads to an endless battle of wits between tax collectors and citizens, in which the rich, with the help of highly paid tax experts, normally do very much better than the poor. In an effort to stop "loopholes" the tax laws become ever more complicated and the demand for—and therefore the income of—tax consultants becomes ever larger. As the taxpayers feel that something they have earned is being taken away from them, they not only try to exploit every possibility of legal tax avoidance, not to mention practices of illegal tax evasion, they also raise an insistent cry in favour of the curtailment of public expenditure. "More taxation for more public expenditure" would not be a vote-catching slogan in an election campaign, no matter how glaring may be the discrepancy between private affluence and public squalor.

There is no way out of this dilemma unless the need for public expenditure is recognised in the structure of ownership of the means of production.

It is not merely a question of public squalor, such as the squalor of many mental homes, of prisons, and of countless other publicly maintained services and institutions; this is the negative side of the problem. The positive side arises where large amounts of public funds have been and are being spent on what is generally called the "infrastructure," and the benefits go largely to private enterprise free of charge. This is well known to anyone who has ever been involved in starting or running an enterprise in a poor society where the "infrastructure" is insufficiently developed or altogether lacking. He cannot rely on cheap transport and other public services; he may have to provide at his own expense many things which he would obtain free or at small expense in a society with a highly developed infrastructure; he cannot count on being able to recruit trained people: he has to train them himself; and so on. All the educational, medical, and research institutions in any society, whether rich or poor, bestow incalculable benefits upon private enterprise—benefits for which private enterprise does not pay *directly* as a matter of course, but only indirectly by way of taxes, which, as already mentioned, are resisted, resented, campaigned against, and often skillfully avoided. It is highly illogical and leads to endless complications and mystifications, that payment for benefits obtained by private enterprise from the "infrastructure" cannot be exacted by the public authorities by a direct participation in profits but only

The principles of the Scott Bader Companies worldwide are developed from our core values embodied in our constitution and founding charter and reflect in our reputation. The values formed the covenant under which the company was entrusted to all employees who qualify for membership. We are thereby committed to develop a radical company, founded upon trust, structured to be a fundamentally co-operative enterprise, eliminating social injustice.

The sustainability of all Scott Bader Companies relies on upholding our reputation for honesty, integrity, service, and quality in all our transactions. We conduct our business by making decisions ethically, managing resources effectively, showing respect to all with whom we come into contact, and not discriminating on grounds of gender, race, age, or religion— recognizing the dignity of all as human beings. ➡

after the private appropriation of profits has taken place. Private enterprise claims that its profits are being earned by its own efforts, and that a substantial part of them is then taxed away by public authorities. This is not a correct reflection of the truth—generally speaking. The truth is that a large part of the costs of private enterprise has been borne by the public authorities—because *they* pay for the infrastructure—and that the profits of private enterprise therefore greatly overstate its achievement.

There is no practical way of reflecting the true situation, unless the contribution of public expenditure to the profits of private enterprise is recognised in the structure of ownership of the means of production.

I shall therefore now present two examples of how the structure of ownership can—or could—be changed so as to meet the two fundamental criticisms made above. The first example is of a medium-sized firm which is actually operating on a reformed basis of ownership. The second example is a speculative plan of how the structure of ownership of large-scale firms could be reformed.

THE SCOTT BADER COMMONWEALTH

Ernest Bader started the enterprise of Scott Bader Co. Ltd. in 1920, at the age of thirty. Thirty-one years later, after many trials and tribulations during the war, he had a prosperous medium-scale business employing 161 people, with a turnover of about £625,000 a year and net profits exceeding £72,000. Having started with virtually nothing, he and his family had become prosperous. His firm had established itself as a leading producer of polyester resins and also manufactured other sophisticated products, such as alkyds, polymers, and plasticisers. As a young man he had been deeply dissatisfied with his prospects of life as an employee; he had resented the very ideas of a "labour market" and a "wages system," and particularly the thought that capital employed men, instead of men employing capital. Finding himself now in the position of employer, he never forgot that his success and prosperity were the achievements not of himself alone but of all his collaborators and

decidedly also of the society within which he was privileged to operate. To quote his own words:

> I realised that—as years ago when I took the plunge and
> ceased to be an employee—I was up against the capitalist
> philosophy of dividing people into the managed on the one
> hand, and those that manage on the other. The real obstacle,
> however, was Company Law, with its provisions for dictator-
> ial powers of shareholders and the hierarchy of manage-
> ment they control.

He decided to introduce "revolutionary changes" in his firm,
"based on a philosophy which attempts to fit industry to human
needs."

> The problem was twofold: (1) how to organise or combine a
> maximum sense of freedom, happiness and human dignity
> in our firm without loss of profitability, and (2) to do this by
> ways and means that could be generally acceptable to the pri-
> vate sector of industry.

Mr. Bader realised at once that no *decisive* changes could be
made without two things: first, a transformation of ownership—
mere profit-sharing, which he had practised from the very start, was
not enough; and, second, the voluntary acceptance of certain self-
denying ordinances. To achieve the first, he set up the Scott Bader
Commonwealth in which he vested (in two steps: ninety per cent in
1951 and the remaining ten per cent in 1963) the ownership of his
firm, Scott Bader Co. Ltd. To implement the second, he agreed with
his new partners, that is to say, the members of the Commonwealth, his former employees, to establish a *constitution* not only to
define the distribution of the "bundle of powers" which private
ownership implies, but also to impose the following restrictions on
the firm's freedom of action:

> *First,* the firm shall remain an undertaking of limited
> size, so that every person in it can embrace it in his mind and

➡ We understand the key
importance of providing the
necessary education so that
the qualities of trust, open-
ness, involvement, and
sharing with those less fortunate are developed in our
worldwide community. We
are a learning enterprise,
committed to personal development, raising the awareness in ourselves and others
to our spiritual potential.
 We believe through
increasing understanding
everyone will recognize the
benefits of building and living
in a more peaceful, intelligent society.
—GODRIC BADER

We have pretty well kept to 350 persons or thereabouts in Wollaston. We are developing companies in other countries that we hope eventually will practice our principles.

At the 1986 general meeting, we voted (albeit by a narrow margin) to drop the fixed pay ratio in favor of the community council deciding whether the highest pay is excessive in relation to the lowest. This happened mainly by pressure of management to adopt comparative market rates for jobs to be able to recruit people with necessary commercial and technical skills and knowledge for higher positions.

The board of the operating company remains accountable to members of the Commonwealth via the community council, the Commonwealth board, and general meetings. The community council has the right to confirm or initiate the removal of the company directors; and the Commonwealth board has the right of approving or removing ➡

imagination. It shall not grow beyond 350 persons or thereabouts. If circumstances appear to demand growth beyond this limit, they shall be met by helping to set up new, fully independent units organised along the lines of the Scott Bader Commonwealth.

Second, remuneration for work within the organisation shall not vary, as between the lowest paid and the highest paid, irrespective of age, sex, function or experience, beyond a range of 1:7, before tax.

Third, as the members of the Commonwealth are partners and not employees, they cannot be dismissed by their co-partners for any reason other than gross personal misconduct. They can, of course, leave voluntarily at any time, giving due notice.

Fourth, the Board of Directors of the firm, Scott Bader Co. Ltd., shall be fully accountable to the Commonwealth. Under the rules laid down in the Constitution, the Commonwealth has the right and duty to confirm or withdraw the appointment of directors and also to agree to their level of remuneration.

Fifth, not more than forty per cent of the net profits of Scott Bader Co. Ltd. shall be appropriated by the Commonwealth—a minimum of sixty per cent being retained for taxation and for self-finance within Scott Bader Co. Ltd.—and the Commonwealth shall devote one-half of the appropriated profits to the payment of bonuses to those working within the operating company and the other half to charitable purposes outside the Scott Bader organisation.

And finally, none of the products of Scott Bader Co. Ltd. shall be sold to customers who are known to use them for war-related purposes.

When Mr. Ernest Bader and his colleagues introduced these revolutionary changes, it was freely predicted that a firm operating on this basis of collectivised ownership and self-imposed restrictions could not possibly survive. In fact, it went from strength to strength, although difficulties, even crises and setbacks, were by no means absent. In the highly competitive setting within which the firm is operating, it has, between 1951 and 1971, increased its sales from £625,000 to £5 million; net profits have grown from £72,000 to nearly £300,000 a year; total staff has increased from 161 to 379; bonuses amounting to over £150,000 (over the twenty-year period) have been distributed to the staff, and an equal amount has been donated by the Commonwealth to charitable purposes outside; and several small new firms have been set up.

Anyone who wishes to do so can claim that the commercial success of Scott Bader Co. Ltd. was probably due to "exceptional circumstances." There are, moreover, conventional private enterprise firms which have been equally successful or even more so. But this is not the point. If Scott Bader Co. Ltd. had been a commercial failure after 1951, it could serve only as an awful warning; its undeniable success, as measured by conventional standards, does not *prove* that the Bader "system" is necessarily superior by these standards: it merely demonstrates that it is not incompatible with them. Its merit lies precisely in the attainment of objectives which lie outside the commercial standards, of *human* objectives which are generally assigned a second place or altogether neglected by ordinary commercial practice. In other words, the Bader "system" overcomes the *reductionism* of the private ownership system and uses industrial organisation as a servant of man, instead of allowing it to use men simply as means to the enrichment of the owners of capital. To quote Ernest Bader:

> Common Ownership or *Commonwealth,* is a natural development from Profit Sharing, Co-Partnership or Co-Ownership, or any scheme where individuals hold sectional interests in a common enterprise. They are on the way to owning things in common, and, as we shall see, Common-Ownership has unique advantages.

While I do not intend to go into the details of the long evolution of ideas and new styles of management and co-operation during the more than twenty years since 1951, it is useful here to crystallise out of this experience certain general principles.

➡ *membership of the Commonwealth. However, management pressure has ensured that these responsibilities are only timidly exercised.*

Profit distribution remains as originally conceived and has settled down recently to 90 percent plow back, five percent to employees, and five percent to charity. We did, however, under some management pressure take advantage of a government scheme for an element of tax-free profit-related pay. This will stop next year and we will have to reconsider the original principle that any surplus profit should be distributed equally to all members with an equivalent sum for charitable and social projects.

We have continued our embargo on supplying materials for war-related purposes, but we have supplied resins for defensive applications such as minesweepers and riot shields, such as for Northern Ireland.
—GODRIC BADER

There are a number of myths surrounding economic globalization. Perhaps foremost among these myths is the idea that globalization is the result of natural evolution. In fact, there is nothing natural or inevitable about the process of globalization. It is the result of human policy choices. Globalization is being driven by "free trade" agreements, government policies, and direct and indirect subsidies to big business. Taxpayers' money is being systematically directed toward creating an economic framework that favors large-scale production and long-distance distribution over more human-scale, culturally sensitive, and environmentally benign economic activities.

It is often said that globalization is being driven by technological advances. What is rarely mentioned is that technology is not neutral, but is itself shaped by economic policy. The clear implication of this is that ⇒

The first is that the transfer of ownership from a person or a family—in this case the Bader family—to a collectivity, the Commonwealth, changes the existential character of "ownership" in so fundamental a way that it would be better to think of such a transfer as effecting the *extinction* of private ownership rather than as establishment of collective ownership. The relationship between one person, or a very small number of persons, and a certain assembly of physical assets is quite different from that between a Commonwealth, comprising a large number of persons, and these same physical assets. Not surprisingly, a drastic change in the *quantity* of owners produces a profound change in the *quality* of the meaning of ownership, and this is so particularly when, as in the case of Scott Bader, ownership is vested in a collectivity, the Commonwealth, and no individual ownership rights of individual Commonwealth members are established. At Scott Bader, it is legally correct to say that the operating company, Scott Bader Co. Ltd., is owned by the Commonwealth; but it is neither legally nor existentially true to say that the Commonwealth members, as individuals, establish any kind of ownership in the Commonwealth. In truth, ownership has been replaced by specific rights and responsibilities in the administration of assets.

Second, while no one has *acquired* any property, Mr. Bader and his family have nonetheless deprived themselves of their property. They have voluntarily abandoned the chance of becoming inordinately rich. Now, one does not have to be a believer in total equality, whatever that may mean, to be able to see that the existence of inordinately rich people in any society today is a very great evil. Some inequalities of wealth and income are no doubt "natural" and functionally justifiable, and there are few people who do not spontaneously recognise this. But here again, as in all human affairs, it is a matter of scale. Excessive wealth, like power, tends to corrupt. Even if the rich are not "idle rich," even when they work harder than anyone else, they work differently, apply different standards, and are set apart from common humanity. They corrupt themselves by practising greed, and they corrupt the rest of society by provoking envy. Mr. Bader drew the consequences of these insights and refused to become inordinately rich and thus made it possible to build a real *community*.

Third, while the Scott Bader experiment demonstrates with the utmost clarity that a transformation of ownership is essential—without it everything remains make-believe—it also demonstrates that the transformation of ownership is merely, so to speak, an enabling act: it is a necessary, but not a sufficient, condition for the attainment of higher aims. The Commonwealth, accordingly, recognised that the tasks of a business organisation in society are not simply to make profits and to maximise profits and to grow and to become powerful: the Commonwealth recognised four tasks, all of equal importance:

(A) The economic task: to secure orders which can be designed, made, and serviced in such a manner as to make a profit.
(B) The technical task: to enable marketing to secure profitable orders by keeping them supplied with up-to-date product design.
(C) The social task: to provide members of the company with opportunities for satisfaction and development through their participation in the working community.
(D) The political task: to encourage other men and women to change society by offering them an example by being economically healthy and socially responsible.

Fourth: it is the fulfillment of the social task which presents both the greatest challenge and the greatest difficulties. In the twenty-odd years of its existence, the Commonwealth has gone through several phases of constitution-making, and we believe that, with the new constitution of 1971, it has now evolved a set of "organs" which enable the Commonwealth to perform a feat which looks hardly less impossible than that of squaring the circle, namely, to combine real democracy with efficient management. I refrain here from drawing diagrams of the Scott Bader organisation to show—on paper—how the various "organs" are meant to relate to one another; for the living reality cannot be depicted on paper, nor can it

➡ *nation-states and their citizens have power to regain control of the economic juggernaut and create a new financial and economic "architecture" directed toward human-scale economies and the maintenance and promotion of cultural and biological diversity.*

—HELENA
NORBERG-HODGE

be achieved by copying paper models. To quote Mr. Ernest Bader himself:

> I would very much prefer to take any interested person on a tour of our forty-five-acre, ancient Manor House Estate, interspersed with chemical plants and laboratories, than to laboriously write [an] article which is bound to raise as many questions as it answers.

The evolution of the Scott Bader organisation has been—and continues to be—*a learning process,* and the essential meaning of what has been happening there since 1951 is that it has enabled everyone connected with Scott Bader to learn and practise many things which go far beyond the task of making a living, of earning a salary, of helping a business to make a profit, of acting in an economically rational manner "so that we shall all be better off." Within the Scott Bader organisation, everybody has the opportunity of raising himself to a higher level of humanity, not by pursuing, privately and individualistically, certain aims of self-transcendence which have nothing to do with the aims of the firm—*that* he is able to do in any setting, even the most degraded—but by, as it were, freely and cheerfully gearing in with the aims of the organisation itself. This has to be learned, and the learning process takes time. Most, but not all, of the people who joined Scott Bader have responded, and are responding, to the opportunity.

Finally, it can be said that the arrangement by which one-half of the appropriated profits must be devoted to charitable purposes outside the organisation has not only helped to further many causes which capitalist society tends to neglect—in work with the young, the old, the handicapped, and the forgotten people—it has also served to give Commonwealth members a social consciousness and awareness rarely found in any business organisation of the conventional kind. In this connection, it is also worth mentioning that provision has been made to ensure, as far as possible, that the Commonwealth should not become an organisation in which individual selfishness is transformed into group selfishness. A Board of Trustees has been set up, somewhat in the position of a constitutional monarch, in which personalities from outside the Scott Bader organisation play a decisive role. The Trustees are trustees of the constitution, without power to interfere with management. They are, however, able and entitled to arbitrate, if there should arise a serious conflict on fundamental issues between the democratic and the functional organs of the organisation.

As mentioned at the beginning of this account, Mr. Ernest Bader set out to make "revolutionary changes" in his firm, but *"to do this by ways and means that could be generally acceptable to the private sector of industry."* His revolution has been bloodless; no one has come to grief, not even Mr. Bader or his family; with plenty of strikes all around them, the Scott Bader people can proudly claim: "We have no strikes"; and while no one inside is unaware of the gap that still exists between the aims of the Commonwealth and its current achievements, no outside observer could fairly disagree when Ernest Bader claims that:

> the experience gained during many years of effort to establish the Christian way of life in our business has been a great encouragement; it has brought us good results in our relations with one another, as well as in the quality and quantity of our production.
>
> Now we wish to press on and consummate what we have so far achieved, making a concrete contribution toward a better society in the service of God and our fellowmen.

And yet, although Mr. Bader's quiet revolution *should be* "generally acceptable to the private sector of industry," it has, in fact, not been accepted. There are thousands of people, even in the business world, who look at the trend of current affairs and ask for a "new dispensation." But Scott Bader—and a few others—remain as small islands of sanity in a large society ruled by greed and envy. It seems to be true that, whatever evidence of a new way of doing things may be provided, "old dogs cannot learn new tricks." It is also true, however, that "new dogs" grow up all the time; and they will be well advised to take notice of *what has been shown to be possible* by The Scott Bader Commonwealth Ltd.

NEW METHODS OF SOCIALISATION

The community land trust concept offers a practical way to take land off the market and place it into a system of trusteeship on a region-by-region basis. The goods created by an individual as a result of labor applied to land—the harvest from a garden, the home built of wood from the forest, the sweater knit from spun wool—is rightfully private property and may appropriately be traded as commodities. However, the land itself and its resources, which are earth-given and of limited supply, should be held in trust by the regional community and their use allocated on a limited basis for present and future generations.

A community land trust is a not-for-profit organization with membership open to any resident of the geographical region or bioregion where it is located. A community land trust acquires land by gift or purchase and then develops a land-use plan for the parcel, identifying ➡

There appear to be three major choices for a society in which economic affairs necessarily absorb major attention—the choice between private ownership of the means of production and, alternatively, various types of public or collectivised ownership; the choice between a market economy and various arrangements of "planning"; and the choice between "freedom" and "totalitarianism." Needless to say, with regard to each of these three pairs of opposites there will always in reality be some degree of mixture—because they are to some extent complementaries rather than opposites—but the mixture will show a preponderance on the one side or on the other.

Now, it can be observed that those with a strong bias in favour of private ownership almost invariably tend to argue that non-private ownership inevitably and necessarily entails "planning" and "totalitarianism," while "freedom" is unthinkable except on the basis of private ownership and the market economy. Similarly, those in favour of various forms of collectivised ownership tend to argue, although not so dogmatically, that this necessarily demands central planning; freedom, they claim, can only be achieved by socialised ownership and planning, while the alleged freedom of private ownership and the market economy is nothing more than "freedom to dine at the Ritz and to sleep under the bridges of the Thames." In other words, everybody claims to achieve freedom by his own "system" and accuses every other "system" as inevitably entailing tyranny, totalitarianism, or anarchy leading to both.

The arguments along these lines generally generate more heat than light, as happens with all arguments which derive "reality" from a conceptual framework, instead of deriving a conceptual framework from reality. When there are three major alternatives, there are 2^3 or 8 possible combinations. It is always reasonable to expect that real life implements all possibilities—at one time or other, or even simultaneously in different places. The eight possible cases, as regards the three choices I have mentioned, are as follows (I arrange them under the aspect of freedom versus totalitarianism, because this is the major consideration from the metaphysical point of view taken in this book):

1. Freedom
   Market Economy
   Private Ownership
2. Freedom
   Planning
   Private Ownership
3. Freedom
   Market Economy
   Collectivised Ownership
4. Freedom
   Planning
   Collectivised Ownership
5. Totalitarianism
   Market Economy
   Private Ownership
6. Totalitarianism
   Planning
   Private Ownership
7. Totalitarianism
   Market Economy
   Collectivised Ownership
8. Totalitarianism
   Planning
   Collectivised Ownership

It is absurd to assert that the only "possible" cases are 1 and 8: these are merely the *simplest* cases from the point of view of concept-ridden propagandists. Reality, thank God, is more imaginative; but I shall leave it to the reader's diligence to identify actual or historical examples for each of the eight cases indicated above, and I should recommend to the teachers of political science that they suggest this exercise to their students.

My immediate purpose, here and now, is to speculate on the possibility of devising an ownership "system" for large-scale enterprise which would achieve a truly "mixed economy"; for it is "mixture" rather than "purity" which is most likely to suit the manifold exigencies of the future, if we are to start from the actual situation in the industrialised part of the world, rather than starting from zero, as if all options were still open.

I have already argued that private enterprise in a so-called advanced society derives very large benefits from the infrastructure—both visible and invisible—which such a society has built up through public expenditure. But the public hand, although it defrays a considerable part of the cost of private enterprise, does not directly participate in its profits; all these profits are initially privately appropriated, and the public hand then has to try to cover its own financial requirements by extracting a part of these profits from private pockets. The modern businessman never tires of claiming and complaining that, to a large extent, he "works for the state," that the state is his partner, inasmuch as profit taxes absorb a

➡ *which lands should remain forever wild and which should support low-impact development. The land trust then leases sites for the identified purposes. The lease runs for 99 years and is inheritable and renewable on the original terms. The leaseholder owns the buildings and any agricultural improvements on the land, but not the land itself. Upon resale, leaseholders are restricted to selling their buildings and improvements at current replacement cost, excluding the land's value from the transfer. The resale restriction ensures that the land will never again be capitalized and will provide affordable access to land for future generations. The land-use plan ensures that the resource base is maintained and enriched, not depleted. By restructuring our formal relationship to the land from one of owner to one of steward, a community land trust encourages proper long-term care for the land.*
—ROBERT SWANN

Since its inception in 1993, the Community Housing Land Trust Foundation (CHLTF) has explored ways to implement the land trust model in British Columbia, Canada. It finds properties already used for affordable housing where residents are threatened with rising rents and unstable tenure, then attempts to negotiate a discounted purchase price with the owner. Once purchased, the properties are offered on a long-term, nonprofit basis to residents. CHLTF supports housing co-ops, with their mixed income and diverse resident populations, and works with residents to establish housing co-ops where appropriate.

Property discounts are achieved in a variety of ways. CHLTF has approached the provincial government, who through the Lands Now policy, can discount lands up to 75 percent to support affordable housing. CHLTF also uses its charitable tax status as incentive to private property owners to discount the price of properties in ➡

substantial part of what he believes to be really due to him alone, or to his shareholders. This suggests that the public share of private profits—in other words, the company profits taxes—might just as well be converted into a public share of the *equity* of private business—in any case as far as large-scale enterprises are concerned.

For the following exposition I postulate that the public hand should receive one-half of the distributed profits of large-scale private enterprise, and that it should obtain this share not by means of profit taxes but by means of a fifty per cent ownership of the equity of such enterprises.

1. To begin with, the minimum size of enterprises to be included in the scheme must be defined. Since every business loses its private and personal character and becomes, in fact, a public enterprise once the number of its employees rises above a certain limit, minimum size is probably best defined in terms of persons employed. In special cases it may be necessary to define size in terms of capital employed or turnover.
2. All enterprises attaining this minimum size—or exceeding it already—must be joint-stock companies.
3. It would be desirable to transform all shares of these companies into no-par shares after the American pattern.
4. The number of shares issued, including preference shares and any other pieces of paper which represent *equity*, should be doubled by the issue of an equivalent number of new shares, these new shares to be held by "the public hand" so that for every privately held old share one new share with identical rights will be held publicly.

Under a scheme along these lines, no question of "compensation" would arise, because there would be no expropriation in the strict sense of the word, but only a conversion of the public hand's right to levy profit taxes into a direct participation in the economic assets from the use of which taxable profits are obtained. This conversion would be an explicit recognition of the undoubted fact that a major role in the creation of "private" economic wealth is in any case played by the public hand, that is to say, by non-capitalist social forces, and that the assets created by the public contribution should be recognised as public, and not private, property.

The questions that would immediately arise may be divided into three groups. First, what precisely is meant by the "public hand"? Where are the newly issued shares to be placed and who is to be the representative of the "public hand" in this context? Second, what rights of ownership should possession of these new shares carry? And, third, questions relating to the transition from the existing system to the new, to the treatment of international and other combines, to the raising of new capital, and so forth.

As regards the first set of questions, I should propose that the newly created shares, representing fifty per cent of the equity, should be held by a local body in the district where the enterprise in question is located. The purpose would be to maximise both the degree of decentralisation of public participation and the integration of business enterprises with the social organism within which they operate and from which they derive incalculable benefits. Thus, the half-share in the equity of a business operating within District X should be held by a local body generally representative of the population of District X. However, neither the locally elected (political) personalities nor the local civil servants are necessarily the most suitable people to be entrusted with the exercise of the rights associated with the new shares. Before we can go further into the question of personnel, we need to define these rights a little more closely.

I therefore turn to the second set of questions. In principle, the rights associated with ownership can always be divided into two groups—managerial rights and pecuniary rights.

I am convinced that, in normal circumstances, nothing would be gained and a great deal lost if a "public hand" were to interfere with or restrict the freedom of action and the fullness of responsibility of the existing business managements. The "private" managers of the enterprises should therefore remain fully in charge, while the managerial rights of the public half-share should remain dormant, unless and until special circumstances arise. That is to say, the publicly held shares would normally carry no voting rights

➡ *exchange for a charitable receipt. Working with municipalities and developers, CHLTF also seeks to be the steward of lands designated for affordable housing as specified in municipal affordable housing policies.*
—MARY FLYNN

but only the right to information and observation. The "public hand" would be entitled to place an observer—or several—on the Board of Directors of an enterprise, but the observer would not normally have any powers of decision. Only if the observer felt that the public interest demanded interference with the activities of the existing management, could he apply to a special *court* to have the dormant voting rights activated. A *prima facie* case in favour of interference would have to be established in front of the court, which would then activate the publicly held voting rights for a limited period. In this way, the managerial rights of ownership associated with the new, publicly owned equity shares would normally remain a mere possibility in the background and could become a reality only as a result of certain specific, formal, and public steps having been taken by the "public hand." And even when in exceptional cases these steps have been taken and the voting rights of the publicly owned shares have been activated, the new situation would persist only for a short time, so that there should be no doubt as to what was to be considered a normal or an abnormal division of functions.

It is often thought that "the public interest" can be safeguarded in the conduct of private business by delegating top or medium-grade civil servants into management. This belief, often a main plank in proposals for nationalisation, seems to me to be both naïve and impractical. It is not by dividing the responsibilities of management but by ensuring public accountability and transparency that business enterprises will be most effectively induced to pay more regard to the "public interest" than they do at present. The spheres of public administration on the one hand and of business enterprise on the other are poles apart—often even with regard to the remuneration and security offered—and only harm can result from trying to mix them.

While the managerial rights of ownership held by the "public hand" would therefore normally remain dormant, the pecuniary rights should be effective from the start and all the time—obviously so, since they take the place of the profits taxes that would otherwise be levied on the enterprise. One-half of all distributed profits would automatically go to the "public hand" which holds the new shares. The publicly owned shares, however, should be, in principle, inalienable (just as the right to levy profit taxes cannot be sold as if it were a capital asset). They could not be turned into cash; whether they could be used as collateral for public borrowings may be left for later consideration.

Having thus briefly sketched the rights and duties associated with the new shares, we can now return to the question of personnel. The general aim of the scheme is to integrate large-scale business enterprises as closely as possible with their social surroundings, and this aim must govern also our solution of the personnel question. The exercise of the pecuniary and managerial rights and duties arising from industrial ownership should certainly be kept out of party political controversy. At the same time, it should not fall to civil servants, who have been appointed for quite different purposes. I suggest, therefore, that it should belong to a special body of citizens which, for the purpose of this exposition, I shall call the "Social Council." This body should be formed locally along broadly fixed lines without political electioneering and without the assistance of any governmental authority, as follows: one-quarter of council members to be nominated by the local trade unions; one-quarter, by local professional associations; and one-quarter to be drawn from local residents in a manner similar to that employed for the selection of persons for jury service. Members would be appointed for, say, five years, with one-fifth of the membership retiring each year.

The Social Council would have legally defined but otherwise unrestricted rights and powers of action. It would, of course, be publicly responsible and obliged to publish reports of its proceedings. As a democratic safeguard, it might be considered desirable to give the existing Local Authority certain "reserve powers" *vis-à-vis* the Social Council, similar to those which the latter has *vis-à-vis* the managements of individual enterprises. That is to say, the Local Authority would be entitled to send its observer to the Social Council of its district and, in the event of serious conflict or dissatisfaction, to apply to an appropriate "court" for temporary powers of intervention. Here again, it should remain perfectly clear that such interventions would be the exception rather than the rule, and that in all normal circumstances the Social Council would possess full freedom of action.

We live in collapsing ecological and socio-economic systems based on developments since the Industrial Revolution that were motivated largely by gain and power. So it is not surprising that such systems are unable to reflect or sustain our true needs—purpose and identity. Trusteeship essentially means having faith and confidence in a process of taking responsibility for assets and social values and administering their rightful and creative usage for the benefit of others—now and in coming generations.

—GODRIC BADER

The Social Councils would have full control over the revenues flowing to them as dividends on the publicly held shares. General guiding principles with regard to the expenditure of these funds might have to be laid down by legislation; but they should insist on a high degree of local independence and responsibility. The immediate objection that the Social Councils could scarcely be relied upon to dispose of their funds in the best possible way provokes the obvious reply that neither could there be any guarantee of this if the funds were controlled by Local Authorities or, as generally at present, by Central Government. On the contrary, it would seem safe to assume that local Social Councils, being truly representative of the local community, would be far more concerned to devote resources to vital social needs than could be expected from local or central civil servants.

To turn now to our third set of questions. The transition from the present system to the one here proposed would present no serious difficulties. As mentioned already, no questions of compensation arise, because the half-share in equity is being "purchased" by the abolition of company profits taxes and all companies above a certain size are treated the same. The size definition can be set so that initially only a small number of very large firms is affected, so that the "transition" becomes both gradual and experimental. If large enterprises under the scheme would pay as dividends to the "public hand" a bit more than they would have paid as profit taxes outside the scheme, this would act as a socially desirable incentive to avoid excessive size.

It is worth emphasising that the conversion of profit tax into "equity share" significantly alters the psychological climate within which business decisions are taken. If profit taxes are at the level of (say) fifty per cent, the businessman is always tempted to argue that "the Exchequer will pay half" of all marginal expenditures which could possibly have been avoided. (The avoidance of such expenditure would increase profits; but half the profits would anyhow go as profit taxes.) The psychological climate is quite different when profit taxes have been abolished and a public equity share has been introduced in their place; for the knowledge that half the company's equity is publicly owned does not obscure the fact that *all* avoidable expenditures reduce profits by the exact amount of the expenditure.

Numerous questions would naturally arise in connection with companies which operate in many different districts, including international companies. But there can be no serious difficulties as long as two principles are firmly grasped: that profit tax is converted into "equity share," and that the involvement of the public hand shall be local, that is, in the locality where the company employees actually work, live, travel, and make use of public services of all kinds. No doubt, in complicated cases of interlocking company structures there will be interesting work for accountants and lawyers; but there should be no real difficulties.

How could a company falling under this scheme raise additional capital? The answer, again, is very simple: for every share issued to private shareholders, whether issued against payment or issued free, a free share is issued to the public hand. At first sight this might seem to be unjust—if private investors have to pay for the share, why should the public hand get it free? The answer, of course, is that the company as a whole does not pay profit tax; the profit attributable to the new capital funds, therefore, also escapes profit tax; and the public hand receives its free shares, as it were *in lieu* of the profit taxes which would otherwise have to be paid.

Finally, there may be special problems in connection with company reorganisations, takeovers, windings-up, and so forth. They are all perfectly soluble in accordance with the principles already stated. In the case of windings-up, whether in bankruptcy or otherwise, the equity holdings of the public hand would, of course, receive exactly the same treatment as those in private hands.

The above proposals may be taken as nothing more than an exercise in the art of "constitution-making." Such a scheme would be perfectly *feasible;* it would restructure large-scale industrial ownership without revolution, expropriation, centralisation, or the substitution of bureaucratic ponderousness for private flexibility. It could be introduced in an experimental and evolutionary manner—by starting with the biggest enterprises and gradually working down the scale, until it was felt that the public interest had been given sufficient weight in the citadels of business enterprise. All the indications are that the present structure of large-scale industrial enterprise, in spite of heavy taxation and an endless proliferation of legislation, is not conducive to the public welfare.

EPILOGUE

IN THE EXCITEMENT over the unfolding of his scientific and technical powers, modern man has built a system of production that ravishes nature and a type of society that mutilates man. If only there were more and more wealth, everything else, it is thought, would fall into place. Money is considered to be all-powerful; if it could not actually buy non-material values, such as justice, harmony, beauty, or even health, it could circumvent the need for them or compensate for their loss. The development of production and the acquisition of wealth have thus become the highest goals of the modern world in relation to which all other goals, no matter how much lip-service may still be paid to them, have come to take second place. The highest goals require no justification; all secondary goals have finally to justify themselves in terms of the service their attainment renders to the attainment of the highest.

This is the philosophy of materialism, and it is this philosophy—or metaphysic—which is now being challenged by events. There has never been a time, in any society in any part of the world, without its sages and teachers to challenge materialism and plead for a different order of priorities. The languages have differed, the symbols have varied, yet the message has always been the same: "Seek ye *first* the kingdom of God, and all these things [the material things which you also need] shall be *added* unto you." They shall be added, we are told, here on earth where we need them, not simply in an after-life beyond our imagination. Today, however, this message reaches us not solely from the sages and saints but from the actual course of physical events. It speaks to us in the language of terrorism, genocide, breakdown, pollution, exhaustion. We live, it seems, in a unique period of convergence. It is becoming apparent that there is not only a promise but also a threat in those astonishing words about the kingdom of God—the threat that "unless you seek first the kingdom, these other things, which you also need, will cease to be available to you." As a recent writer put it, without reference to economics and politics but nonetheless with direct reference to the condition of the modern world:

> If it can be said that man collectively shrinks back more and more from the Truth, it can also be said that on all sides the Truth is closing in more and more upon man. It might almost be said that, in order to receive a touch of It, which in the past required a lifetime of effort, all that is asked of him now is not to shrink back. And yet how difficult that is![I]

We shrink back from the truth if we believe that the destructive forces of the modern world can be "brought under control" simply by mobilising more resources—of wealth, education, and research—to fight pollution, to preserve wildlife, to discover new sources of energy, and to arrive at more effective agreements on peaceful coexistence. Needless to say, wealth, education, research, and many other things are needed for any civilisation, but what is most needed today is a revision of the ends which these means are meant to serve. And this implies, above all else, the development of a life-style which accords to material things their proper, legitimate place, which is secondary and not primary.

The "logic of production" is neither the logic of life nor that of society. It is a small and subservient part of both. The destructive forces unleashed by it cannot be brought under control, unless the "logic of production" itself is brought under control—so that destructive forces cease to be unleashed. It is of little use trying to suppress terrorism if the production of deadly devices continues to be deemed a legitimate employment of man's creative powers. Nor can the fight against pollution be successful if the patterns of production and consumption continue to be of a scale, a complexity, and a degree of violence which, as is becoming more and more

Consciences are being stirred across the world. Ethics are being taught in business schools. Market economics, currency speculation, soil vitality, air pollution, the destruction of historic social cultures and marginalization of human relationships are all under intense discussion in the media and elsewhere. The continuing violence to the human condition and its environment is being challenged, but often the answer is to apply further violence as a restraint.

Possibly even more insidious is the violence that results from the pressure for more intensive growth via capitalism and the many forms of privatization. The real fact of economic life is that the world's resources (notably fossil fuels, minerals and the land, dependent on sun, rain, and wind) are the seedbed of the future, and must be husbanded, recycled, and replaced as one conserves capital, not expended as income.

—GODRIC BADER

*One of the crucial tasks of
the new century will be to so
shape our economic system
so that environmental and
social safeguards are built
into its design. Advocacy for
better working conditions
and non-polluting methods
of production will certainly
play a part in this reshaping,
but theoretical knowledge
by itself will not necessarily
stimulate a change in our
consumer habits. Rather, we
need to be able to picture the
manufacturing processes so
clearly that we are compelled
to demand secure conditions
for the workers, and to
restore the waters poisoned
by toxic waste.*

*By intentionally narrowing
our choices of consumer
goods to those locally made,
local currencies allow us to
know more fully the story of
items purchased, stories that
include the human beings
that made them and the
minerals, rivers, plants, and
animals that gave of their
substance to form them.
Such stories, formed from
real life experience, work in
the imagination to foster* ➡

apparent, do not fit into the laws of the universe, to which man is just as much subject as the rest of creation. Equally, the chance of mitigating the rate of resource depletion or of bringing harmony into the relationships between those in possession of wealth and power and those without is non-existent as long as there is no idea anywhere of enough being good and more-than-enough being evil.

It is a hopeful sign that some awareness of these deeper issues is gradually—if exceedingly cautiously—finding expression even in some official and semi-official utterances. A report, written by a committee at the request of the Secretary of State for the Environment, talks about buying time during which technologically developed societies have an opportunity "to revise their values and to change their political objectives." It is a matter of "moral choices," says the report; "no amount of calculation can alone provide the answers.... The fundamental questioning of conventional values by young people all over the world is a symptom of the widespread unease with which our industrial civilisation is increasingly regarded."[3] Pollution must be brought under control and mankind's population and consumption of resources must be steered towards a permanent and sustainable equilibrium. "Unless this is done, sooner or later—and some believe that there is little time left—the downfall of civilisation will not be a matter of science fiction. It will be the experience of our children and grandchildren."[4]

But how is it to be done? What are the "moral choices"? Is it just a matter, as the report also suggests, of deciding "how much we are willing to pay for clean surroundings?" Mankind has indeed a certain freedom of choice: it is not bound by trends, by the "logic of production," or by any other fragmentary logic. But it is bound by truth. Only in the service of truth is perfect freedom, and even those who today ask us "to free our imagination from bondage to the existing system"[5] fail to point the way to the recognition of truth.

It is hardly likely that twentieth-century man is called upon to discover truth that has never been discovered before. In the Christian tradition, as in all genuine traditions of mankind, the truth has been stated in religious terms, a language which has become well-nigh incomprehensible to the majority of modern men. The language can be revised, and there are contemporary writers who have done so, while leaving the truth inviolate. Out of the whole Christian tradition, there is perhaps no body of teaching which is more relevant and appropriate to the modern predicament than the marvellously subtle and realistic doctrines of the Four Cardinal Virtues—*prudentia, justitia, fortitudo,* and *temperantia.*

The meaning of prudentia, significantly called the "mother" of all other of all virtues—*prudentia dicitur genitrix virtutum*—is not conveyed by the word "prudence," as currently used. It signifies the opposite of a small, mean, calculating attitude to life, which refuses to see and value anything that fails to promise an immediate utilitarian advantage.

> The pre-eminence of prudence means that realisation of the good presupposes knowledge of reality. He alone can do good who knows what things are like and what their situation is. The pre-eminence of prudence means that so-called "good intentions" and so-called "meaning well" by no means suffice. Realisation of the good presupposes that our actions are appropriate to the real situation, that is to the concrete realities which form the "environment" of a concrete human action; and that we therefore take this concrete reality seriously, with clear-eyed objectivity.[6]

This clear-eyed objectivity, however, cannot be achieved and prudence cannot be perfected except by an attitude of "silent contemplation" of reality, during which the egocentric interests of man are at least temporarily silenced.

Only on the basis of this magnanimous kind of prudence can we achieve justice, fortitude, and *temperantia,* which means knowing when enough is enough. "Prudence implies a transformation of the knowledge of truth into decisions corresponding to reality." What, therefore, could be of greater importance today than the study and cultivation of prudence, which would almost inevitably lead to a real understanding of the three other cardinal virtues, all of which are indispensable for the survival of civilisation?[8]

Justice relates to truth, fortitude to goodness, and *temperantia* to beauty; while prudence, in a sense, comprises all three. The type of

➡ responsible consumer choices and re-establish a commitment to the community. In this sense, local currencies become a tool not only for economic development but for cultural renewal.

The multi-layered nature of local currencies has captivated and energized an informal network of practitioners who are issuing scrip in their own communities. When these activists get together, there is no mistaking the positive dynamic at work. The movement has all the energy, idealism, and mobility of young adulthood—still experimenting to find the right form, not afraid to take risks, able to alter direction as needed, and determined to change the economic system to reflect deeply held social and environmental values.

—SUSAN WITT

realism which behaves as if the good, the true, and the beautiful were too vague and subjective to be adopted as the highest aims of social or individual life, or were the automatic spin-off of the successful pursuit of wealth and power, has been aptly called "crackpot-realism." Everywhere people ask: "What can I actually *do*?" The answer is as simple as it is disconcerting: we can, each of us, work to put our own inner house in order. The guidance we need for this work cannot be found in science or technology, the value of which utterly depends on the ends they serve; but it can still be found in the traditional wisdom of mankind.

NOTES AND ACKNOWLEDGEMENTS

This third edition has been prepared under the guiding eye of editorial advisor David Rousseau and the steady hand of coordinating editor Sharon McCann.

Special thanks are extended to Hazel Henderson, George McRobie, Mark Roseland, Peter Warshall, and Susan Witt for their continuous support, encouragement, and advice.

The publishing house also wishes to extend its thanks to all the contributors of the third edition, for not only their commentaries on Schumacher's legacy, but also for their personal dedication to sustaining the planet for generations to come.

PART I—THE MODERN WORLD

1. *The Problem of Production*
   Based on a lecture given at the Gottlieb Duttweiler Institute, Rüschlikon, Nr. Zürich, Switzerland, 4 February 1972.

2. *Peace and Permanence*
   First published in *Resurgence,* Journal of the Fourth World, Vol. III, No. 1, May/June 1970.
   1. *Towards New Horizons* by Pyarelal (Navajivan Publishing House, Ahmedabad, India, 1959).
   2. *Creed or Chaos* by Dorothy L. Sayers (Methuen & Co. Ltd., London, 1947).

3. *The Role of Economics*

Partly based on The Des Væux Memorial Lecture, 1967, "Clean Air and Future Energy—Economics and Conservation," published by the National Society for Clean Air, London, 1967.

4. *Buddhist Economics*

First published in *Asia: A Handbook,* edited by Guy Wint, published by Anthony Blond Ltd., London, 1966.

1. *The New Burma* (Economic and Social Board, Government of the Union of Burma, 1954).
2. Ibid.
3. Ibid.
4. *Wealth of Nations* by Adam Smith.
5. *Art and Swadeshi* by Ananda K. Coomaraswamy (Ganesh & Co., Madras).
6. *Economy of Permanence* by J.C. Kumarappa (Sarva-Seva Sangh Publication, Rajghat, Kashi, 4th edn., 1958).
7. *The Affluent Society* by John Kenneth Galbraith (Penguin Books Ltd., 1962).
8. *A Philosophy of Indian Economic Development* by Richard B. Gregg (Navajivan Publishing House, Ahmedabad, India, 1958).
9. *The Challenge of Man's Future* by Harrison Brown (The Viking Press, New York, 1954).

5. *A Question of Size*

Based on a lecture given in London, August 1968, and first published in *Resurgence,* Journal of the Fourth World, Vol. II, No. 3, September/October 1968.

PART II—RESOURCES

6. *The Greatest Resource—Education*

1. *Note:* Incidentally, the Second Law of Thermodynamics states that heat cannot of itself pass from a colder to a hotter body, or, more vulgarly, that "You cannot warm yourself on something that is colder than you"—a familiar though not very inspiring idea, which has been quite illegitimately extended to the

pseudo-scientific notion that the universe must necessarily end in a kind of "heat death" when all temperature differences will have ceased.

> *Out, out brief candle!*
> *Life's but a walking shadow; a poor player*
> *That struts and frets his hour upon the stage*
> *And then is heard no more; it is a tale*
> *Told by an idiot, full of sound and fury,*
> *Signifying nothing.*

The words were Macbeth's when he met his final disaster. They are repeated today on the authority of science when the triumphs of that same science are greater than ever before.

2. Charles Darwin's *Autobiography*, edited by Nora Barlow (Wm. Collins Sons & Co. Ltd., London, 1958).

7. The Proper Use of Land

1. *Topsoil and Civilisation* by Tom Dale and Vernon Gill Carter (University of Oklahoma Press, Norman, Okla., 1955).
2. *Man and His Future*, edited by Gordon Wolstenholme (A Ciba Foundation Volume, J. & A. Churchill Ltd., London, 1963).
3. *The Soul of a People* by H. Fielding Hall (Macmillan & Co. Ltd., London, 1920).
4. *Our Accelerating Century* by Dr. S.L. Mansholt (The Royal Dutch/Shell Lectures on Industry and Society, London, 1967).
5. *A Future for European Agriculture* by D. Bergmann, M. Rossi-Doria, N. Kaldor, J.A. Schnittker, H.B. Krohn, C. Thomsen, J.S. March, H. Wilbrandt, Pierre Uri (The Atlantic Institute, Paris, 1970).
6. Ibid.
7. Ibid.
8. Ibid.
9. Ibid.
10. Our Synthetic Environment by Lewis Herbert (Jonathan Cape Ltd., London, 1963).
11. Ibid.
12. Op. cit.
13. Op. cit.

8. Resources for Industry

Long quotation from *Prospect for Coal* by E.F. Schumacher, published by the National Coal Board, London, April 1961.

1. *The Economic Journal,* March 1964, p. 192.

9. Nuclear Energy—Salvation or Damnation?

Based on The Des Væux Memorial Lecture, 1967, "Clean Air and Future Energy—Economics and Conservation," published by the National Society for Clean Air, London, 1967.

1. *Basic Ecology* by Ralph and Mildred Buchsbaum (Boxwood Press, Pittsburgh, 1957).
2. "Die Haftung für Strahlenschäden in Grossbritannien" by C.T. Highton in *Die Atomwirtschaft: Zeitschrift für wirtschaftliche Fragen der Kernumwandlung,* 1959.
3. *Radiation: What It Is and How It Affects You* by Jack Schubert and Ralph Lapp (Viking Press, New York, 1957). Also, *Die Strahlengefährdung des Menschen durch Atomenergie* by Hans Marquardt and Gerhard Schubert (Hamburg, 1959); and Vol. XI of *Proceedings* of the International Conference on the Peaceful Uses of Atomic Energy, Geneva, 1955; and Vol. XXII of *Proceedings* of the Second United Nations International Conference on the Peaceful Uses of Atomic Energy, Geneva, 1958.
4. "Changing Genes: Their Effects on Evolution" by H.J. Muller in *Bulletin of the Atomic Scientists* (Chicago, 1947).
5. Statement by G. Failla, Hearings before the Special Sub-Committee on Radiation, of the Joint Committee on Atomic Energy, 86th Congress of the United States, 1959. "Fallout from Nuclear Weapons," Vol. II (Washington, D.C., 1959).
6. "Oceanic Research Needed for Safe Disposal of Radioactive Wastes at Sea" by R. Revelle and M.B. Schaefer; and "Concerning the Possibility of Disposing of Radioactive Waste in Ocean Trenches" by V.G. Bogorov and E.M. Kreps. Both in Vol. XVIII of *Proceedings,* Geneva Conference, 1958.
7. "Biological Factors Determining the Distribution of Radioisotopes in the Sea" by B.H. Ketchum and V.T. Bowen in Vol. XVIII of *Proceedings,* Geneva Conference, 1958.
8. Conference Report by W.H. Levi in *Die Atomwirtschaft,* 1960.
9. U.S. Atomic Energy Commission, Annual Report to Congress, Washington, D.C., 1960.

10. U.S. Naval Radiological Defense Laboratory Statement in *Selected Materials on Radiation Protection Criteria and Standards: Their Basis and Use.*

11. *Friede oder Atomkrieg* by Albert Schweitzer, 1958.

12. *The Hazards to Man of Nuclear and Allied Radiations* (British Medical Research Council).

13. Lewis Herber, op. cit.

14. "Summary and Evaluation of Environmental Factors That Must Be Considered in the Disposal of Radioactive Wastes" by K.Z. Morgan in *Industrial Radioactive Disposal,* Vol. III.

15. "Natürliche und künstliche Erbanderungen" by H. Marquardt in *Probleme der Mutationsforschung* (Hamburg, 1957).

16. Schubert and Lapp, op. cit.

17. "Today's Revolution" by A.M. Weinberg in *Bulletin of the Atomic Scientists* (Chicago, 1956).

18. *Must the Bomb Spread?* by Leonard Beaton (Penguin Books Ltd., in association with the Institute of Strategic Studies, London, 1966).

19. "From Bomb to Man" by W.O. Caster in *Fallout,* edited by John M. Fowler (Basic Books, New York, 1960).

20. Op. cit.

21. Op. cit.

22. "The Atom's Poisonous Garbage" by Walter Schneir in *Reporter,* 1960.

23. Lewis Herber, op. cit.

24. *On Peace* by Albert Einstein, edited by O. Nathan and H. Norden (Schocken Books, New York, 1960).

25. *Pollution: Nuisance or Nemesis?* (HMSO, London, 1972).

10. *Technology with a Human Face*
Based on a lecture given at the Sixth Annual Conference of the Teilhard Centre for the Future of Man, London, 23 October 1971.

PART III—THE THIRD WORLD

11. *Development*
Based on the Anniversary Address delivered to the general meeting of the Africa Bureau, London, 3 March 1966.

12. *Social and Economic Problems Calling for the Development of Intermediate Technology*

First published by UNESCO, Conference on the Application of Science and Technology to the Development of Latin America, organised by UNESCO with the cooperation of the Economic Commission for Latin America, Santiago, Chile, September 1965.

1. "A Plan for Full Employment in the Developing Countries" by Gabriel Ardant (*International Labour Review,* 1963).

2. "Wages and Employment in the Labor-Surplus Economy" by L.G. Reynolds (*American Economic Review,* 1965).

3. *Industrialisation in Developing Countries,* edited by Ronald Robinson (Cambridge University Overseas Studies Committee, Cambridge, 1965).

4. Ibid.

5. Ibid., quoted from "Notes on Latin American Industrial Development" by Nuño F. de Figueiredo.

6. Ibid.

7. "Technologies Appropriate for the Total Development Plan" by D.R. Gadgil in *Appropriate Technologies for Indian Industry* (SIET Institute, Hyderabad, India, 1964).

13. *Two Million Villages*

First published in *Britain and the World in the Seventies: A Collection of Fabian Essays,* edited by George Cunningham (Weidenfeld & Nicolson Ltd., London, 1970).

14. *The Problem of Unemployment in India*

A talk given to the India Development Group, London, 1971.

1. *The New Industrial State* by John Kenneth Galbraith (Penguin Books Ltd., in association with Hamish Hamilton Ltd., London, 1967).

PART IV—ORGANISATION AND OWNERSHIP

15. *A Machine to Foretell the Future?*

Lecture delivered at the First British Conference on the Social and Economic Effects of Automation, Harrogate, June 1961.

1. *The Economics of 1960* by Colin Clark (Macmillan Co., Toronto, 1941).

16. *Towards a Theory of Large-Scale Organisation*
    First published in "Management Decision," *Quarterly Review of Management Technology,* London, Autumn 1967.
    1. Encyclical "Quadragesimo Anno."
    2. *Selected Works* by Mao Tse-tung, Vol. III.

17. *Socialism*

18. *Ownership*
    All quotations in this chapter are from *The Acquisitive Society* by R.H. Tawney.

19. *New Patterns of Ownership*

    Epilogue
    1. *Ancient Beliefs and Modern Superstitions* by Martin Lings (Perennial Books, London, 1964).
    2. *Pollution: Nuisance or Nemesis?* (HMSO, London, 1972).
    3. Ibid.
    4. Ibid.
    5. Ibid.
    6. *Prudence* by Joseph Pieper, translated by Richard and Clara Winston (Faber & Faber Ltd., London, 1960).
    7. *Fortitude and Temperance* by Joseph Pieper, translated by Daniel F. Coogan (Faber & Faber Ltd., London, 1955).
    8. *Justice* by Joseph Pieper, translated by Lawrence E. Lynch (Faber & Faber Ltd., London, 1957). No better guide to the matchless Christian teaching of the Four Cardinal Virtues could be found than Joseph Pieper, of whom it has been rightly said that he knows how to make what he has to say not only intelligible to the general reader but urgently relevant to the reader's problems and needs.

BIOGRAPHIES OF CONTRIBUTORS

Godric Bader—life president of the Scott Bader Company Ltd. in Wellingborough, England. He is the son of Ernest Bader, who, in 1920, founded the company that became one of the few business examples of Gandhi's trusteeship principle in action. Godric co-founded the Commonwealth, which holds in trusteeship this unique corporation.

Robert Bateman—distinguished Canadian wildlife artist, naturalist, and spokesman for environmental and preservation issues. He has been featured in numerous books and films, and was honored as an Officer of the Order of Canada.

Tom Bender—architect, teacher, and strategic planner. He has been a leader and international award winner in the development of sustainable design and economics. His four books and over one hundred articles span the technical, community, psychological, and spiritual dimensions of how we relate to our surroundings.

David Brower—a leader in conservation battles since 1938, he was the first executive director of the Sierra Club (1952–69), and founder of Friends of the Earth (now in 63 countries), the League of Conservation Voters, and Earth Island Institute, where he still serves as chairman.

Herman Daly—professor at the University of Maryland, School of Public Affairs and former senior economist at the World Bank. A prolific writer about economic development, population, resources, and the environment, his books include *For the Common Good* (with John Cobb, Jr.), *Valuing the Earth*, and *Beyond Growth*. He also co-founded the journal *Ecological Economics*.

David Ehrenfeld—professor of biology at Rutgers University where he teaches ecology. His books include *The Arrogance of Humanism* and *Beginning Again: People and Nature in the New Millennium*. He is also founding editor of the international scientific journal, *Conservation Biology*.

Bill Ellis—physicist, futurist, farmer, and former science policy consultant for UNESCO, the World Bank, National Science Foundation, and the U.S. Congress. For the last two decades, he and his wife Margaret have facilitated TRANET, a transnational network of local developers participating in the alternative and transformational movements.

Pliny Fisk—architect, long-time member of the U.S. appropriate technology movement, and co-director of Center for Maximum Potential Building Systems. From the 1970s to 1990s, he has innovated systems for materials, alternative energy, water harvesting, and wastewater; small-scale economic development projects; sustainable city plans; and sustainable building guidelines.

Mary Flynn—chief executive officer of the Community Housing Land Trust Foundation and executive director of the Co-operative Housing Federation of B.C. for the past 16 years. She serves on many boards and has earned numerous awards, including the Canada Mortgage and Housing Award for Outstanding Contribution to Co-op Housing.

Avi Friedman—architect, associate professor, and director of the Affordable Homes Program of McGill University, School of Architecture, Montreal, Canada. His three housing prototypes, the Grow Home (a narrow-front rowhouse), the Next Home (for a community development), and La Casa a la Carta (for Latin America), have led to numerous awards for technological innovation.

Paul Hawken—environmentalist, author, entrepreneur, and consultant. Author of five books (most recently *Natural Capitalism: Creating the Next Industrial Revolution* with Amory and Hunter Lovins), his books have been published in over 50 countries. As co-chair of The Natural Step International, he assists business and government leaders worldwide in committing to environmental sustainability.

Hazel Henderson—an independent futurist and lecturer, author of five books, a worldwide syndicated columnist, and consultant on sustainable development. She serves numerous editorial boards and organizations advocating ecologically sustainable human development and socially responsible business and investment.

Wes Jackson—president of The Land Institute and former professor at Kansas Wesleyan and California State University. His numerous publications include *Becoming Native to This Place*, *Altars of Unhewn Stone*, and *New Roots for Agriculture*, which outlines the basis for agricultural research at his institute.

Jane Jacobs—writer and critic of urban planning. Although her ideas are unconventional, they are well respected. She is an icon to a new generation of city planners, urban activists, and all those who care deeply about what makes a city healthy and livable. Her books include *The Death and Life of Great American Cities* and *Cities and the Wealth of Nations*.

Charles Komanoff—economist and activist who deconstructed nuclear power economics in the 1970s and 1980s as an expert witness and author *(Power Plant Cost Escalation)*. Currently he is a campaigner for pedestrians and bicyclists as researcher-author of *Bicycle Blueprint* and *Killed By Automobile,* and founded the New York City activist group, Right Of Way.

Satish Kumar—a founder of the Schumacher Society (UK) and leading promoter of Schumacher's vision of human-scale society. He is also program director at Schumacher College, editor of the ecological economics magazine, *Resurgence*, and author of *Path Without Destination*.

Winona LaDuke—campaign director for White Earth Land Recovery Project, co-chair of the Indigenous Women's Network, and program director of Honor the Earth Fund, advocating for Native environmental groups. A member of the Mississippi Band Anishinabeg, she is also author of *Last Standing Woman*.

Amory Lovins—co-CEO of Rocky Mountain Institute. He holds an Oxford MA and six honorary doctorates, a MacArthur Fellowship, and a 1997 Heinz Award. The *Wall Street Journal* named him one of 28 people most likely to change the course of world business in the 1990s.

John McClaughry—a founder and current board chairman of the E.F. Schumacher Society, created in 1980 to expand appreciation of the decentralist and human-scale tradition. He is president of the Institute for Liberty and Community, and has also been a Vermont state senator and senior policy advisor in the Reagan White House.

George McRobie—co-founder (and later chairman) of the Intermediate Technology Development Group in 1965 with E.F. Schumacher, with whom he worked for 20 years. In the 1980s he taught appropriate technology at the University of Pennsylvania, and now serves on the boards of Intermediate Technology, Technology Exchange, Soil Association, New Economics Foundation, and the India Development Group.

David Morris—author of *Neighborhood Power and Self-Reliant Cities*, editor-in-chief of *The New Rules Journal*, and vice-president of the Minneapolis and Washington, D.C. Institute for Local Self-Reliance.

Helena Norberg-Hodge—director of the International Society for Ecology and Culture, which promotes ecological regeneration and community renewal while raising awareness of the impact of economic globalization. She is also author of *Ancient Futures: Learning from Ladakh,* which has been translated into 30 languages.

David Orr—professor and chair of the Environmental Studies Program of Oberlin College in Ohio, best known as an environmental educator and pioneer in environmental literacy and campus ecology. His books include *Earth in Mind* and *Ecological Literacy.* He is also the education editor for *Conservation Biology.*

William Rees—ecologist and professor at the University of British Columbia, School of Community and Regional Planning. He teaches and researches the necessary ecological conditions for sustainable socioeconomic development. Much of his work is in ecological economics and human ecology, including advancing his ecological footprint concept. He also grows perfect tomatoes.

Karl-Henrik Robèrt—one of Sweden's foremost cancer scientists who, in 1989, initiated an international environmental movement for dialogue between scientists and policy-makers called "The Natural Step." His research on damaged human cells provided a platform for his interest in environmental questions. In 1995, he was appointed adjunct professor of resource theory at the University of Gothenburg, Sweden.

James Robertson—former policy-maker for Prime Minister Harold Macmillan and director of British banking research who collaborated with Schumacher in the 1970s. He later co-founded The Other Economic Summit (TOES) and New Economics Foundation. Japanese, Russian, and Swedish editions of his *Schumacher Briefing, Transforming Economic Life: A Millennial Challenge* (1998) are now in preparation.

Mark Roseland—director of the Community Economic Development Centre at Simon Fraser University and a professor of geography. His publications include *Toward Sustainable Communities: Resources for Citizens and Their Governments* and *Eco-City Dimen-*

sions: *Healthy Communities, Healthy Planet.* He is currently North American editor of the international journal, *Local Environment.*

Wolfgang Sachs—writer and researcher at the Wuppertal Institute for Climate, Environment and Energy in Wuppertal, Germany. His most recent, co-authored publication is *Greening the North, A Post-Industrial Blueprint for Ecology and Equity.*

Kirkpatrick Sale—a founding board member of the E.F. Schumacher Society, USA and author of eight books, including *Human Scale, Dwellers in the Land: The Bioregional Vision,* and *The Conquest of Paradise: Christopher Columbus and the Columbian Legacy.*

Catherine Sneed—founder and director of The Garden Project, which helps former offenders of the San Francisco County Jail through job training in gardening, counseling, and assistance in continuing education. The Garden Project plants trees and gardens, and teaches nutrition and local environmental issues.

Robert Swann—carpenter by trade and president of the E.F. Schumacher Society, USA, founding director of the Institute for Community Economics, and "father" of the Community Land Trust movement. He has worked tirelessly for small communities, peace, social justice, affordable access to credit, social investment, worker ownership, and land reform.

Nancy Jack Todd—writer, editor, and founder of New Alchemy Institute and Ocean Arks International, which disseminates the ideas and practice of ecological sustainability throughout the world. She edits Ocean Arks' publication, *Annals of Earth,* contributes to environmental journals and anthologies, and has authored several books.

Peter Warshall—editor of the quarterly *Whole Earth,* the magazine of *Whole Earth Catalog.* He is also a consultant on water resources and wildlife conservation with the UN, US AID, many local and indigenous communities, as well as multinational corporations. He is a maniacal naturalist, especially in love with birds.

Susan Witt—executive director of the E.F. Schumacher Society, USA since 1980. She founded the SHARE micro-credit program, administers the Community Land Trust in the Southern Berkshires, co-edits *Local Currency News*, and actively serves her local community. Her essays on regional economics appear in books and publications.

RESOURCES

Center for Maximum Potential Building Systems has worked from the 1970s on appropriate technology and sustainable community and regional planning, spanning highly technical development of alternative cements to community-scaled ecological footprint games that enable people to plan a community. The Center attempts to balance life-cycle issues (such as water use and wastewater treatment; food growing and waste treatment; energy production and use) and building systems. Contact Center for Maximum Potential Building Systems 8604 FM 969, Austin, Texas, USA 78724; tel: 512-928-4786; fax: 512-926-4418.

Community Economic Development Centre at Simon Fraser University was established in 1989 to bring university resources and talents together to further the understanding and practice of community economic development. Its goal is to encourage accountable, sustainable, and appropriate community economic development in British Columbia. Contact Community Economic Development Centre, Simon Fraser University, Burnaby, British Columbia, Canada V5A 1S6; tel: 604-291-5850; fax: 604-291-5473; email: psimpson@sfu.ca; web site: www.sfu.ca/cedc/.

Community Housing Land Trust Foundation was established in 1993 to preserve and increase affordable housing opportunities in British Columbia for seniors, people with special needs, and those with low incomes. The Foundation's aim is to acquire land currently used for affordable housing, but threatened by economic pressures to convert to other uses or become part of the market-priced housing stock. Additionally, the Foundation seeks to acquire undeveloped land on which new affordable units can be built. Contact Community Housing Land Trust Foundation, 133 E. 8th Ave., Vancouver, British Columbia, Canada V5T 1R8; tel: 604-879-5111; fax: 604-879-4611.

E.F. Schumacher Society, USA was founded in 1980 to promote the ideas of the decentralist tradition and to implement them in practical programs for local economic self-reliance, stewardship of natural resources, and community renewal. The Society's regional programs in micro-lending, community land trusts, local currencies, and consumer-supported farming have gained national media attention and have been replicated throughout the world. The Society's extensive library includes Schumacher's personal books and papers, computer-indexed and accessible over the Internet. Selected talks from the Society's highly regarded Annual E.F. Schumacher Lecture series are collected in the book, *People, Land, and Community*. Contact E.F. Schumacher Society, 140 Jug End Rd., Great Barrington, Massachusetts, USA 01230; tel: 413-528-1737; web site: www.schumachersociety.org.

Institute for Local Self-Reliance (ILSR), founded in 1974, works to decentralize authority, responsibility, and productive capacity. ILSR publishes *The New Rules Journal* and maintains a web site (www.newrules.org) that report on policies encouraging strong local economies. ILSR staff also provide technical assistance for local, state, and national governments and small businesses. Contact ILSR, 1313 5th St. SE, Minneapolis, Minnesota, USA 55414; tel: 612-379-3815; fax: 612-379-3920; web site: www.ilsr.org.

Intermediate Technology Development Group was founded in 1965 by Fritz Schumacher and his associates to develop and introduce low-cost, small-scale technologies that can be owned and operated by poor people in poor countries. Much of the Group's work is now done by IT centers in developing countries, with headquarters in the U.K. There are now similar organizations around the world, including AT International in Washington, D.C., the International Development and Research Centre in Ottawa, Canada, and others in Germany, Holland, and Switzerland. The Group also operates a commercial consulting service and IT Publications. Contact Intermediate Technology Development Group, Bourton Hall, Bourton-on-Dunsmore, Rugby, Warwickshire, UK CV2 39QZ; tel: 0178-866-1100; fax: 0178-866-1101; email: itdg@itdg.org.uk; web site: www.oneworld.org/itdg.

International Society for Ecology and Culture (ISEC) is an international nonprofit organization working to promote critical discussion about the impacts of industrial development and economic globalization. ISEC helps local communities worldwide resist the consumer monoculture and explore alternative systems based on their own cultures. ISEC is the parent organization of the Ladakh Project, which has been running "hands-on" programs on the Indian subcontinent since 1975. The Society's directors form the editorial board of *The Ecologist* magazine. Contact ISEC, Apple Barn, Week, Dartington, Devon, UK TQ9 6JP; tel: 0180-386-8650; fax: 0180-386-8651; email: isecuk@gn.apc.org; web site: www.isec.org.uk.

New Economics Foundation, founded in 1986, is a leading, independent think-tank to promote a new economy focused on social justice, human scale, and sufficiency. With 25 full-time staff and 2000 new economics activists, the Foundation works from the village level to the United Nations. Current programs include how to reshape the global economy; how to build corporate accountability, in which the Foundation's work on social auditing has a central role; how to promote financial services that support healthy, local economies; and how to build a truly participatory democracy. Contact New Economics Foundation, Cinnamon House, 6–8 Cole St., London, UK SE1 4YH; tel: 0171-407-7447; fax: 0171-407-6473; email: info@neweconomics.org; web site: www.neweconomics.org.

Ocean Arks International was incorporated in 1983 to disseminate the ideas and practice of ecological sustainability. Its principal focus is bioremediation of polluted waters using ecologically designed living technologies and living machines, which teach ecosystem dynamics to primary, secondary, and university students. Ocean Arks also publishes *Annals of Earth*, a journal about economic and ecological solutions to local and global social problems. Contact Ocean Arks International, 176 Battery St., 3rd Floor, Burlington, Vermont, USA 05401; tel: 802-860-0011; fax: 802-860-0022; web site: www.oceanarks.org.

Resurgence **magazine**, to which E.F. Schumacher contributed regularly, continues to support his vision and attracts well-known writers to contribute. A selection of Schumacher's writing in *Resurgence* was published in the book, *This I Believe*, by Green Books. For free sample copies of the magazine and subscription details, contact: Ford House, Hartland, Bideford, Devon, UK EX39 6EE; tel: 0123-744-1293; fax: 0123-744-1203; email: ed@resurge.demon.co.uk.

Rocky Mountain Institute, founded by Hunter and Amory Lovins in 1982, is an independent, nonprofit resource policy center whose 50 staff foster the efficient and sustainable use of resources as a path to global security. Its research, outreach, and implementation, serving corporations, communities, and citizens, often examine optimal scale. Its latest work is summarized in the book with Paul Hawken, *Natural Capitalism: Creating the Next Industrial Revolution*. Contact Rocky Mountain Institute, 1739 Snowmass Creek Rd., Snowmass, Colorado, USA 81654-9199; tel: 970-927-3128; fax: 970-927-4178; email: ablovins@rmi.org; web site: www.rmi.org.

Schumacher Institute of Appropriate Technology and Rural Development was established by E.F. Schumacher and Mansur and Surur Hoda in 1970 as the India Development Group. In 1985 the Group established a training center in India. It trains people to help poor rural communities, with special attention given to the self-employed and women. Courses include management of micro-enterprises, maintenance and repair of rural equipment, welding, plumbing, tailoring, and knitting. Contact The Schumacher Institute, Village Malhaur, P.O. Chinhat, Lucknow–227 105 Uttar Pradesh India; tel: 91-522-315-873; fax: 91-522-222-061.

Schumacher Society, UK holds annual lectures in Bristol, Liverpool, and Manchester. The Society also publishes a newsletter and *Schumacher Briefings,* exploring current issues to influence policy makers to consider human-scale values in social and national affairs. Contact Schumacher Society, Foxhole, Dartington, Totnes, Devon, UK TQ9 6EB; tel: 0180-386-5051.

Schumacher College is an internationally known center for the study of an ecological and spiritual world view. Some of the world's best thinkers, writers, and activists in new paradigms lead courses and explore holistic ideas in depth—in particular, ecological economics and environmental science. Contact The Old Postern, Dartington, Devon, UK TQ9 6EA; tel: 0180-386-5934; fax: 0180-386-6899; email: schumcoll@gn.apc.org.

Soil Association was formed in 1946 to ensure safe, healthy food, an unpolluted countryside, and organic farming in Britain and the world. Fritz Schumacher was president from 1970 until his death in 1977. The Association's symbol is awarded to organic products that conform to its quality standards, which are backed by national and European law. The Association is currently campaigning for the removal of genetically modified organisms in the food chain, a more responsible use of farm antibiotics, a ban on organophosphate pesticides, and a revival of the local food economy. Contact Soil Association, Bristol House, 40–56 Victoria St., Bristol, England BS1 6BY; tel: 0117-929-0661; fax: 0117-925-2504; email: info@soilassociation.org.

Technology Exchange began in 1985 as a spin-off from the IT Group. It has three specialized data bases on technological, commercial, and international opportunities: the first listing 10,000 technologies from 35 countries; the second has 18,000 commercial offers and requests; and the third specializes in commercial opportunities in developing countries. Contact Technology Exchange,

Wrest Park, Silsoe, Bedfordshire, England MK45 4HS; tel: 0152-886-0333; fax: 0152-886-0664; email: info@uktech.net; web site: www.uktech.net.

The Land Institute was founded in 1976 as a nonprofit research and education organization dedicated to ecological sustainability. Its programs are Natural Systems Agriculture to develop grains for food using perennial plants and save soils by mimicking native ecosystems; Sunshine Farm, a 10-year project in energy accounting for a small diversified farm; and Rural Community Studies, including a public school consortium to reform rural education with a place-based, interdisciplinary curriculum. Contact The Land Institute, 2440 East Water Well Road, Salina, Kansas, USA 67401; tel: 785-823-5376; fax: 785-823-8728; email: landinst_development@midkan.net.

TRANET (TRANsnational NETwork) was created in 1976 at the UN Conference on Human Settlements by grassroots activists who, rejecting a formal organization on appropriate technology, opted for a network to share information. For 20 years, Bill and Margaret Ellis produced a newsletter-directory on publications, products, programs, projects, and people. Since 1997, TRANET has been an on-line service only. Contact TRANET, PO Box 567, Rangeley, Maine, USA 04970-0567; email: tranet@rangeley.org; web site: www.nonviolence.org/tranet.

Wuppertal Institute, founded in 1992, has a staff of 80 who research policy regarding energy, transport, climate, resource flows, and new models of wealth. Twenty-five years after *Small is Beautiful* was first published, the Institute attempts to sketch out what Schumacher called for—an economics as if people (and nature) mattered. Contact Wuppertal Institute, P.O.B. 100480, D-42004, Wuppertal, Germany; tel: 49-202-2492-0; email: info@wupperinst.org; web site: www.wupperinst.org.

INDEX